The Bay of Pigs

ALSO BY HOWARD JONES

PIVOTAL MOMENTS
IN AMERICAN HISTORY

Series Editors
David Hackett Fischer
James M. McPherson

James T. Patterson
Brown v. Board of Education:
A Civil Rights Milestone and Its Troubled Legacy

Maury Klein
Rainbow's End: The Crash of 1929

James McPherson
Crossroads of Freedom: Antietam

Glenn C. Altschuler
All Shook Up: How Rock 'n' Roll Changed America

David Hackett Fischer
Washington's Crossing

John Ferling
Adams vs. Jefferson: The Tumultuous Election of 1800

Colin G. Calloway
The Scratch of a Pen:
1763 and the Transformation of North America

Joel H. Silbey
Storm over Texas:
The Annexation Controversy and the Road to Civil War

Raymond Arsenault
Freedom Riders: 1961 and the Struggle for Racial Justice

Sally G. McMillen
Seneca Falls and the Origins of the Women's Rights Movement

The

BAY *of* PIGS

Howard Jones

OXFORD
UNIVERSITY PRESS
2008

OXFORD
UNIVERSITY PRESS

Oxford University Press, Inc., publishes works that further
Oxford University's objective of excellence
in research, scholarship, and education.

Oxford   New York
Auckland   Cape Town   Dar es Salaam   Hong Kong   Karachi
Kuala Lumpur   Madrid   Melbourne   Mexico City   Nairobi
New Delhi   Shanghai   Taipei   Toronto

With offices in
Argentina   Austria   Brazil   Chile   Czech Republic   France   Greece
Guatemala   Hungary   Italy   Japan   Poland   Portugal   Singapore
South Korea   Switzerland   Thailand   Turkey   Ukraine   Vietnam

Published by Oxford University Press, Inc.
198 Madison Avenue, New York, NY 10016

www.oup.com

Oxford is a registered trademark of Oxford University Press

Library of Congress Cataloging-in-Publication Data
Jones, Howard, 1940–
The Bay of Pigs / Howard Jones.
p. cm.
Includes bibliographical references and index.
ISBN 978-0-19-517383-3
1. Cuba—History—Invasion, 1961.
2. Counterrevolutionaries—Cuba—History—20th century.
3. United States—Foreign relations—Cuba.
4. Cuba—Foreign relations—United States.
5. United States—Foreign relations—1953–1961.   I. Title.
F1788.J615 2008
972.9106—dc22   2008001591

9 8 7 6 5 4 3 2 1

Printed in the United States of America
on acid-free paper

For my mom and dad, who wanted to read it, and for

my best friend Mary Ann, daughters Debbie and Shari,

and grandchildren Tim, Ashley, Lauren, Tyler,

and Katelyn, who I hope will do so.

[Richard] Bissell's high purpose, unbounded energy,

and unswerving devotion to duty are benchmarks in the

intelligence service. He leaves an enduring legacy.

—President John F. Kennedy, March 1, 1962

Contents

Editor's Note

On April 18–19, 1961, Americans awoke to the news that President John F. Kennedy had secretly mounted an invasion of Cuba. Rumors of its imminence had been circulating in the media. But when the Bay of Pigs actually happened, the initial reaction was shock.

As more news arrived, shock turned to disbelief. The invasion was a complete disaster. Worse, the Cubans and Americans whom President Kennedy had sent into combat were almost immediately abandoned by the United States. Admiral Arleigh Burke had a powerful carrier task group standing by. When it was clear that the invasion was failing, Burke interrupted the president at a social event and demanded authority to rescue survivors.

"We just can't become involved," President Kennedy said.

"Goddamn it, Mr. President," Burke replied, "we *are* involved, and there is no way to hide it."

In 1961, many Americans thought that their country did not make war in such a way. They genuinely believed that the United States took up arms when an enemy had fired the first shot, fought in an open and honorable fashion, stood by its soldiers, and never lost a major war. Some wars had happened otherwise, but this idea was an important reality in the United States and one of its oldest traditions. The Bay of Pigs was different in every respect. It was a covert action, conceived as a preemptive strike against Cuban dictator Fidel Castro—a brutal tyrant, but one who had given the

United States little cause to go to war under international law. The invasion had not been led by uniformed armed forces but by high officers in the Central Intelligence Agency who wanted to ensure "plausible deniability." And it failed in scenes of unimaginable incompetence at every level of command.

How did so many things go wrong? Howard Jones draws on primary sources—some of which have only recently been made available—to reconstruct the history of the invasion itself. The result is a story of high drama, strong characters, strange choices, and instructive results. Jones also examines the broader context of the event and finds that the Bay of Pigs was part of a larger operation to assassinate Fidel Castro and destroy his regime. These two operations were closely linked, and they produced odd bedfellows. An attempt was made by the CIA to recruit the Mafia as hit men in Cuba at the same time as other government agencies were trying to send them to jail in the United States.

The Kennedy administration did not invent these dark methods. From the early days of the cold war, unfriendly heads of state had been murdered by American agents and others working with them in Iran, Central America, Africa, and Southeast Asia. President Kennedy and Attorney General Robert Kennedy went farther. Howard Jones provides evidence that from its earliest days, the Kennedy administration had "taken steps toward establishing a program of assassination that targeted any leader who seemed threatening to American security." After the Bay of Pigs, they became even more obsessed with Castro. Despite frequent denials, many covert attempts were made to assassinate him. Other assassinations were attempted in Brazil and succeeded in Vietnam, where President Ngo Dinh Diem and his brother were murdered on November 1, 1962, with the participation of American officials. After the revelations of the Church Committee in 1975, President Gerald Ford issued an executive order against the use of assassination. Since then, some high officials have sought to revive that practice.

Some of these early actions succeeded in their immediate goals. They were thought at first to be tactical successes, but subsequent events proved them to be strategic disasters. Later we are still living with their consequences in Iran, Africa, Latin America, and Asia. Policies based on the assumption that criminal means are justified by exalted ends have had an ironic way of eventually failing. Moreover, criminal means are contagious in international affairs. When we use them against others, they are turned against us. Howard Jones found a CIA report in 1967 that noted, "At the very moment President Kennedy was shot a CIA officer was meeting with a Cuban agent in Paris and giving him an assassination device for use against Castro."

Jones's book also provides new evidence that the United States, with its long traditions of open government, the rule of law, and a free press, is the unfittest nation on earth to conduct preemptive attacks, covert operations, and criminal activities under a cloak of "plausible deniability. These actions have done grave injury to America's standing in the world. Yet it is a lesson that many leaders still have not learned. Marine Colonel Jack Hawkins, who worked on the Bay of Pigs invasion and other secret operations, observed thirty years later that civilian leaders in Washington "continue to harbor unrealistically overblown ideas about what can be accomplished by covert, deniable means."

The Bay of Pigs was indeed a pivotal moment, as this important book clearly reveals. Howard Jones's research is full of warnings for us all.

David Hackett Fischer

Acknowledgments

A book is often the product of many people, and in this case especially so. To the Earhart Foundation, I extend my gratitude for once again believing in my work and providing research support. For reading all or parts of the manuscript and making numerous helpful suggestions, I express deepest appreciation to David Beito, Don Bohning, Larry Clayton, Brian Latell, Pete Maslowski, and Stephen Schwab. To Brian and Steve, I owe special thanks for sharing their insights gained from many years of experience in the CIA; and to Don, who was a young reporter and then Latin America editor for the *Miami Herald* through these tumultuous years and wrote a splendid account of covert actions against Cuba, I convey my heartfelt gratitude for his encouragement, incisive advice, and willingness to provide assistance regarding the principals in this story, many of whom he met. James K. Galbraith again offered sound counsel on the years in which his father, John Kenneth Galbraith, served the Kennedy administration with distinction. Several of my former and present graduate students at the University of Alabama encouraged me by their interest in the topic: Carol Jackson Adams, Becky Bruce, Ryan Floyd, Trent Given, Jon Hooks, Timothy Johnson, Steven McCullough, Charity Rakestraw, Donald Rakestraw, Justin Turner, Ham Walters, Christian McWhirter, and David Zimov. Steve Bunker and Steve Schwab invited me to explore my ideas before their classes, Teresa Golson of the University of Alabama's Imagery Services provided priceless help in arranging photographs for the book, and Kay Branyon, Ellen Moon,

Julie Moore, and Fay Wheat in the History Department's office expressed continued interest in the project and took on many tasks that facilitated its completion.

Archivists and research assistants are critical to anyone's research, and I consider myself extremely fortunate to have had the guidance and help of James Mathis and John Taylor at the National Archives and of James Hill, Stephen Plotkin, and Stephanie Waters at the John F. Kennedy Library. Ian Drake, a graduate student at the University of Maryland, proved particularly adept at locating key CIA materials.

Once again, I have experienced the warm and accommodating atmosphere of the good people associated with Oxford University Press. The late Sheldon Meyer gave me my first opportunity to publish with Oxford, and Susan Ferber and Peter Ginna (since moved to another press) invited me to contribute this work to the Pivotal Moments in American History series. Timothy Bent brought his extraordinary editorial expertise and equally amazing patience to the project as he and the series editors, David Hackett Fischer and James M. McPherson, gently convinced me of the need to bring more focus to the manuscript. Dayne Poshusta furnished invaluable assistance in its final stages of production, Joellyn Ausanka once again proved enormously helpful in facilitating the publication process itself, and India Cooper provided superb copy editing, confirming the fine reputation she enjoys. Alice Thiede did an excellent job preparing the maps, as did Peter Brigaitis and Marie S. Nuchols in compiling the index.

It is impossible to convey the depth of my appreciation, admiration, and respect.

Last, and most important, I dedicate this work to Mary Ann, my longtime friend and partner in life, who continues to return my love and devotion to her in ways beyond measure.

Howard Jones
Northport, Alabama
Fall 2007

The Bay of Pigs

CENTRAL AMERICA
AND THE
CARIBBEAN

UNITED STATES

• Jacksonville

FLORIDA

• Tampa

Gulf of Mexico

• Miami

ATLANTIC OCEAN

BAHAMAS

Key West

ESCAMBRAY
MTS.

Havana

Isle of Pines

Zapata
Peninsula

• Trinidad

Bay of Pigs

CUBA

ORIENTE

DOMINICAN
REPUBLIC

PUERTO
RICO

MEXICO

GRAND
CAYMAN
ISLAND

Guantánamo
Naval Base

HAITI

Vieques
Island

BRITISH
HONDURAS
(now BELIZE)

Great Swan Island
(Honduras)

JAMAICA

GUATEMALA

SIERRA
MADRE

• Retalhuleu

HONDURAS

• Puerto Cabezas

CARIBBEAN SEA

EL SALVADOR

NICARAGUA

PACIFIC
OCEAN

COSTA RICA

PANAMA

VENEZUELA

COLOMBIA

0   100   200 Miles

0   100   200 Kilometers

Prologue

At 6:00 A.M. on April 17, 1961, a lone B-26 roared out of the dim light of the distant western horizon to challenge the Cuban brigade as it hurried to complete a night-time landing at Red Beach in southern Cuba. The pilot, one of Fidel Castro's best, circled the *Barbara J* before zeroing in on the huge gunboat with rhythmic blasts of machine-gun fire that disabled two engines and almost sank it on a return assault. But those on board the ship returned the volleys with the steady hammer of BARs and machine guns, hitting the plane on its third pass and sending it down in a fiery crash beyond the dense mangrove trees and into the swamp.

Within minutes, however, three more planes burst onto the scene, including another B-26 that repeatedly missed both the *Barbara J* and the *Houston*, and a Sea Fury fighter that rolled and dived while strafing the *Houston*.

Then came the third and deadliest challenge—a T-33 jet that streaked across the sky, firing a bevy of rockets at the ships, two of them ripping into the stern of the *Houston* and threatening to send it to the bottom as its men jumped into the shark-infested water. The blazing speed with which the Cuban pilot maneuvered his T-33 around the invasion force made it virtually impossible for the cannon on the heavy landing vessels to hit their mark. The sleek plane's wave of bombs and rockets somehow missed the *Barbara J*, but their percussion loosened the plates protecting the hull, ripping open jagged passageways that allowed huge volumes of water to rush inside the crippled vessel.

The bright morning sky had become a hazy pastel of smoke and debris as the *Barbara J* fired back in an effort to protect the fifteen hundred forces on the ground attempting to establish a beachhead at the Bay of Pigs.

President John F. Kennedy had specifically prohibited American involvement in the invasion, and yet two Americans stood in the midst of the conflagration, watching the battle unfold while in charge of the *Blagar* and *Barbara J*, then shepherding a retired U.S. naval vessel and three merchant ships frantically unloading both men and matériel on two beaches. Grayston "Gray" Lynch from Texas furiously paced the deck of the flagship *Blagar* a few miles away at Blue Beach, a husky veteran of the World War II invasion at Normandy, who must have had flashbacks while transfixed on an approaching B-26 soon followed by two Sea Furies, all taking aim at the Cuban forces struggling in their own D-Day to gain a foothold in the sand. Fellow Texan William "Rip" Robertson, a grizzled marine from World War II as well, likewise seethed with anger at Red Beach as he watched the fighting from on board the companion ship *Barbara J*.

Both men were CIA case officers who had been involved in the operation from its beginning, leading two small groups of frogmen ashore in the pre-dawn hours to place a half-dozen lighted markers in the sand to guide the ships through the deadly rings of razor-like coral rimming much of the bay. Gray and Rip had already had a taste of the fighting, exchanging fire with Cuban militia who had discovered the frogmen in the darkness. Now they could do nothing but encourage their comrades in arms as they tried to join dissidents on the island in overthrowing Castro.

The two chief antagonists in this Caribbean conflict—Kennedy and Castro—closely followed these events, one as an observer from afar, the other soon to be a direct participant. The president waited anxiously at his post in Washington, absorbing every piece of information from the battlefront about an assault that had not been of his making but had won his reluctant approval. His highly revered predecessor in the White House, Dwight D. Eisenhower, had put in motion a CIA-engineered overthrow of Castro and left the program in its developmental stages on his departure from office. Kennedy had become so tempted by the opportunity to score an early victory in the Cold War that he ignored his instincts warning against such action and followed the advice of his experts in the CIA and Joint Chiefs of Staff in approving the amphibious operation. The other leading character in this drama, Fidel Castro, had been awakened at 2:30 in the morning at his Havana home with word that his country was under the long-expected attack. Knowing the odds—that his ward was an island taking on a continent—he rushed to the beaches to orchestrate the defense.

Poorly planned and executed, driven by self-deception and political spin, the Bay of Pigs—almost always routinely referred to as a "fiasco" in later years—marked the first United States–sponsored regime change that relied on a combination of military force and assassination. The resort to pre-emptive and covert action not only raised serious ethical questions in a self-professed democracy, but it focused on leaders of countries that were not at war with the United States and had not raised arms against Americans. Yet in the midst of a burgeoning Cold War, fear and suspicion often guided Washington's thinking, conjuring up images of threats to the national in-terest that were more perception than reality. At a time when to question U.S. policy was to oppose it, the White House decided to simply eliminate troublesome leaders such as Patrice Lumumba in the Congo, Rafael Trujillo in the Dominican Republic, Ngo Dinh Diem in South Vietnam, and, most urgently, Fidel Castro in Cuba.

By the time Kennedy became president, the United States sat on the cusp of the tumultuous 1960s, ready to face the challenges of the Cold War. Its relations with the Soviet Union had hardened in the wake of their bitter rivalry over winning the allegiances of the many new nations sprouting up throughout the Third World in the aftermath of World War II. The wide-spread fear of Communism fueled by the ugly excesses of McCarthyism had not yet run its course, leading many Americans to believe that a Communist monolith headquartered in the Kremlin had devised a blueprint for world conquest that threatened the Free World and forced the United States to take the lead in a war on all fronts. Consequently, foreign state leaders who did not agree with the United States on important matters were automat-ically suspect of being at the least Communist sympathizers and at the most outright Communists—subject to removal by whatever means necessary. Lumumba, Trujillo, and Diem either leaned toward Communism or pur-sued dangerously independent or destructive policies that encouraged un-rest at home and invited Communist infiltration. But it was Castro who proclaimed himself a socialist and allied with the Soviet Union.

Such simplistic analyses of foreign leaders set the tone of Presi-dent Kennedy's foreign policy and provided a model for succeeding administrations dealing with other places throughout the world. Intervention by force became predictable, justified by claims that these figures constituted threats to the Free World and hence to American security. A policy of regime change seemed in order.

The United States in April 1961 embarked on a new and more aggressive Cold War policy that did not become evident until a congressional investigation published its findings fifteen years later. In the bitter aftermath of the Vietnam War and the Watergate scandal, Americans became irate over growing claims that the CIA, in an effort to bring down unfavorable leaders, had engaged in several assassination attempts in the 1960s—charges confirmed by a blue-ribbon Senate investigation in 1975 chaired by Idaho Democrat Frank Church. The Church Committee had followed the work of the Rockefeller Commission, a special "Commission on CIA Activities Within the United States" that Vice President Nelson Rockefeller headed and that came under heavy public criticism for not going far enough in its inquiry into government conduct. In appointing the Rockefeller Commission, according to the charge, President Gerald Ford attempted to circumvent the volatile assassination question by confining the investigation to domestic matters. The Rockefeller Commission, however, recorded numerous allegations and collected considerable evidence pointing to CIA assassination plots. The Church Committee's six Democrats and five Republicans conducted a broadly based inquiry into the CIA, the FBI, and other federal agencies, trying to determine whether the attempts to assassinate Castro and other foreign leaders were attributable to either CIA-instigated domestic upheavals or outright assassinations by CIA-sponsored accomplices. Most unsettling, the investigators asked, was the White House behind these actions?

The Church Committee uncovered no proverbial smoking gun, but the CIA answered directly to the president, and the evidence compiled by the committee along with additional materials later uncovered points to White House involvement in pre-emptive action in the form of both regime change and assassination. The committee conducted sixteen months of closed-session hearings that resulted in nearly ten thousand pages of testimony from more than one hundred witnesses and former advisers in the Eisenhower, Kennedy, and Lyndon B. Johnson administrations, and it examined thousands of documents from the CIA, the FBI, the White House, various government agencies, and all three presidential libraries. But a wave of collective amnesia appeared to descend on those government officials providing testimony, for most of them claimed to have no recollection of any discussions of assassination. These tactics did not convince the committee. Its interim report, published in 1976 under the suggestive title of *Alleged Assassination Plots Involving Foreign Leaders*, proved so explosive that President Ford issued an executive order specifically prohibiting U.S. involvement in assassination.[1]

For the purposes of this study, the Church Committee's findings showed that the CIA's primary interest lay in killing Castro and that this particular project continued for almost six years, beginning in late 1959, reaching its zenith in the Bay of Pigs era, and coming to a close in the autumn of 1965. The proposed schemes—at least eight in number—included poisoned pills, pens, darts, and cigars; telescopic rifles; giving him a diving suit containing a deadly contaminant; placing an exotic seashell filled with explosives in the waters where he went snorkeling; a standard gangland-style execution; a military coup that would doubtless lead to Castro's death; and, most shocking to the American public, securing the services of the Mafia.[2]

Especially disturbing to many observers was that neither moral concerns nor legal considerations had discouraged assassination and that to attempt assassination was to invite retaliation in kind. Few contemporaries questioned the necessity of gathering intelligence intended to help the White House make informed decisions on foreign matters, but many feared that the CIA had gone astray from its original mission of compiling information to delve into the dark and dangerous world of shadow warfare. Covert action in an open, democratic system, the use of pre-emptive attacks on governments not friendly to the United States, and assassination—all violated basic constitutional principles, traditional American beliefs, the fundamental ethics of a republic, the nation's own neutrality laws, and at minimum the peacekeeping mission of the UN Charter. An assassination policy, more than a few Americans worried, put their own state leaders at risk. Indeed, some asked whether there was any connection between the attempts to kill Castro and the assassination of President Kennedy in November 1963.

The United States had taken a new direction in foreign policy at the Bay of Pigs that its proponents considered vital to the republic's survival but was certain to escalate international tensions and incense the American public. Such aggressive action, of course, depended on secrecy, and secrecy invited sinister activities, cover-ups, the use of euphemisms to hide lies in accordance with the guidelines of plausible deniability, and the temptation of resorting to any method under the shroud of national security—including assassination. United States policy in Cuba set a precedent by combining the two elements of assassination and military force in going farther than any corrective previously considered at the highest level of government. Even though such a venture presented the tantalizing possibility of an immediate and decisive victory in the sharply escalating Cold War, it also carried the risk of a devastating defeat whose repercussions would shape policy for years afterward.

Thus the United States in April 1961 pursued a foreign policy fraught with danger and uncertainty. The Eisenhower administration had successfully employed the CIA in devising clandestine operations that undermined unfriendly regimes in Iran, Laos, and Guatemala. And in its waning days it turned to assassination in trying to manipulate the same outcomes in the Congo and the Dominican Republic. But Cuba posed a special case: a fledgling Communist state lying less than a hundred miles off America's southernmost shore. Ironically, three presidents—Eisenhower, Kennedy, and Johnson—found it critical to mesh assassination with military action in an attempt to topple a government that had come to power in January 1959 with the promise of reform, after throwing out the dictator Fulgencio Batista and claiming to be a revolutionary force emanating from the people.

But it was John F. Kennedy who made the critical decision to launch the assault on the Bay of Pigs. Why?

For reasons that remain perplexing, the new president adopted a course of pre-emptive and covert action that he *hoped* would work. Here was, it appeared, his first real opportunity to strike a blow at the Communist world when to do otherwise would be an admission to defeat having serious long-range consequences. Kennedy was in a hurry to make his mark and earn the respect of his Soviet counterparts who considered him too young and inexperienced for the job. A product of the Munich syndrome of appeasing aggressors and of the McCarthy era's warning against appearing soft on Communism, he could not permit an aggressive Communist state to thrive so close to Florida, free to spread its insidious and violent doctrines throughout the hemisphere while openly flaunting its alliance with the Soviet Union.

But perhaps more was involved—personal considerations that compounded the Cold War problems of pre-emption and covert action.

In an almost paradoxical sense, the two new leaders were remarkably similar while profoundly different. Both men, Kennedy forty-three years of age and Castro ten years younger, were charismatic, handsome, intelligent, and inspiring, just entering the highest stages of their professional careers that would end fatally short for the president and, despite all manner of obstacles, continue for the Maximum Leader to the day of this writing. Both were Roman Catholic and came from wealthy and dominating fathers, and both were athletic, idealistic, ambitious, sophisticated, and sexually voracious. They were also highly adept at working the media and public with a wit and charm that exuded confidence, knowledge, and an infectious sense of humor. Interestingly, both leaders developed an inordinate attraction for guerrilla warfare, with Castro using such tactics to take office and Kennedy welcoming the revival of this ancient art of war as a matching of wits on a global chessboard.

But their differences quickly overcame their similarities and led to a bitter and almost personal feud. Whereas Kennedy came from an urban, cosmopolitan life, went to Harvard, and felt comfortable working with the brightest minds possible, Castro had emerged from the rugged rural confines of Oriente province on the eastern side of the island, went to law school at the University of Havana, appeared less self-confident, and preferred to have lesser intellectuals around him.[3] As if a special chemistry were at work, the two leaders soon engaged in fierce and bitter competition, with Castro infuriating the president by fiery and derisive attacks on the United States as the colossus from the north, and Kennedy becoming obsessed with eliminating his southern neighbor despite a host of rational arguments that he posed no threat to U.S. security.

Powerful egos confronted each other from across the Caribbean, and one suspects that by April 1961 Kennedy had been drawn into a nearly personal conflict with a rival state leader who had masterfully goaded him into irrational actions that played themselves out at the Bay of Pigs and left an enduring legacy.

1

Genesis

Assassination was intended to reinforce the plan. There was the thought that Castro would be dead before the landing, [making the invasion] either unnecessary or much easier. —Richard Bissell, post–April 17, 1961

Throughout the 1950s the Eisenhower administration sought to maintain economic and political stability in Cuba as a means for promoting both U.S. commerce and security in the Caribbean world. To facilitate these objectives, the White House supported Fulgencio Batista's iron rule by providing arms and military advisers through the Mutual Security Program until congressional pressure cut off military assistance in the latter part of the decade. On the surface U.S. aid efforts underscored a resounding success, for the very mention of Havana conjured up images of booming and risqué nightclubs, packed and festive gambling casinos, and streets overrun by rollicking tourists with wads of money to spend. The reality was profoundly different. Years earlier the Mafia had forged a virtual alliance with Batista that gave it control over the casinos, drug traffic, and brothels. Furthermore, American businesses owned much of the prime land, and the Cuban government callously ignored its people's welfare. The number of large Cuban landholders had increased greatly after World War II, and the island's middle classes were large, sophisticated, internationally connected, and rapidly growing in the 1950s. Trouble was predictable. Those in Cuba's power circles were filthy rich; the great masses of peasants were dirt poor. Batista's rule took a sharp downspin, most ominously marked by his loss of popularity among his people and the army. His 1952 coup ironically became the critical turning point in legitimizing violent opposition and making revolution a matter of time.[1]

I

Out of this groundswell of discontent emerged Fidel Castro, a charismatic young lawyer and reform advocate who at first attracted little attention when he and his small band of supporters, bolstered by widespread sentiment in the towns and cities, began guerrilla operations against the Batista regime in early 1957. But their numbers grew over the next couple of years, driven by the brilliant politico-psychological strategy Castro pursued, the brutal violence perpetrated by Batista, and the weakness and gradual collapse of his armed forces. When Batista's rule seemed increasingly shaky, the United States withdrew its support, curtailing arms shipments and ensuring his demise. In the ensuing "26th of July Movement," Castro's forces drove Batista into exile and on January 1, 1959, seized control of the government. The Eisenhower administration quickly extended recognition to the fledgling regime, praising its assurances of democratic elections and fundamental freedoms.

But the romantic aura that some observers in Washington wishfully cast over the new leader soon faded. Kangaroo courts meted out mass executions of Batistianos at the *paredón* (the wall), leading many Cubans to seek asylum in the United States, and Castro then forced U.S. interests off the island as a prelude to resurrecting the Cuban economy and putting it under his exclusive control. A pattern of events strongly suggested Castro's allegiance to Communism. More likely, he steered away from the island's small and weak Communist Party because it too carefully avoided confrontational politics and was not likely to become revolutionary. But his suspected tilt toward Communism appeared certain to Washington as he announced an agrarian reform program hinging on the expropriation of more than $1 billion of American properties.[2]

Two weeks after taking over, Castro proclaimed his intention to end American violations of Cuba's integrity. "The Platt Amendment is finished," he declared in referring to the 1901 pact awarding the United States a small patch of land that now housed its naval base at Guantanamo. The new leaders would "neither sell themselves, nor falter nor become intimidated by any threat." To American complaints about the regime's brutal attempts to flush out the Batistianos, Castro shot back: "What do Americans know about . . . a tyrant's atrocities, except in the novels and movies?" Why hadn't they expressed moral indignation over Batista's murderous actions? Before a large public gathering, he accused the United States of mass-murdering Japanese at the end of World War II. "What was done at Hiroshima and Nagasaki? In the name of peace two cities were bombed and more than three hundred thousand human beings killed. We have shot no child, we have shot no woman, we have shot no old people . . . . We are shooting the assassins so that they will not kill our children tomorrow, and when all is said and done the total of assassins we shoot will not be more than four hundred, which is about one assassin for every thousand men, women, and children assassinated in Hiroshima and Nagasaki."[3]

In a move having more repercussions than were recognized at the time, Castro shut down the Mafia's flourishing gambling operations. "We are not only disposed to deport the gangsters," he declared, "but to shoot them." Less than a week later, however, he relented to the pressure of tourist trade advocates and reopened the casinos, although to non-Cuban patrons only. To send a message to the underworld, Castro ordered Cuba's gaming leaders to pay exorbitant taxes, prohibited slot machines as what he derided as mechanical thievery, and, in a masterly piece of political theater, required letters from the U.S. embassy swearing to the "good reputation" of casino workers.[4]

The Eisenhower administration slowly moved toward upending a regime seemingly veering toward Communism. In April 1959, Castro visited Washington, leading the president to leave town rather than have to talk with him. Vice President Richard Nixon met with Castro for three hours and, after finding him "either incredibly naïve about Communism or under Communist discipline," thought him the former. The administration would need to "orient him in the right direction." But this approach seemed insufficient with two well-known Communists who were part of the new regime: Fidel's brother Raúl and the already fabled guerrilla chieftain and Argentine physician Ernesto (Che) Guevara. The new U.S. ambassador in Havana, Philip Bonsal, had desperately tried to forge good relations and argued that no evidence suggested that Castro had come under Communist influence. But CIA director Allen Dulles considered Castro a threat. "Cuba was drifting toward Communism," he told the National Security Council in early December. At another NSC meeting about a week later, Nixon presided with the president out of the country and now took a similar position, insisting that Cuba "was being driven toward Communism more and more." The CIA's deputy director of plans, Richard Bissell, agreed, asserting (mistakenly) that every top officer in that government but one had a Communist connection.[5]

Castro called himself a "utopian Socialist" and never became a member of the Communist Party, but he engaged in strident anti-American harangues and pursued militant efforts to export the revolution to other Latin American countries. If not a Marxist, according to Robert Hurwitch from the State Department, Castro had a "general Marxist orientation" along with the political savvy to realize that popularity at home lay in denouncing America, especially in view of Batista's past relationship with Washington. This predisposition pushed him into "a pro-Soviet, anti-American stance" that ultimately forced him to make a choice between the Cold War adversaries. Cuba had always been a profitable American market, and "through Marxian eyes" he felt confident that Washington would maintain the trade regardless of his actions. Thus Castro could "romp along," counting on Soviet protection while publicly criticizing the United States. The truth remains elusive, but it appears that the Eisenhower administration's heavy-handed tactics encouraged Castro to follow a path he had chosen in his earlier days as a student at the University of Havana. Cuba, it seemed to anxious analysts in Washington, was poised to become a Communist headquarters inside the Western Hemisphere for spreading the violent revolutionary party gospel throughout the Americas.[6]

The White House's initial attempts to undermine the new Cuban regime consisted of an amateurish CIA program designed to discredit Castro before his people and the world. Such schemes included mounting an aerosol assault on his chief radio station intended to leave the mind-blurring impact of LSD on its victims, giving him chemically laced cigars to disorient him before he delivered a speech, and sprinkling thallium salts in his shoes to make his facial hair fall out and thereby undermine his virile reputation as "El Barbudo," or "the Bearded One." No evidence suggests that any of these plans reached the desks of higher officials or that they amounted to much more than back office scheming that never materialized.[7]

By the end of 1959 the White House had escalated its efforts, now determined to *remove* Castro either by covert means or, perhaps, by assassination. In December the CIA considered two programs intended to prepare Cubans for paramilitary operations aimed at overthrowing the regime. The first proposal called for recruiting a small number of Cubans, preferably with military experience, for intensive guerrilla training. These new trainees would then secretly groom small teams of fellow Cubans to infiltrate areas inhabited by Castro's opponents. But the second option promised quicker results. In a handwritten note, supported by Bissell, Dulles approved a mid-December recommendation by the head of the agency's Western Hemisphere Division, Colonel Joseph C. King, to consider "the elimination of Fidel Castro."[8]

Bissell believed that Dulles had actually approved assassination as a last resort but shrewdly covered his real intentions by referring to "elimination," a euphemism that permitted plausible deniability by seeming to condone Castro's overthrow by a general action that did not necessarily result in his death. Bissell knew that his superior was well versed in methods intended to convey meaning without seeming to do so. A wink, a nod, a smile, a shrug, a knowing glance, a moment of silence—all were parts of a tactical arsenal capable of signaling a subtle proposal or approval of an assassination plan never evident in either verbal or written form. Dulles appeared to be a pipe-smoking professorial type not given to violence, and yet he had approved several brutal approaches that included undermining regimes in Iran and Guatemala. And he was not averse to assassination. His first important intelligence assignment had been to kill Adolf Hitler, and in the period just after World War II he delivered a major speech to the New York Bar Association in which he declared that assassination might be "the only means left of overthrowing a modern tyrant."[9]

Bissell also was not what he appeared to be. A Yale-trained economist known for his brilliance, he had left his alma mater's teaching ranks during World War II to take various government positions, including one with the War Shipping Administration that facilitated his attendance at the Quebec, Yalta, and Potsdam conferences, and to work closely with the CIA's predecessor, the Office of Strategic Services. After the war, he became assistant administrator of the Marshall Plan in Germany before heading the collection of classified information on Europe for the Economic Cooperation Administration. He then worked with the Ford Foundation before accepting a CIA position in 1954 as Dulles's special assistant, where he helped develop the U-2 spy plane and four years later, although inexperienced in covert warfare, became deputy director of plans and hence in charge of "black" operations. To Bissell, Castro's assassination offered a realistic solution to a major problem. "My philosophy during my last two or three years in the agency," he wrote in his memoirs, "was very definitely that the end justified the means." Questions of morality did not bother him in high policy; "assassinations are as old as history," he snorted. Snuffing out the life of a dangerous demagogue was far better than toppling a regime by military actions leading to widespread collateral damage. King's first recommendation for "incapacitating" Castro was appealing, but should that measure fail, assassination would become necessary "if we can't do anything else."[10]

Assassination became more than a possibility when Bissell instructed the chief of the CIA's Technical Services Division, Dr. Sidney Gottlieb (aka "Dr. Death"), to develop the means for either disabling or getting rid of the target figure. In the late spring or early summer of 1960, Bissell asked him to make an inventory of the substances in the agency's laboratories that would facilitate the "capability of the clandestine service in the field of incapacitation and elimination." Gottlieb understood his task: Assassination, he later confirmed, was one of the "capabilities" Bissell asked him to study.[11]

II

Pressure for a regime change in Havana continued to mount in the White House as Nixon emerged as an ardent supporter. This position was not surprising, given his zealous search for Communists in the government during the McCarthy hysteria in the earlier part of the decade. If the Communist danger had spread to neighboring Cuba, Nixon was just as ready to provide the needed corrective. "I was the strongest and most persistent advocate for setting up and supporting such a program," he asserted. Bonsal agreed, calling him 'the father of the operation," and Nixon's military aide, Marine Brigadier General Robert Cushman, referred to him as "the project's action officer in the White House." At a National Security Council meeting the day following Dulles's approval of King's proposal, the vice president insisted that the administration should not handle Cuba "through normal diplomatic channels." Both political parties in Congress would soon publicly attack the administration's Latin American policy and force the White House to pursue "a few dramatic things" to show its refusal "to be kicked around completely."[12]

This interventionist task went to a subcommittee of the National Security Council, the "Special Group" established by NSC 5412 in 1955 to deal with clandestine activities. The four-member Special Group met on a weekly basis and included a deputy undersecretary of state, the deputy secretary of defense, the CIA director, and the special assistant to the president for national security affairs. Dulles termed the NSC 5412 directive "one of the most secret documents in the U.S. government," for it authorized the Special Group (sometimes called the 5412 Committee, Forty Group, or Forty Committee) to review covert action proposals and submit them to the president for approval or disapproval. Under NSC oversight, the CIA intended to use its successes in Iran and Guatemala as models for engaging in paramilitary operations aimed at overthrowing Castro.[13]

In the meantime, other signs suggested a quietly jelling CIA program to kill him. Years afterward, U.S. Air Force Colonel L. Fletcher Prouty, then Defense Department liaison with the CIA, claimed that in late 1959 or early 1960 he was privy to a discussion of assassination in a meeting of the Cuba Committee working under the auspices of the NSC's 5412 Committee. This was "the only time I ever sat in a meeting where the object was direct assassination." Most notably, among those present were later high-ranking agency officials Richard Helms and Desmond FitzGerald, both involved in assassination efforts then and later. Helms was probably the highest authority because the meeting, with pictures of the small landing area in Cuba on the table and the gun described, took place in his office in the Air Division at the temporary navy structures next to the Reflecting Pool in Washington. That same night, Prouty received orders to pilot a light plane—an L-28 Helio Courier that needed only 120 feet to land—to transport two Cubans home along with a high-powered rifle fitted with a telescope for assassinating Castro. Considerable circumstantial evidence supports Prouty's assertion. Files from this period confirmed great interest in procuring an air force plane, though making no reference to Cuba as its destination, and they mentioned the air drop of Springfield rifles with telescopic sites.[14]

The new aggressive direction in American foreign policy became evident to some advisers outside the CIA, for at a Pentagon meeting in early January 1960, Livingston Merchant from the State Department termed the Cuban situation "extremely grave" but warned against reckless action. The threat was military and strategic in that it jeopardized the U.S. naval base at Guantanamo and portended the establishment of a "Soviet satellite" capable of influencing the political direction of other Latin American states. In addition, the regime endangered the lives of eight thousand Americans on the island along with American investments in Cuba. But any remedy, Merchant warned, required a "delicate operation" in that the "precipitous disappearance" of Castro could spawn leaders who would be worse yet. The United States had to be sure that a new government acted in America's interests. "In summary, a scalpel is called for; not a meat axe."[15]

The necessity for an immediate corrective had become plain to the president by early 1960. Eisenhower cultivated the image of a genial grand-fatherly type, but his military leadership in World War II more accurately demonstrated a hard-nosed and sometimes hot-tempered disposition that brooked no insults or threats to his country and made the new Cuban leader an almost natural enemy. Castro was hysterically abusive of the United States from his first weeks in office, and his tirades only increased in volume and vitriol. Eisenhower had no need for a "natural" enemy, and he never had a real interest in Latin America or the Caribbean. But the new Cuban leader's public attacks made him impossible to ignore. The previous October, Castro eliminated moderates from his regime and in an all-night address castigated his real and imagined enemies—those "enemies" who were seeking a democratic Cuba and who had believed him committed to it, as he had said repeatedly. Soon afterward, Eisenhower laid the basis for a regime change by approving an anti-Castro propaganda campaign both inside Cuba and throughout Latin America. The State Department and the CIA sought presidential authority to secretly funnel in help to opposition groups in Cuba while making it appear that Castro's ultimate collapse came from his own inept rule. Admiral Arleigh Burke, the chief of naval operations, called for direct military action. The island was about to go Communist, he insisted. For now, however, his remedy remained a distant option.[16]

In mid-January 1960, Dulles followed the president's wishes by urging the Special Group to begin "contingency planning" of a covert project intended to unseat Castro. When the State Department warned that "timing was very important so as to permit a solidly based opposition to take over," Dulles artfully dodged any hint of assassination by insisting that the CIA wanted only to help the Cuban opposition overthrow the regime. It did not contemplate "a quick elimination of Castro."[17]

United States military intervention threatened to become a viable alternative when the State Department reported on the weakness of Castro's opposition and called for "drastic action of a political or economic sort." The chair of the Joint Chiefs of Staff, General Lyman Lemnitzer, direly noted that Castro sought arms from various countries, and Burke observed that the regime could easily secure oil from the Soviet Union because its ships were already transporting the product to regional neighbors Brazil and Uruguay. Cuba under international Communist control would endanger American interests in the Panama Canal and Guantanamo. The United States should prepare for unilateral military action as a "last resort." The Defense Department asserted that "Communist control of Cuba—either by the USSR or indirectly—would be intolerable." That concern in mind, the Joint Chiefs recommended "a program of positive action to re-establish a stable, friendly, non-communist government in Cuba."[18]

From the Eisenhower administration's perspective, the final bits of proof of Castro's Communist allegiance fell into place in February 1960 when, shortly after extending recognition to the People's Republic of China, he signed a treaty with the Soviet Union. Nearly eleven years after the Communists took over the Chinese mainland in October 1949, Cuba joined a host of countries, both Communist and non-Communist, in recognizing the new Beijing regime. Americans discerned a pattern of global Communist conquest, orchestrated by the Kremlin in Moscow. Castro had drawn Soviet acclaim by launching radio and television diatribes against the United States and demanding the surrender of Guantanamo. The Soviet-Cuban pact now posed a direct threat to the United States. It guaranteed arms to Cuba over the next five years, in exchange for sugar, which meant that the island would be stronger militarily.[19]

That same February the White House imposed an embargo on U.S. arms shipments to Cuba, and on March 4 relations sharply deteriorated when a French vessel filled with Belgian arms, the *La Coubre*, mysteriously blew up in Havana harbor, killing more than a hundred people on the ship and shore. At the funeral the next day, Castro accused the United States of the act, distorting the historical record by comparing it with the destruction of the USS *Maine* in 1898 as a pretext for provoking war and justifying United States intervention. "We have reason to believe," he proclaimed, "that this was a premeditated attempt to deprive us of the possibility to get weapons." The charge remains unproven of whether the CIA was responsible, but Castro expected further terrorist acts by the United States. That thought in mind, he prepared to nationalize all American property, mobilized his regular and militia forces, and looked to the Soviets for some friendly reaction to the incident.[20]

Soviet premier Nikita Khrushchev soon responded, heightening American concern by boasting to the international press in Moscow of his new Communist comrade while issuing a dark warning to the United States. The short and rotund leader soon made clear that he was capable of overly dramatic if not unbalanced behavior, constantly searching for that chink in the American armor he might exploit in the growing Cold War. Seeing this opportunity with an equally rash Castro, Khrushchev promised support to any Cuban attempt to close the U.S. base at Guantanamo and warned the United States against threatening the Havana regime. The Monroe Doctrine had "died a natural death and should be buried as every dead body is." It was "sheer iniquity that the United States should be maintaining its Cuban naval base...without a time limit." The U.S. claim that the Soviets wanted a military base in Cuba was "a silly fabrication." The Cubans themselves had asserted that "the best base is the Soviet Union, whose rockets can hit any sector in any part of the globe." Privately Khrushchev exulted over the first request from Castro for more than economic aid and assured him of Soviet and Czech weapons.[21]

Castro's bitter reaction to the La Coubre's explosion had further pushed the United States toward intervention, for five days afterward King warned the recently established CIA Task Force on Cuba that he appeared ready to attack Guantanamo and called for an immediate leadership change. The alternative to military force was to eliminate Castro, his brother Raúl, and Che Guevara "in one package," even though the prospect of success in such a sweeping action was "highly unlikely." The day following King's warning, the National Security Council held a long meeting on how to "bring another government to power in Cuba." Burke wanted a Cuban leader who could attract a large following, but Dulles argued that the island lacked effective anti-Castro figures, and President Eisenhower cautioned against creating "another Black Hole of Calcutta in Cuba." When Dulles suggestively announced that the CIA was working on a solution, Burke came closer to specifics by reiterating the point that "any plan for the removal of Cuban leaders should be a package plan, since many of the leaders around Castro were even worse than Castro." His "disappearance," warned Undersecretary of State Douglas Dillon, could lead to "a Communist take-over."[22]

The inferences of assassination were readily discernible in the discussion, even though no one mentioned the word. Burke claimed that the subject did not come up at the NSC meeting and that President Eisenhower never would have permitted such talk or action. General Andrew Goodpaster, President Eisenhower's staff secretary and defense liaison officer, insisted he never heard any discussion of assassination. And General Gordon Gray, the president's special assistant for national security affairs and his representative on the Special Group, asserted that Eisenhower never discussed assassination and that the subject never came before the Special Group or anyone else. In a curious attempt to distinguish between killing Castro in an outright assassination and killing him in the course of an invasion, Gray insisted that Dulles's reference to a plan under way meant an *invasion* by Cuban exiles and *not* "a targeted attempt on Castro's life." Gray admitted, however, that some advisers at the March 10 meeting may have had assassination in mind, but he said it never came under serious discussion as a "program of action by the President or even the Forty Group."[23]

President Eisenhower decided against the Joint Chiefs' call for military action and supported instead a covert program run by the CIA. The U.S. Country Team in Havana had opposed White House intervention, slowing the move toward a military solution and contributing to this decision. On March 17 the president approved "A Program of Covert Action Against the Castro Regime," which Bissell had developed and the Special Group supported. The program, code-named Operation Pluto, sought to overthrow Castro by organizing an opposition group outside Cuba, spreading anti-regime propaganda among the Cuban people, establishing a covert group inside Cuba to foment unrest and build underground connections with dissidents, and developing a paramilitary contingent outside Cuba to engage in covert actions on the island. The CIA Task Force would report to Bissell as head of clandestine operations, who was answerable to his two superiors, Dulles and his deputy director, General Charles Cabell. And the CIA, of course, was directly responsible to the president.[24]

Immediately after the White House meeting, the CIA made preparations for implementing the program. It called for three hundred recruits for guerrilla training outside the United States, established "Radio Swan" on Great Swan Island off Cuba to begin the propaganda effort, and took the first steps toward creating the Frente Revolucionario Democrático (FRD), a front organization of Cubans on the island who would employ guerrilla tactics, provide cover for the preparation of a small-scale military force to instigate uprisings, and facilitate air drops of guns and other materials. The CIA also acquired a number of safe houses in Miami, instituted paramilitary training in that city's Coral Gables business area under the cover of a job placement company, and began a similar preparation program in Panama in June. The following month the first thirty Cubans recruited by the FRD arrived in a jungle area in Mexico to begin military training.[25]

But these measures did not seem sufficient, and pressure soon grew to change the small-scale guerrilla focus to a military contingent large enough to attack Cuba. During the summer of 1960 the CIA Task Force expressed little confidence in the guerrillas' capacity to throw out Castro and suggested that a Cuban strike force of up to three hundred infantrymen hit Cuba in coordination with the paramilitary contingent. The task force also called for a small Cuban rebel air force comprised of discarded U.S. fighter-bombers—lightweight, fast-strike twin-engine Douglas B-26 Invaders that would, as in World War II, engage in close ground-support bombing and strafing missions. Their particular attractions were their ready availability in surplus quantities in Arizona and the ease with which they could be disguised as part of Castro's force, because he also had B-26s. To facilitate what was fast becoming an amphibious operation, the CIA opened an army communications center at the former Richmond Naval Air Station then under lease by the University of Miami.[26]

In mid-August, the president approved a $13 million budget and the use of Defense Department personnel and equipment but specifically ruled out U.S. soldiers in a combat role. Furthermore, the training center would move to Guatemala because of the growing publicity about activities in Miami and Panama. Dulles noted that about thirty instructors had completed their paramilitary training in the Panama Canal Zone and would soon relocate in Guatemala to prepare for an operation that had grown to *five hundred* Cubans. When Secretary of Defense Thomas Gates expressed concern about U.S. military personnel appearing on the Cuban beaches, Bissell shrugged away that fear. Approximately twenty U.S. Air Force trainers would concentrate only on the transports hauling men and supplies, and they would wear civilian clothes, assume bogus names, and work for the CIA. "There would be no conceivable hazard involved and they would get no closer to paramilitary operations than the airstrip in Guatemala."[27]

III

Concurrent with this growing military effort ran an unspoken idea that soon became an integral part of the invasion—the assassination of Castro. There can be little doubt that the Eisenhower administration's repeated references to Castro's "elimination," "removal," and "disappearance" were synonymous with assassination, but the real meaning of the terms remained obscured by euphemistic language. Indeed, the president used the same wording when he told the National Security Council in late July that Dominican leader Rafael Trujillo had infuriated other Latin American states with his brutal and sadistic rule and that he would have to be "eliminated" before they would support U.S. policy in Cuba. And in Africa, Dulles thought he had the president's support in ordering the CIA to "eliminate" Congo leader Patrice Lumumba for his alleged Communist leanings. Trujillo died at the hands of Dominican dissidents armed with weapons provided by the CIA, and Lumumba was killed by someone having no connection with the agency, but it is most revealing that *Bissell* had devised and managed the CIA's efforts (even if not carried out by its operatives) to eliminate the two leaders. In the case of Cuba, the CIA—likewise through Bissell—was in charge of the overthrow operation and naturally assumed control over assassination as well. Thus the same CIA officer crafted both the assassination plot and the invasion plan, making it unlikely that he separated the two overthrow approaches into two tracks of action that paralleled each other but never met. Bissell viewed assassination as the proper predecessor to the landing and reported directly to Dulles, who likewise considered assassination an appropriate part of the project. "Assassination was intended to reinforce the plan," Bissell insisted. "There was the thought that Castro would be dead before the landing, [making the invasion] either unnecessary or much easier."[28]

In August 1960, after the Eisenhower administration approved the program to overthrow Castro, Bissell approached Colonel Sheffield Edwards, the CIA's director of the Office of Security, to propose a "gangster-type action" based on identifying potential Cuban assassins. Edwards, Bissell knew, was a hard-line, highly experienced agency figure who had a wide range of "assets" or contacts, appointed case officers to agency projects, and could provide guidance and damage control if the scheme leaked to the press. They pondered the most vital prerequisite: an anti-Castro group in Cuba that had, first, motive for killing the new chieftain and, second, a web of connections throughout the island that would facilitate contacts with dissidents and establish the basis for a popular uprising. The answer became evident as Bissell and Edwards winnowed their options to the Mafia.[29]

Their reasoning seemed impeccable. After Castro's ascension to power, he had enraged the Mafia by shutting down the casinos and terminating its control over prostitution and the drug traffic. The Mafia, Bissell and Edwards realized, needed no greater motive for vengeance. Moreover, its well-known desire to regain control of gaming provided the CIA with a sound cover story by making it appear that the Mafia was acting out of vengeance and on its own. With the CIA's ingenuity and the mob's contacts in Cuba, the two organizations could collaborate in Castro's assassination without arousing suspicions of U.S. involvement.[30]

To avoid direct CIA contact with the underworld, Bissell and Edwards hired a "cut-out"—Washington private investigator and former FBI agent Robert Maheu—to acquire the Mafia's services in arranging a contract hit on Castro for $150,000. Maheu was a devoutly religious man who wrestled with some of his actions for the government but reconciled them as vital to national security. He had performed a number of tasks for the CIA on a contract basis, including bugging rooms, arranging female companionship for clients, and, in one imaginative scheme, securing the help of actor-singer Bing Crosby and his brother Larry in producing a brief Cold War propaganda film depicting neutralist President Achmed Sukarno of Indonesia having sex with a Soviet-planted "honey-trap" (a woman hired to acquire intelligence by providing sexual favors). The CIA denied using the film; Maheu insisted that the agency circulated stills from the film that helped to discredit Sukarno.[31]

More important, however, was Maheu's friendship with one Johnny Roselli, an *advocato* for the Mafia whose responsibility was to arbitrate or mediate disagreements within the organization. "Uncle Johnny," as he was affectionately known in the Maheu household, was what Maheu termed "one of the most powerful mob figures in the country" and "had access to the highest levels of the Mafia." A handsome and flamboyant Los Angeles–Las Vegas–based troubleshooter, Roselli was an illegal Sicilian émigré known to the underworld as "Don Giovanni." Self-indulgent and a master of seduction, he was usually decked out in a dark tailored suit and custom-made shirt with diamond cuff links—in short, a tall and silver-maned *impresionado* who commanded attention by his presence. Roselli had worked for Chicago gangland leader Al Capone and enjoyed a reputation for "fixing" problems by making offers his patrons could not refuse.[32]

Beneath Roselli's affable and sparkling exterior lay a hardened and deadly Mafioso who could be brutally efficient in closing deals for his friends. Perhaps the most vivid illustration of this trait was his success in landing struggling actor-singer Frank Sinatra a leading role in Columbia Pictures' 1953 blockbuster movie *From Here to Eternity.* Its producer-director, Roselli's former employer Harry Cohn, not only hated the singer but thought him wrong for the part. Roselli interceded on Sinatra's behalf, making Cohn an offer he could not refuse. Sinatra won the Academy Award as best supporting actor, an outcome that made his career. Indeed, according to some accounts, Cohn's conversion became the basis for the fictional account of singer-actor Johnny Fontane in Mario Puzo's best-selling novel *The Godfather,* which immortalized the horse-head-in-the-bed scene in one of Hollywood's all-time most popular movies.[33]

A high-risk venture to be sure, but without Roselli's assistance, Maheu knew, there could be no plan.

In the late summer of 1960, Maheu met with Roselli at the Brown Derby Restaurant in Beverly Hills, California, where he appealed to his friend's patriotism in enlisting his help in killing Castro. They had had numerous lunches after their first meeting a year earlier, and Maheu had grown accustomed to Roselli's sharp and snazzy look as he slid into the booth. There, surrounded by Hollywood celebrities and other dream-makers in Tinseltown, Maheu unveiled a proposal over coffee that he emphasized must remain top secret. The CIA needed his assistance against Communism by getting rid of Castro "any which-way we could." Before Roselli could speak, Maheu continued. "Nobody could know the details—not even the rest of the U.S. government. This was a 'cut-out' operation, and the Agency must have total deniability."[34]

After a few moments of silence, Roselli broke out in laughter. "Me? You want *me* to get involved with Uncle Sam? The Feds are tailing me wherever I go. They go to my shirt maker to see if I'm buying things with cash. They go to my tailor to see if I'm using cash there. They're always trying to get something on me. Bob, are you sure you're talking to the right guy?" When Maheu insisted that he was "serious, *very* serious," Roselli sat in stunned disbelief, staring at his friend while tapping his fingers on the table. Roselli was skeptical, leery of a government sting intended to subject him to deportation for illegally entering the country while a child. Hadn't he undergone intense questioning in 1950 by the crime investigative committee led by Senator Estes Kefauver? Hadn't a second and still ongoing congressional committee inquiry headed by Senator John McClellan shown extraordinary acuity in exposing organized crime?[35]

Maheu pushed harder. "It's up to you to pick whom you want, but it's got to be set up so that Uncle Sam isn't involved—ever. If anyone connects you with the U.S. government, I will deny it," he declared. "If you say Bob Maheu brought you into this, that I was your contact man, I'll say you're off your rocker, you're lying, you're trying to save your hide. I'll swear by everything holy that I don't know what in hell you're talking about." Furthermore, Maheu continued, this was "a one-shot deal. I won't ever do business with you again." He assured Roselli of total confidentiality. "I won't ever reveal the content of any private conversations I may overhear while I'm in your company. It's none of my business or anyone else's."[36]

Roselli continued to sit quietly, brooding over his friend's proposal but clearly beginning to come around. It must be a "government project," Roselli finally declared in breaking the stiff silence. "Otherwise, I wouldn't be interested." Authority came from "high-level sources," Maheu assured him—the CIA. Still suspicious of a trap by his old nemesis—the Feds—Roselli insisted on verifying the claim with a government representative. Maheu complied, arranging a meeting in mid-September with the CIA's case officer assigned to the Mafia project, "Big Jim" O'Connell (whom Roselli had met in Maheu's Virginia home), at the Plaza Hotel in New York City. There, in a luxurious guest room, Roselli accepted the job, and the three conspirators laid out plans for taking Castro's life—in a meeting ironically taking place at the same time the Cuban leader was at the United Nations in New York and the press was highlighting the U.S. government's efforts to protect him.[37]

Maheu later insisted that Roselli agreed to the arrangement because of loyalty to country and *not* to worm his way into a deal with the U.S. government to avert deportation. The truth was, "as corny as it may sound," Roselli "down deep...thought it was his 'patriotic' duty." Like Maheu, Roselli legitimized Castro's assassination as a "patriotic" act and agreed to find the right people "to perform the desired project." As he attested years afterward, "I did it for honor and dedication."[38]

Roselli now opened doors to the underworld. As part of Mafia protocol, he facilitated Maheu's connection with Sam Giancana, the hotheaded and psychopathic yet charming and affable godfather of the Chicago organization known as "the Outfit," who was Roselli's boss and had also trained under Capone, and with the cool-mannered, sinister-looking Santo Trafficante from Florida, who had followed his father into the underworld, worked with Roselli in managing one of Cuba's hotel casinos, and was godfather of the Mafia's southern branch.

The two principals in the operation, Roselli and Giancana, refused any compensation. All four men later claimed that they joined the assassination operation for patriotic reasons, but it could not have been coincidental that the three crime dons' cooperation with the U.S. government might protect them from jail sentences for past and future crimes.[39]

The conspirators first had to clear a major snag—the method for killing Castro. Before Trafficante joined the group, Maheu had related the CIA's recommendation for a mob slaying with machine guns. "A gangland-style killing!" exclaimed Giancana as he and Roselli stared at Maheu in disbelief. The three sat across from each other in the bar of one of Giancana's investment ventures, Miami Beach's swank Fontainebleu Hotel, all dumbfounded by the suggestion. Who would kill for money, knowing he had no chance for escape? Poison was preferablè, Roselli insisted—"nice and clean, without getting into any kind of out-and-out ambushing." Yes, Giancana agreed—no "ambush or shootout but a slow-acting pill slipped into Castro's food or drink that left no trace and gave the assassin time to get away."[40]

That issue resolved, the band of conspirators turned to finding someone who could recruit a potential assassin. Roselli suggested one Rafael "Macho" Gener, a Cuban exile in Miami who had been an official in the Carlos Prío Socarrás regime that Batista had ousted in 1952. Gener had initially aligned with Castro during his rise to power but later turned against him and worked with the underworld. Gener had trusted contacts within the Castro regime who were also disenchanted and would eagerly participate in a patriotic effort that promoted both U.S. and Cuban interests—as well as his own. Trafficante spoke Spanish and would serve as translator.[41]

About three weeks later, at a late September 1960 meeting in a Cuban's home in the Venetian Causeway area of Miami, Maheu, Roselli, and Trafficante discussed the matter for hours with a number of Cuban dissidents, including Gener and prominent exile leader Antonio Varona, prime minister under Batista's predecessor. Varona owned an insurance company with a branch in Puerto Rico and was among the few who had stayed on with Batista and soon developed links with the Mafia and its casinos.

Varona had created the Revolutionary Rescue Movement (Rescate) as a step toward acquiring the Cuban presidency for himself and was now civilian head of the revolutionary group FRD. Sharply critical of Castro's land laws, Varona appeared arrogant and unlikable but found support in the CIA and the State Department in conspiring against the revolutionary regime. Yet he exercised great care in dealing with these officers, particularly those from the CIA. "They were neither friends nor enemies," he cynically remarked. "They were Americans."

At the meeting, Maheu and Roselli assured the would-be assassin of ample money and poison for the job. Varona suggested two choices: Either plant a bomb in Castro's desk or poison his food at a restaurant he frequented. Gener, however, offered a third option. He had contacted a prospective assassin in Cuba—Juan Orta, a former recipient of kickbacks from the gambling syndicate who was embittered over having lost that income after Castro's rise to power. Orta held a high position in the office of the prime minister as his private secretary, giving him direct access to Castro. Maheu and Roselli preferred this proposal. Trafficante would assure delivery of the poison pills.[42]

If the underworld sought immunity from prosecution as its reward, such recompense must have seemed to Bissell and Edwards a small price to pay for its service to national security. They considered the Mafia's role so integral to Castro's overthrow that they ignored the dangers of working with a crime organization. Bissell intended to stage the landing at the same time as Castro's assassination to assure a widespread insurrection. "Covert intervention," Bissell later told the Council on Foreign Relations in Washington, was "probably most effective in situations where a comprehensive effort is undertaken with a number of separate operations designed to support and complement one another and to have a cumulatively significant effect." And in his posthumously published memoirs, Bissell asserted that "as I moved forward with plans for the brigade, I hoped the Mafia would achieve success."[43]

Further evidence for the connection between assassination and a successful brigade landing came from the project chief of the CIA Task Force on Cuba, Jacob Esterline (aka Jake Engler), who was well schooled in the art of covert warfare and a longtime veteran of the agency. After serving the OSS as a guerrilla commander in Burma during World War II, he became the first chief instructor at Fort Benning's Guerrilla Warfare School in Georgia in the early 1950s. Then, in a career-making move, he headed the task force for the overthrow of Guatemalan president Jacobo Arbenz in 1954. As his reward, Esterline became CIA station chief in Guatemala, staying there for three years before taking the same position in Venezuela, where he remained until 1960, when he began working for the Cuba Task Force and played a key role in drafting the March 1960 plan for overthrowing Castro. On the Cuban matter, he noted that beginning in the autumn of 1960 about $200,000 for the assassination effort came from money earmarked for the overthrow. "All of a sudden," he explained in an interview years afterward, "I started getting requests to authorize big payments, $60,000, $100,000, and [not knowing what they were for] I refused them." A call came from Colonel King in the CIA's Western Hemisphere division, telling him in no uncertain terms that "you're going to have to sign these things." Esterline adamantly refused to release any funds without an explanation.

"J.C., I'm not going to sign this thing. If it's something you can't tell me about, then you better get somebody here that you tell about it."

"I can't because you're not cleared," explained King.

"Get someone else to sign them," Esterline shot back.

"Oh no, we can't do that," King asserted as the conversation abruptly ended with his assurance that he would get back to Esterline.[44]

A few days later, Esterline received a call informing him that "you're going to be briefed." Edwards soon arrived, accompanied by O'Connell. When the two emissaries revealed the assassination plot involving the Mafia, Esterline was mystified. "So all of a sudden the agency gets sucked into being a part of it, which I never could understand how this made any sense." Going back to King, Esterline asked, "J.C., do you realize that this is going to make people take this whole thing less seriously if somebody thinks there's an easy way out with Castro being killed?"

"Nobody's going to find out," King assured him.

"What are we going to tell Bissell?" asked Esterline.

"Don't tell Bissell," King replied, deadpan. "Bissell's not cleared."[45]

Not until years afterward did Esterline discover Bissell's central role in the assassination program. "I found out Bissell was the guy behind it," Esterline declared with disgust. Though a hardened veteran of the CIA's wars, he found this plan repulsive and "absolutely immoral."[46]

With the Mafia in place by late September 1960, Bissell and Edwards briefed Dulles and Cabell on the plan, and they approved. The discussion focused on "an intelligence operation," Bissell recalled, but "the objective of the operation was made unmistakably clear." Edwards talked in "somewhat circumlocutious terms" about "the plan that he had discussed with syndicate representatives." Edwards later concurred, asserting that he and Bissell avoided "bad words" such as "assassination" but "conveyed the message to Mr. Dulles." Edwards told the two top officers of the CIA that "a plan had been prepared for their use." In late June 2007, the CIA released the "Family Jewels," a collection of top-secret documents that for the first time publicly and explicitly tied the CIA director to the plan by noting that he "gave his approval" of the "gangster-type action" to assassinate Castro. Dulles, Edwards recalled, "merely nodded, presumably in understanding and approval."[47]

Did the CIA's senior officers share this plan with the White House? Bissell thought that Dulles told President Eisenhower of the assassination operation and that the president approved, "perhaps only tacitly." This claim did not rest on "hard evidence," Bissell admitted, but on "pure personal opinion" based on his knowledge of the "command relationship, of Allen Dulles as an individual, and of his mode of operations." If so, Bissell continued, Dulles would have used a "circumlocutious approach" in an effort "to protect the President" from covert actions. But General Goodpaster thought Bissell's guesses about vague language "completely unlikely," declaring Dulles no confidant of President Eisenhower. In another defense of the president, Thomas Parrott, who was Dulles's assistant working as secretary of the Special Group, dismissed Bissell's claim by testifying that Dulles always gave specific authorization for projects and not "tacit approval." Later CIA director Richard Helms probably came closer to the truth when he declared that if Dulles knew of the plot, he would never have privately informed the president of its details, for this would have violated the doctrine of plausible deniability.[48]

Some years later, Bissell remarked that his greatest concern about working with the Mafia to kill Castro was the "unfavorable publicity, if by chance it leaked out." His worst fears almost came to pass in late October 1960 when the CIA became involved in an illegal wiretapping episode in Las Vegas that threatened to expose the assassination plan and tie it to the White House. During the initial CIA-Mafia discussions in Miami, Giancana learned that his mistress, singer Phyllis McGuire of the highly popular McGuire Sisters Trio, might also be having an affair with Dan Rowan of the Rowan and Martin comedy team. Maheu arranged CIA assistance in bugging Rowan's hotel room, but a private detective firm hired to do the job bungled the operation by using illegal wiretaps that local authorities discovered. Potential felony charges led to FBI involvement and a successful

CIA plea that the Justice Department not prosecute, on the grounds that it would expose the Cuba project and jeopardize national security. Bissell could never have imagined such a scenario, but he was not naïve. "I knew it was serious. I knew these were Mafia leaders. And I knew they were in a position to make very damaging revelations about the agency. But we thought it was all under control."[49]

2

Trinidad

Guatemala does not need nor is it offering sites for
foreign bases. Neither has any friendly nation requested
permission to establish bases on national territory.
—Guatemalan president Miguel Ydígoras Fuentes,
October 1960

[President Kennedy insisted that] the United States
cannot allow the Castro Government to continue to exist
in Cuba. —Robert McNamara, January 24, 1961

Washington's policymakers meanwhile shifted the emphasis from infiltration to invasion by developing Operation Trinidad, a plan that moved
forward almost in concert with their concern that Castro would attack the
American naval base at Guantanamo and force a war. From the moment
Castro came to power, the United States feared that he would try to nullify
or renounce the 1903 treaty granting America's hold on that small piece of
land. An attack, the Joint Chiefs grimly asserted, would constitute an act of
war. Burke assured his Pentagon and State Department colleagues that the

navy had movie cameras ready to record all events along the base perimeter. If Castro's forces hit Guantanamo, declared Merchant from the State Department, "that is it—we are at war."[1]

I

Not everyone believed Castro would risk war over the base. Admiral Robert Dennison, the commander in chief of the Atlantic Command (CINCLANT) in Norfolk, Virginia, told the State Department that sabotage posed the greatest threat. President Eisenhower was dubious about going to war "merely because Cuba attacked Guantanamo." Americans "did not want to destroy the Cuban people whom, we believe, are friendly to the U.S."[2]

Castro's military buildup nonetheless alarmed Washington, particularly if armed with Soviet missiles. In early October the Defense Department recommended U-2 reconnaissance flights to determine whether missile sites were under construction. A thousand anti-Castro guerrillas operated in the Escambray Mountains, but they were poorly armed and supplied and lacked unity and leadership. Soviet military goods continued to flow into the country, including jeeps, machine guns, anti-aircraft artillery, and perhaps tanks. Although the CIA said nothing about missile sites and could not be certain whether the Soviets had sent jet-powered MIGs, it reported Cuban pilots and maintenance people undergoing training in Czechoslovakia.[3]

Radio Swan meanwhile stepped up its anti-Castro campaign. The Catholic Welfare Bureau in Miami had launched Operation Peter Pan, which its founders declared was an effort to save Cuban children from Communist indoctrination by relocating them in the United States. Havana denounced it as a U.S.-sponsored program aimed at destabilizing Cuban families and undermining Castro's rule; Radio Swan defended the operation as humanitarian, alleging that like the mythical Peter Pan, who took three children to Never-Never Land, the Communists intended to steal the nation's children at the age of five and keep them in indoctrination programs until they were eighteen. The parents must seek guidance from the Catholic clergy in Florida.[4]

Washington's growing apprehension about the Cuban threat led to a policy change in mid-November. The concern over Guantanamo; the Soviet-sponsored military buildup in Cuba; the spread of Communism throughout the hemisphere—all these factors dramatically intensified the pressure for decisive action. After months of "patience and forbearance," Robert Hurwitch declared from the State Department, the administration considered the Castro regime Communist and "beyond redemption." As forerunner to the overthrow, the CIA in the previous spring of 1960 had helped small teams of guerrillas wielding weapons and explosives to infiltrate Cuba and join the insurgents in the Escambrays. But when the Special Group met in November to reassess the overthrow project, it received a State Department report showing that the guerrilla program was not succeeding because of the difficulty in air-dropping supplies. Merchant noted "the changing concept of the operation" as a consensus developed that covert operations should give way to overt measures.[5] The Special Group recommended a middle ground between continuing guerrilla tactics based on infiltration and resorting to direct U.S. military action: an amphibious invasion—code-named Bumpy Road—by an enlarged Cuban force trained and supplied by the United States.

The CIA Task Force took the first step toward an invasion by arranging the construction of what was, at best, a substandard air strip in Guatemala about eight hundred miles from Cuba that would serve both bombers and transports, all without U.S. markings. An American firm soon completed a five-thousand-foot airfield as part of a military installation at Retalhuleu on two huge coffee plantations owned by Robert Alejos, the brother of Carlos, who was Guatemala's ambassador to the United States. Carlos had secured permission from President Ydígoras Fuentes for the CIA to set up a training center known as Camp Trax, located about thirty miles from Retalhuleu and resting high in the Sierra Madre Mountains on the Pacific side of the coast. The airstrip was barely passable, having only a few feet of clearance from the parking ramp and a runway extending a scant four feet on each side of the landing gear. And it was highly vulnerable to attack. Communist guerrillas from the hills could easily sabotage the planes, given the poor defensive capabilities of the Guatemalan guards, the run-down fence encasing the area, and the possibility of disabling the first plane on the narrow runway and thereby bottling up the others.[6]

Furthermore, the site was almost impossible to access by land and had no training provisions and hardly any living accommodations. It took several months to construct buildings and maritime and air bases, and to bring in supplies and matériel. In the meantime tropical rain pelted the area, food and other supplies ran short, and the failure to screen all recruits allowed troublemakers to slip in among the trainees and disrupt the program. The base was anything but secret. Workers on trucks carrying coffee beans from the plantations joined passengers on a nearby railway in gawking at the strange activities on the base.[7]

Problems in Guatemala continued to mount as the November decision for an invasion created mammoth space problems due to the projected influx of Cubans for training. Furthermore, the Americans on site had not received word of the potential shift in plans and would soon have to cope with a great number of recruits. When the State Department noted the problems in Guatemala, the marine officer in charge of paramilitary training, Colonel Jack Hawkins, argued that the best airfield was at the deserted Opa-Locka Naval Air Base near the Everglades at the northwest fringe of Miami. The Special Group had no solution but firmly rejected a suggestion to establish a base in the United States. Not until later that month were ten seven-man guerrilla teams ready for dispatch to Cuba, only to have to wait until infiltration plans arrived.[8]

On November 29 President Eisenhower resolved that final problem by approving the operation's new military direction. Sixty men were to work as guerrillas with the Cuban resistance while the great mass of remaining forces began training in conventional warfare. The critical factor remained the same: igniting an internal insurrection.[9]

The Guatemalan base was no secret. The Soviet news agency Tass announced in late October that an American arms buildup was under way in Guatemala in preparation for invading Cuba. That same day a student group less than a hundred miles from the base made the same charge, and the following month Cuban intelligence informed the Soviet Union that CIA officers were training Cuban exiles in Guatemala. President Fuentes tried to cloud the facts by vigorously denying the allegation. "Guatemala does not need nor is it offering sites for foreign bases. Neither has any friendly nation requested permission to establish bases on national territory." The air base at Retalhuleu "was one of several established in a program designed to re-orient military training in Guatemala toward guerilla warfare." The charge that his country had become a training center for a Cuban invasion was a "lot of lies."[10]

Amid the denials, Guatemala became a veritable armed camp. Seventeen World War II–vintage B-26 bombers sat alongside the runway, each fitted with eight machine guns in the metal nose but vulnerable to rear attack because of the removal of its tail guns to lighten the plane's weight and enable it to carry extra fuel on the wings for the long flight to the target.

Outside the armory sat an assortment of armaments that included more than a thousand fragmentation bombs, each one 250 pounds of deadly shrapnel; 500 demolition bombs weighing 500 pounds each that burrowed into the ground and blew up everything in a broad area; nearly a thousand five-inch rockets; and more than 300 napalm bombs weighing 750 pounds each and containing a gelatinous mixture of gasoline and white powder that burst into liquid fire on impact. Inside the armory were hundreds of boxes packed with hand grenades, pistols, machine guns, and Browning automatic rifles. The bombs would turn Castro's airfields into "baseball fields," boasted Edward Ferrer, a former Cuban commercial airline pilot now working for the CIA in dropping weapons to fellow insurgents.[11]

The Guatemalan camp sat too far from Cuba for the planes to make a round-trip, so the CIA secured permission from Nicaraguan president Luis Somoza to use an airstrip and nearby docks at Puerto Cabezas on the Caribbean coast, about five hundred miles from the target point in central Cuba and within flight range. Strategists estimated seven hours of flying time, including one hour over Cuba. From Guatemala eleven huge transports—four twin-engine C-46s and seven four-engine C-54s (the latter used for military action in the Korean War)— would fly the trainees and their supplies to the "Tide," their recently acquired staging area at Happy Valley in Puerto Cabezas. The B-26s lacked the maneuverability and speed necessary for air-to-air fighting and were particularly vulnerable to enemy attack from their unprotected rear, but their machine guns, rockets, bombs, and napalm gave them the capacity to hit key Cuban military targets prior to the invasion, and to provide air cover on D-Day. The assault force would board covered trucks and leave the docks at night for the final leg of the journey by sea to Cuba. In overthrowing Castro, Somoza told the CIA, "I'm willing to support you, but be sure you get rid of that son of a bitch, or you are going to live with him the rest of your life."[12]

II

Meanwhile, back in Washington the Special Group pondered other supportive steps in the plan, including a triple assassination intended to incite an uprising on the eve of invasion. At an early November meeting, Livingston Merchant from the State Department carefully skirted the word *assassination* by asking whether planning had begun about "taking direct positive action" against the two Castros and Che Guevara. Admittedly, the move must accomplish the nearly impossible task of taking out all three men at the same time, but it was worth the gamble because their fall would leave the Cuban government "leaderless and probably brainless." The CIA deputy director, General Charles Cabell, was well aware of the secret Mafia arrangement and recognized the problems in recruiting *one* assassin. He declared it "beyond our capabilities" to find enough qualified Cubans who could simultaneously kill all three leaders.[13]

There can be no doubt that "direct positive action" meant assassination. The Defense Department's deputy assistant for special operations, Edward Lansdale, thought the three killings part of the broader program of overthrowing the regime by "joint political-military-economic action." Castro's continued rule was "absolutely intolerable," making it incumbent on the administration to "bring about a desired change." Gray admitted that the "positive action" under discussion "could include assassination," but Thomas Parrott disagreed. In taking the minutes of the meeting, he insisted that "direct positive action" was *not* a euphemism for assassination and that he did not use euphemisms in recording Special Group discussions except in matters involving the president. Bissell, however, assumed that since Cabell knew of the CIA-Mafia program, he considered the term a euphemism for assassination. He also found it "difficult to understand" why Cabell considered it impossible to eliminate all three Cuban leaders at the same time. Furthermore, Bissell thought it significant that the idea of assassination came up in a Special Group meeting. This meant that this action "in that context was not unthinkable, even to ... well-trained and experienced Foreign Service Officers." Particularly noteworthy is the CIA's "Official History" of this period. Its author, Jack Pfeiffer, insisted that "the white-hatted guys" in Washington would not have objected to a successful assassination and noted "a number of such activities" under way. "Only someone ... in omphaloskepsis would have a problem understanding the meaning to be anything other than assassination."[14]

A change in Washington's leadership did not alter the progression of events regarding Cuba. That same month of November, Democratic Senator John F. Kennedy narrowly defeated Republican Vice President Richard Nixon for the presidency. In the heated campaign, both candidates took a hard line on Cuba, with Nixon having to remain silent on the invasion plan and thereby unable to counter his adversary's charge that the administration was soft on Castro. President Eisenhower had another two months in office, and even though a lame duck he continued the Cuban preparations until turning over the government to his successor.

In a curious development, Antonio Varona, one of the assassination conspirators at the Venetian Causeway talks, met with Hurwitch and three others from the State Department in Washington to discuss anti-Castro measures in Cuba. Assassination, of course, never appeared in the minutes of this late November 1960 meeting, but Varona's plea for direct military action did. Castro was hurting American prestige throughout Latin America, Varona warned, and anti-Castro groups in Cuba had become impatient with Washington's policy of nonintervention, particularly in view of the rapidly growing Soviet presence. Castro only had about 30 percent support on the island, but this number included workers and peasants, who were "the most combative type." Of those great numbers who opposed him, only about 20 percent of them were willing to fight. His hundred thousand militia forces had Soviet and Czech weapons but were not yet trained in their use. Within three months, however, they would master the cannon, tanks, and other military apparel, meaning that each passing day made his overthrow more difficult. An invasion force of about three thousand in number could seize an operating area and declare itself the new government of Cuba, thereby attracting enough defectors to convince the United States to grant recognition and support. Soviet tanks and heavy weaponry made U.S. armed intervention "unavoidable."[15]

Perhaps running against this clock, the following December the CIA Task Force developed a detailed invasion plan code-named Operation Trinidad, the target area a town of eighteen thousand inhabitants on Cuba's southeastern coast chosen for the amphibious landing. Trinidad lay less than three miles from the Escambray Mountains to the west and near the Casilda docks on the southern side of the island. The potential landing zone had superb beaches located near hills running as high as four thousand feet and providing an excellent habitat for nearly a thousand anti-Castro guerrillas. According to Hawkins, Trinidad offered the distinct military advantage of isolation from the enemy. Mountains ridged the west, a river impossible to ford ringed the north, and only two bridges to the east permitted passage of Castro's tanks and other vehicles. Castro thus had no access from the north, for the main throughway came out of Santa Clara and ran south across the two bridges that the Cuban invasion force would destroy. The only other approach was from Cienfuegos in the west along the coast, and the bridges along the way were also susceptible to destruction. The area thus provided isolation and, since Trinidad had a reputation for anti-Castro sentiment, was a veritable hotbed of local assistance and recruits that the CIA could arm. Guerrilla control of the territory would cut Cuba in half and inflict a death blow on the regime.[16]

Admittedly, the landing force at Trinidad would encounter more than nominal opposition. Castro had a police battalion and forty thousand militia, along with five thousand regulars around the Escambray Mountains. But the militiamen were of poor fighting quality and had put up only token resistance to the guerrillas. Furthermore, he had never deployed his planes against the guerrillas in the Trinidad area, and the rough terrain prohibited the use of tanks and artillery. After the invasion forces secured the area, they intended to arm up to twenty-five hundred anti-Castro civilians (according to one CIA officer's estimate), take over the hospital and other buildings, work closely with local leaders while establishing contact with the guerrillas, and use the airport for replenishing supplies. Although the airfield was not large enough to accommodate B-26s, the chief advantages of the Trinidad Plan lay in the chances for a popular uprising and the refuge afforded by the mountains. If the landing force failed to hold the beaches, it could escape into the Escambrays and ally with the indigenous guerrillas while dependent on air-dropped supplies.[17]

The White House had just received a generally favorable assessment of the invasion force from Lieutenant Colonel Frank Egan, the CIA operations officer sent to organize the Cubans training in Guatemala. He and five American trainers and Cuban officers had selected leaders based on a rigid field performance and by early December had begun seven weeks of training nearly six hundred forces. These stipulations were vital to the program but caused political infighting when it became clear that no one had special rights and that place in rank lasted only as long as the officer handled his responsibilities. The Cuban brigade, Egan declared, possessed "adequate leadership and training," even though only 20 percent of its forces had military experience. They were nonetheless confident that massive firepower would scatter Castro's militia and lead to a wave of defections crucial to victory.[18]

Egan was particularly impressed by José Pérez San Román (Pepe), "a natural born leader" who became the captain and leader of the brigade. The son of a former general in the Cuban army, Pepe graduated with honors from the Cadet School of the military academy and studied combat engineering in the United States. After undergoing U.S. Army officer training at

Fort Belvoir in Virginia, he accepted an invitation to the U.S. Army Infantry Center at Fort Benning, Georgia, where he graduated from an infantry program for field officers and then returned to Cuba to lead a company against guerrillas in 1957 before becoming professor at the military academy. Pepe went to prison for resisting Batista but became free on Castro's ascension to power, only to return to prison for opposing the growing Communist influence in the new regime. Later released, he defected to the United States and joined the early infiltration units before a rapid rise to the top as head of the invasion.[19]

In retrospect, the new paramilitary approach provided a blueprint for future U.S. actions in other countries threatened by Communist takeover. While sixty to eighty guerrillas infiltrated the island, air strikes originating out of Nicaragua would target Cuban military holdings. Then would follow the amphibious landing of up to 750 men, all armed with heavy weaponry. Air assaults and supply drops would continue after the invasion, with the objective of seizing a parcel of land to establish the group's presence and set off a widespread insurrection. Hawkins praised the exiles' drive and abilities, confident in their capacity to stand up against a much bigger Cuban force. The Special Group encouraged the CIA to proceed with the preparation. Years afterward, Richard Goodwin from President-elect Kennedy's speechwriting staff observed that "in some ways Latin America was considered a kind of training ground for Southeast Asia."[20]

III

In its final days, the Eisenhower administration broke relations with Cuba and confronted a rapidly escalating crisis. Castro had ridiculed the CIA's "Cuban mercenaries" for thinking they could take over Cuba, and Khrushchev bitingly proclaimed from Moscow that "the most aggressive American monopolists" were preparing to attack the island. After parading thirty-five of his recently acquired Soviet tanks through Havana, Castro ordered the U.S. embassy in Havana to reduce its staff of three hundred to eleven. The embassy was a "nest of spies," he hotly declared, and indignantly asserted that the American delegation in Havana must be no larger than Cuba's representation in Washington. Indeed, if *all* Americans left his country, he remarked, that would be "perfectly all right with us." After all, "90 percent of functionaries are spies anyway." The U.S. embassy had forty-eight hours to cut its personnel. The chargé recommended breaking relations.[21]

After considerable discussion in the White House, President Eisenhower approved the proposed action and, recognizing the daily worsening situation, directed the Joint Chiefs to expand the training sites to accommodate a doubling of recruits to fifteen hundred. The White House on January 3 notified the Cuban embassy of the decision to terminate relations, and that same day the president released the news to the press. Cuba's demand to reduce the size of the U.S. embassy in Havana, he charged, could have "no other purpose than to render impossible the conduct of normal diplomatic relations with that Government" and was "the latest of a long series of harassments, baseless accusations, and vilification." Secretary of State Christian Herter explained to his incoming successor, Dean Rusk, that it was preferable to end relations rather than to maintain a staff so small that it could not act effectively. In another change of course, the president authorized military preparations in the event of either a Cuban attack on Guantanamo or a threat to American citizens on the island.[22]

President Eisenhower's decision to break relations drew a fiery retort from Cuba's representative in the UN Security Council. Foreign Minister Raúl Roa Garcia angrily accused the United States of engaging in a "sinister plan" aimed at an invasion. In response, America's UN ambassador, James Wadsworth, admitted that Cuban exiles in the United States wanted to throw out Castro but, in a declaration that he doubtless believed to be true, said that "the United States Government has been in no way associated with such activities." Roa's accusation was "false and hysterical" and made his regime look "ridiculous" by crying wolf over an imagined invasion. "It is the same midnight brew, dipped from the same cauldron of hysteria."[23]

As Wadsworth made his defense in good faith, the air dimension of the invasion plan steadily took shape. In early January the Special Group approved the CIA's employment of American contract pilots and seamen to train the Cubans, emphasizing that any use of Americans in piloting the planes required a separate decision. In addition to the new hires, three American contract pilots moved over from another project, along with several present and former members of the Alabama Air National Guard operating under cover of a commercial company. Albert C. "Buck" Persons was one of eighteen U.S. airmen who worked with the Cuban brigade. After serving with the Seaforth Highlanders, the Royal Canadian Air Force, and the U.S. Army Air Corps in World War II, he became a journalist but maintained his skills by flying a DC-3 for a construction company in Birmingham. He and the other pilots received $2,200 a month along with $600 a month for expenses, $15,000 of life insurance, and a $550 monthly indemnity for life to the spouse of anyone killed on the mission.[24]

To protect the brigade, the CIA advocated two waves of air strikes on Cuban planes, ships, and military apparatus, the first on the day before the amphibious operation, and the second on D-Day to cover the invasion. Fifteen B-26s would be sufficient to safeguard the landing if the pre-invasion strikes eliminated Castro's dozen or so workable planes, which included six B-26s, four T-33s, or T-Birds (jet trainers with two .50-caliber machine guns for gunnery training), and two to four Sea Fury props. No one expressed concern about the T-33s. Although jets, they were few in number and only lightly armed, and the pre-invasion air strikes would dispose of them. The D-Day air assault must begin no later than dawn.[25]

The State Department, however, objected to the air assaults on political grounds, arguing that such a "spectacular" event would make it impossible to attribute these attacks to Cuban planes, especially if Americans piloted any of them. The numbers bore out this warning. Only five Cubans were capable by early January of manning a B-26 attack force of fifteen, and of the eleven C-54 and C-46 transports, the former had only a single qualified crew and the latter had three. Former ambassador Whiting Willauer sought American jets to protect the landing forces, but he failed to attract administration support because the planes would have to fly out of U.S. bases and thus make it impossible to deny involvement.[26]

The U.S. presence became difficult to hide once the American pilots began preparations for a possible leading role. They trained at night near Miami, their planes landing and leaving the abandoned Opa-Locka air base as onlookers gaped at the strange activities in a field enveloped in darkness save for a single flare-pot marking the center of the runway's approach. For nearly two weeks, the pilots landed with no lights and flew a bare two hundred feet off the ground in preparation for the low night flights expected over Cuba. When a reporter asked the head of the American border patrol about the planes, he blandly replied, "Nothing has come to my attention."[27]

After the initial air strikes, the planes would provide cover for the landing force on D-Day as it fought for a beachhead, preferably one with an airstrip and access to the sea. Some units from the newly christened 2506 Assault Brigade (or Cuban Expeditionary Force), named for the serial number of the first man in the group to die in an accident while training at Camp Trax, would supply Cuban guerrillas, engineer sabotage missions, and dispense agents all over the island. The invasion force would remain in its enclave unless a general insurrection broke out or U.S. military forces intervened. If no uprising occurred, the site could host a provisional government that the United States recognized as a prelude to sending military aid.[28]

Other problems in strike capacity quickly became evident. Barely a third of the projected fifteen hundred Cubans were training in Guatemala, indicating that FRD recruitment was not going well and necessitating the hurried dispatch of recruitment teams to Miami. For the assault brigade to reach the desired numerical and performance level, it had to be ready by February, which required the immediate departure of the U.S. Special Forces earlier approved for Guatemala. Indeed, in mid-January 1961 the U.S. Army dispatched thirty-eight Special Forces to the training base. Hawkins felt confident about a popular uprising after his "agents" assured him that great numbers of islanders were pleading for arms. Although Castro had enhanced his military strength, his supporters had reportedly dropped in number from their onetime high of 75 percent. The best time for the attack was no later than March 1, Hawkins declared, but this was unlikely for reasons he did not recognize. This target date meant that, because of logistical considerations, President Eisenhower would have to approve the operation no later than mid-January—thus saddling the United States with a potential long-range commitment *before* Kennedy took office. Eisenhower would not do that.[29]

The maritime situation was somewhat better. Three LOUs (limited official use) and four LCVPs (landing craft, vehicle, personnel) were at Vieques in Puerto Rico, and the *Barbara J*, an LCI (landing craft, infantry), had left the United States for that destination but required two weeks of repairs before the operation. Its companion ship, the *Blagar*, was preparing for departure from Miami, meaning that both LCIs from World War II should be ready by mid-January. Troops and supplies would arrive on the *Rio Escondido*, a converted LCT (landing craft, tank), along with another steamship, both from a Panamanian corporation under the control of a family in Cuba supporting the project.[30]

The mission now went on a rushed schedule. Unfavorable publicity led the Guatemalan government to want the Cubans out of the country, and camp morale had plummeted because of deteriorating conditions. Castro's pilots were training in Czechoslovakia and, combined with the introduction of radar throughout the island, could soon have year-round jet capability. Soviet allies had also sent tanks, artillery, mortars, and anti-aircraft weapons, and he had made great strides toward building "a Communist-style police state" that only direct U.S. military intervention could counter. Furthermore, it appeared that the entire world knew of the imminent secret invasion. "U.S. Helps Train an Anti-Castro Force at Secret Guatemalan Air-Ground Base," ran the headlines of a *New York Times* front-page article on January 10. The administration, however, continued to deny the undeniable. In response to a news correspondent's question about Guatemala that same day, the State Department's press officer bluntly asserted, "As to the report of a specific base, I know absolutely nothing about it."[31]

Some Washington officials pushed for direct American military intervention, even if it entailed manufacturing an incident as justification. The CIA and the Joint Chiefs met in early January to establish a task force drawn from the Joint Chiefs, the CIA, and the State and Defense departments, which would draft contingency plans based on the use of U.S. forces. In response to a State Department request, the Defense Department prepared a study of possible military actions, including a fabricated Cuban attack on Guantanamo that required an appropriate U.S. response. Propaganda could manipulate world opinion or make the facts so "muddled" that U.S. forces could hit the island under the guise of self-defense.[32]

The Defense Department's estimates of Castro's military strength suggested that an amphibious landing was not enough and that U.S. military intervention was essential to success. His numbers were impressive: a thirty-two-thousand-man army, a police force of nine thousand, a militia of perhaps three hundred thousand, a navy of five thousand, and an air force that would soon include up to a hundred Czech-trained pilots. In the last five months he had received at least twenty thousand tons of Soviet arms and military apparel, including artillery, armored vehicles, personnel carriers, helicopters, trainer planes, small arms, and ammunition. Without a mass uprising, the CIA warned, the invasion force would need at least five thousand men to hold a sector of land for a lengthy period. The Defense Department concluded that the only actions guaranteeing success were either a unilateral U.S. assault or a combined U.S. and Cuban invasion force. In a statement that resonated in the period afterward, General Gray warned in mid-January that the 750 men then in training could not stand up to Castro's forces.[33]

Given the wealth of warning signs, why did the White House continue the project? The imminent change in administrations contributed to the outgoing president's reluctance to change course, whether to cancel (out of the question) or to escalate the military thrust (a decision fittingly left to his successor). It made sense to give the invasion program a chance, particularly because its hopes rested on air assaults, U.S. military goods and training, and a popular eruption ignited by the landing of the Cuban brigade. Hadn't the CIA proved its mettle by combating Communism in both Iran and Guatemala?[34] And didn't some of the military advocates quietly affirm that their solution remained a ready option in the unlikely event that the invasion failed? But this was a needless concern. The invasion would succeed because of the careful planning, the drive of the Cuban invasion force, and the widespread popular hatred of Castro—all mixed with some luck and ingenuity. As the chief guardian of democracy, the United States could not allow the Communist ideology to engulf Cuba and the rest of Latin America.

On January 19, the day before Kennedy's inauguration, President Eisenhower informed his successor that anti-Castro forces were training in Guatemala for an invasion and recommended that the incoming administration speed up the process. This was not Kennedy's first introduction to the project. Two weeks after the election of 1960, Dulles and Bissell had briefed him in Palm Beach, Florida, emphasizing the intent to land a force sizable enough to incite a revolution in Cuba. In a later discussion at Palm Beach, Dulles privately met with the incoming president, who, Dulles later recounted, asked only about the timetable of the invasion but readily accepted the challenge. According to Robert McNamara, soon to be secretary of defense, Kennedy insisted that "the United States cannot allow the Castro Government to continue to exist in Cuba."[35]

Was the president-elect made aware of the assassination part of the plan by Dulles or anyone else? "I do not believe he was," asserted Bissell. Dulles bore the responsibility of telling Kennedy, but more appropriately *after* he had taken office. The focus in Florida was on the political planning of the invasion, and the incoming president expressed no opposition.[36]

Thus when Kennedy took the oath of office on January 20, 1961, he inherited the ongoing Cuban project from the Eisenhower administration, which had developed all aspects of the overthrow plan and shoulders primary responsibility for one of the most unusual schemes ever to emerge from the CIA.

3

Zapata

Never mention word assassination. —William Harvey,
January 25–26, 1961

Don't forget that we have a disposal problem.
—Allen Dulles, March 15, 1961

There will not be, under any conditions, an intervention
in Cuba by the United States Armed Forces.
—President John F. Kennedy, April 12, 1961

The airfield requirement was what led us into Zapata.
—Richard Bissell, April 24, 1961

[Zapata] had less than a fair chance of success.
—General Earle Wheeler, May 3, 1961

President John F. Kennedy promised Americans a "New Frontier" in both
foreign and domestic policy, but he soon followed the hard-line path of his

predecessor by supporting a regime change in Cuba. Such daring behavior captivated the young president, whether matching wits with the guerrillas in Southeast Asia by sending the Green Berets to Vietnam or approving covert paramilitary operations in Cuba. The James Bond mystique particularly intrigued him, leading to long conversations with CIA director Allen Dulles, who was also an avid reader of Ian Fleming's fictionalized accounts of the British spy licensed to kill. Indeed, at the November briefing in Florida, Jacqueline Kennedy gave Dulles a copy of *From Russia with Love*; later she passed on Fleming's succeeding novels to the new president and his brother and attorney general, Robert Kennedy. It should come as no surprise that the new administration showed strong interest in overthrowing Castro to gain an early victory in the Cold War.[1]

I

The Kennedy White House focused on Cuba within a week of taking office. Two days after the inauguration, the chair of the Joint Chiefs of Staff, General Lyman Lemnitzer, arrived at the State Department with a packet of measures aimed at overthrowing Castro, which he presented in a meeting of several advisers, including Dulles, Rusk, McNamara, Undersecretary of State Chester Bowles, and Attorney General Robert F. Kennedy. No one discussed a plan of action, except that Rusk mentioned the possibility of landing the exiles on the Isle of Pines below Havana. His colleagues, however, added a new twist to the proposal by emphasizing the necessity of direct U.S. military support.[2]

On January 28 Dulles formally briefed President Kennedy on the Cuba project. In a meeting attended by Rusk, McNamara, Lemnitzer, Vice President Lyndon B. Johnson, National Security Adviser McGeorge Bundy, Assistant Secretary of State for Inter-American Affairs Thomas Mann, Assistant Secretary of Defense for International Security Affairs Paul Nitze, and the CIA's assistant deputy director (plans) for covert action, Tracy Barnes, Dulles warned that Castro was converting Cuba into a Communist state and furnished details of a U.S.-run operation aimed at toppling his regime. A lengthy discussion ensued, followed by the president's approval of the plan on a contingency basis only. He authorized a Defense Department study of the CIA's recommendation to use the island's anti-Castro Cuban forces in an overthrow as well as a State Department effort to isolate Castro's regime by securing its condemnation by the Organization of American States. Most important, his contingency approval meant that the CIA continued preparations for the invasion.[3]

But something more decisive lay beneath the surface discussions: *assassination* as not only integral to the invasion but as an instrument of American foreign policy.

Presidential adviser and historian Arthur Schlesinger remained silent on the subject in his Pulitzer Prize–winning memoir of the period, *A Thousand Days*, but he later publicly admitted that even though he did not realize it at the time, "the assassination project was initially an integral part of the invasion scheme." He nonetheless insisted that President Kennedy never knew of the CIA's efforts to kill Castro and that the agency believed it had acquired "permanent" authorization in 1960—perhaps from Dulles after getting some "green light" from Nixon. But evidence now shows that the new administration not only regarded Castro's death as essential to the plan but had earlier taken steps toward establishing a program of assassination that targeted any foreign leader deemed threatening to American security. Within three days of Kennedy's inauguration—hence *before* his January 28 briefing on the Cuban invasion—Bissell received two White House calls that "urged" him to establish an executive action capability inside the CIA. Dulles was doubtless aware of this proposal from the start, for it makes no sense to think the White House caller bypassed the CIA director (and his deputy) in asking Bissell to take on this assignment. More important, Bissell talked about the matter with Bundy, the president's liaison with the CIA, making it certain that the president approved exploratory discussions.[4]

The ultimate objective was assassination, as Bissell indicated in later explaining the program ultimately code-named ZR/RIFLE. He was to create "a small, special unit, and highly compartmented from the rest of the organization," whose purpose was "to secure the removal from office or to render powerless or in some other way to frustrate figures, usually political figures, ... whose activities are considered contrary to the interests of the United States." Executive action covered a "wide spectrum of actions" intended to "eliminate the effectiveness" of foreign leaders, with assassination as the "last resort."[5]

The two conversations, Bissell insisted, could not have taken place without President Kennedy's approval. Bissell had the "uncertain impression" of having received encouragement to plan the operation, but he remembered no "specific authorization that it should go forward." Bundy acknowledged that he did not discourage Bissell. "I am sure I gave no instruction. But it is only fair to add that I do not recall that I offered any impediment either." Amazingly, Bundy could not recall whether he discussed this matter with the president.[6]

Bundy's story raises a number of questions about both its veracity and its legal standing. At one point, he recalled no "plans" that "went beyond the contingency state," which was technically true. On another occasion, however, he disclaimed any knowledge of executive action before abruptly changing course and acknowledging that "someone" (he could not recall who) had told him of that capability but within the context of "a study of assassination methods, and . . . not targeted against any particular individual or country." A few moments later, he suddenly remembered having talked with Bissell, even though insisting that nothing said could have left the impression of an "authorization to proceed with a Castro assassination plot." He had no power to do this. In a statement raising serious questions about his understanding ˌof criminal law, Bundy suggested that on the highest governing level, murder became a legal instrument of policy. "No one but the President," Bundy confidently asserted, "had authority to give such an order in a valid way."[7]

Questions also arise about Bundy's claimed failure to remember whether he informed the chief executive of the conversation. It is highly unlikely that a person of such sharp mind would have forgotten whether he mentioned this sensitive topic to the new president. It is equally inconceivable that Bundy would have approved such an initiative without the president's knowledge—especially so early in the fledgling administration when excitement ran high and fast-paced events left indelible marks on memory. Assuming that Bundy discussed the matter with the president either before or after the initial exploratory conversation with Bissell (and probably both), it necessarily follows that Kennedy gave a favorable response. If the president had opposed the program, Bundy would have had no discussion with Bissell. But the two conversations took place, understandably encouraging Bissell to think that the president supported executive action and that the ongoing Cuba operation made Castro the prime target.

Armed with the Kennedy administration's tacit sanction, Bissell immediately directed William Harvey as head of the CIA's foreign intelligence staff to develop the assassination program. Harvey came to the job with a reputation as a hard-drinking, gunslinging desperado from the Wild West who acted solely on impulse but got things done. His most storied achievement came in postwar West Berlin, where in the rapidly intensifying Cold War he masterminded the construction of a tunnel connecting the divided city that facilitated the escape of Germans from East to West and permitted Americans to eavesdrop on Soviet telephone lines into East Berlin. As a crafty and hardened CIA veteran, he considered executive action a euphemism for "direct elimination, assassination," and insisted that "done in the presence of an imminent and mortal threat to the United States [such action] falls within the province of the President's power to defend the Republic under the Constitution itself." Harvey was convinced that the idea "had been fully approved, including at least in principle, by the White House."[8]

For two days, on January 25 and 26, Harvey discussed the executive action program with two CIA co-workers deeply involved in the Mafia project, O'Connell and Gottlieb. Harvey's hastily scrawled notes on the lengthy meeting leave no uncertainty about the three men's purpose and thereby violated the most basic canon of plausible deniability: "Exec Action," "the Magic Button," the "Last resort beyond last resort & a confession of weakness," and, most revealing, "Never mention word assassination."[9]

Castro's assassination remained the lynchpin of the overthrow and was seemingly well under way, but the invasion track was in flux, with the Joint Chiefs arguing that his recent military buildup required direct U.S. military intervention, and the CIA wanting to stay with the broadly based covert action plan. Lemnitzer insisted that the Cuban rebels must first invade the island, establish a government in exile, and begin guerrilla operations. "At that point we would come in and support them." The CIA countered that the invasion would combine with infiltration and air protection to establish a beachhead having a provisional government, airstrip, and access to the sea. "It is not a military operation," the CIA repeatedly told the Joint Chiefs. "You will not become involved in this; the United States military will be kept out of this; you will not tell anybody in your service."[10]

The Joint Chiefs warned that Castro's growing military power threatened the Western Hemisphere and necessitated a more forceful approach than outlined in the Trinidad Plan. A brigade of eight hundred men now in training was not enough for an invasion, Lemnitzer insisted. In the Pentagon shortly after that day's White House meeting, he and McNamara called for a new and more aggressive plan.[11]

Lemnitzer and his colleagues meanwhile conducted a detailed study of the Trinidad Plan and found it generally acceptable but a high-risk proposition.

Success depended on tight coordination and centralized control over the labyrinthine complexities inherent in an amphibious operation. If the brigade pulled off a surprise landing and current estimates of Castro's air defense were accurate, the limited air strikes should prove effective. At present, however, the number of people earmarked for the invasion and the plans for logistic support were insufficient. If Castro's forces did not suffer a crippling air or ground assault, they could mount a formidable opposition within two days of the landing. Vital to success was either a popular uprising or "substantial follow-on forces." The Joint Chiefs recommended a firsthand inspection of the brigade's combat capabilities and a thorough assessment of the logistics plan by army, navy, and air force representatives.[12]

The Joint Chiefs then sent a confusing message in which they concluded that the plan's advantages outweighed its shortcomings. There was no reserve force, no logistic support apparatus, and no freedom to maneuver once on the beaches. They also noted two critical and yet unknown considerations: strength of popular support and capacity of Cuban army resistance. But several factors worked in favor of the invasion: the pre-invasion air strikes to disable Castro's ground and air opposition, sufficient air cover during the landing, and help from the guerrillas on the island. The plan therefore had "a fair chance of success."[13]

President Kennedy came under great pressure to move forward, but he too had reservations about an approach that so blatantly exposed U.S. involvement. He did not want to undermine an opportunity to overthrow Castro, but he had to be concerned about its feasibility when Bissell echoed the Joint Chiefs in arguing that the invasion plan had only "a fair chance of success" in holding a beachhead and attracting popular support. And yet, Bissell warned, a small-scale infiltration would not have the "psychological effect" necessary to ignite both a popular uprising and a wide revolt among Castro's military forces. If the invasion failed to produce these conditions, the only way to overthrow the regime lay in direct U.S. military intervention. The worst outcome, he assured the president, would find the invaders fighting their way into the Escambray Mountains and engaging in guerrilla operations. The president, however, feared the domestic and foreign political consequences of U.S. attribution and wanted options other than an all-out invasion supported by American planes, ships, and supplies. Was it possible to have a quiet, night-time landing that appeared to be indigenous by coming from the mountains? The consensus of the meeting was the need for further study aimed at having the invasion take shape "as a Cuban force within Cuba, not as an invasion force sent by the Yankees."[14] The implication was ominous: The president sought to impose stringent political restrictions on a military operation.

Even though Lemnitzer also had qualms about the limited nature of the air strikes, he hesitated to say anything *at the time* because of the Joint Chiefs' assigned *non*-leadership role of "appraisal, evaluation, offering of constructive criticism, and assisting [the] CIA in looking at the training and detailed plan." Lemnitzer thought the plan potentially effective, but only if the landing party received air support. The pre-invasion air strikes must significantly reduce Castro's air force. "We didn't intend to stop with just the strike on D-Day." An uprising *had* to erupt throughout the island. The D-Day assault was "one of the critical aspects of the whole operation" in that it must provide air cover for the landing. "Absolutely vital to success," emphasized Lemnitzer, was air control. But Castro's overthrow depended on "the invasion serving as a catalyst for further action on the part of the anti-Castro guerrillas or elements throughout Cuba." The CIA, complained Burke, had assumed control over military operations and left the Joint Chiefs as virtual bystanders.[15]

Lemnitzer's colleagues did not think the Trinidad Plan's limited conception of pre-invasion strikes militarily sound but remained silent because most of them conceded the political importance of plausible denial. The CIA appeared less interested in destroying the Cuban air force than in leaving the impression that the assaults had originated inside Cuba. Lemnitzer had grave concerns about the longtime battle between political and military objectives. "You have to be very careful about diluting military considerations in order to attain nonattribution and nonassociation with the United States." The State Department, however, wanted to be in a position to deny that the attacks had come from either the United States, Guatemala, or Nicaragua, and it did not want to alienate other Latin American nations by directly assaulting a fellow OAS member. General George Decker, army chief of staff, saw through this political fog and insisted that the pre-invasion strikes must knock out Castro's planes before the landing. "It never occurred to me that we could disown supporting this operation."[16]

Thus, despite a host of uncertainties now seriously aggravated by restricted air operations, the Joint Chiefs by early February had quietly relented to the CIA's insistence on Trinidad. Success could still come *as long as* a general uprising followed the invasion. If the landing force failed to secure the beachhead, it could fade into the hills and join the guerrillas already there. More likely, the Joint Chiefs shared the Cuban brigade's belief that the White House could not permit a failure and, if no popular insurrection occurred, would approve U.S. military intervention.[17]

The Trinidad Plan still drew mixed reviews. If evacuation became mandatory, argued Gray, the landing force could break through Castro's forces and make it back to the sea. Colonel King assured his fellow CIA advisers that the local populace would join the guerrillas from the hills in supporting the landing. No Americans would be part of the invading force, although they would participate in the landing process. Some American pilots would take part in the air strikes, but only those working on a contract basis and thus having no direct connection with the CIA. Thomas Mann from the State Department was less confident, agreeing with the Joint Chiefs that U.S. military involvement might become necessary. Once the landing force hit the beaches, the U.S. government was "committed" and "would have to underwrite the success of the venture even if it meant the employment of U.S. naval and military forces."[18]

Lack of combat readiness forced the administration to delay the strike a month, providing time for more questions to arise about the wisdom of going ahead. President Kennedy appeared to frown on the venture, opposing an all-out invasion supported by U.S. military assistance, while also dubious about the possibility of launching a quiet landing aimed at establishing a base in the mountains. Bundy noted that the Defense Department and the CIA were very optimistic, arguing that at the least the landing force would make it to the mountains and at best the result would be a civil war in which the United States could openly help Castro's opposition. The State Department, however, expressed concern about the regional and global political ramifications of an assault and preferred diplomatic efforts aimed at isolating Cuba before resorting to military action. Bundy thought the State Department assessment correct and agreed with Goodwin that the White House must explore all peaceful avenues before approving an invasion.[19]

Schlesinger (according to Robert Kennedy "the one person who was strongly against" an invasion) warned the president to assess the plan within the political context of the hemisphere and the world. The United States could not escape responsibility, meaning that the invasion would destroy the goodwill presently enjoyed by the administration and give it "a malevolent image." Wouldn't it be wiser to manufacture "a black operation" in

Haiti and "induce Castro to take offensive action first?" The administration could then justify a military response on moral principles.[20]

Bissell repeated that infiltration would not work and that an invasion was necessary. Only two areas in Cuba contained rugged mountainous terrain suitable for guerrilla operations: the Sierra Escambray of Las Villas Province in the central part of the island, and the Sierra Maestra of Oriente Province on the eastern side. The Sierra Escambray was a better landing area, because the mountains in the east were too distant from air bases in Latin America for supplying the operation. Furthermore, the guerrillas in the Sierra Maestra were ill trained and poorly equipped. Thus a small-scale infiltration program was not capable of inciting the widespread popular uprisings so critical to success. Indeed, such action would lead to a heavy loss of life, whether during the infiltration attempts or by "drum-head justice and firing squad execution of those captured." Only an invasion could stir up anti-Castro elements in Cuba. "*These conditions must be produced before the Castro Government can be overthrown by any means short of overt intervention by United States armed forces* [emphasis in original]."[21]

President Kennedy remained perplexed about what to do and in March asked his friend Senator George Smathers of Florida, as they walked on the White House lawn, what South America's reaction would be to Castro's assassination. The CIA, Kennedy declared, led him to believe that Castro would be dead by the time of the invasion—that it "would be no problem." Smathers thought it a "bad idea." Regardless of who killed Castro, the United States would shoulder the blame, and the president's credibility would plummet throughout Latin America. "I disapproved of it," Smathers later insisted, "even though I disliked Fidel Castro more than he did. And he completely disapproved of the idea . . . . That I am positive about." Smathers thought the president "was responding to a suggestion that had been made to him. Who made it, I don't know." The senator's "impression" was that in consulting him, Kennedy was asking a friend who "knew a little bit" about South America and had a sizable Latin American constituency.[22]

But the pressure clearly began to wear on the president. One evening he invited Smathers to the White House for a private dinner. He had sent the help home and prepared the food and brought it to the table himself just before Smathers mentioned Cuba. Kennedy "cracked the plate"—one of the First Lady's better plates—with his fork while blurting out, "For Godssakes, quit talking about Cuba."[23]

II

The Joint Chiefs were not comfortable with Operation Trinidad and, in accordance with their February recommendation, assigned three Joint Staff representatives to evaluate the military potential of the strike force training in Guatemala. Their report, based on a three-day visit later that month and sent to the defense secretary, concluded that the odds were "about 85 to 15" *against* achieving one of the essential ingredients in success, a surprise assault, because of the well-publicized preparations under way in both Guatemala and Nicaragua. The U.S. involvement was unmistakable. About twenty Americans ran the training site in Guatemala, and of the 316 personnel in Nicaragua, 159 were Americans. Moreover, the air contingent was problematic, consisting of only twenty-two Cubans, including seventeen B-26 crew members and five C-46 crews. To alleviate this problem, six American B-26 pilots would join the operation, all having combat experience in World War II and Korea or both. The plan could achieve "initial success," but the final outcome depended on whether the invasion triggered a popular uprising. The air strikes could fail if the CIA proved wrong about Castro's having no jet craft. Indeed, without a surprise landing, a single enemy plane fitted with .50-caliber machine guns could sink the invading force.[24]

The Joint Chiefs' inspection team had detected many weaknesses in the training program in Guatemala, particularly the lack of centralized control and planning that its superiors had emphasized in their review of the Trinidad Plan. The trainees received first-rate instruction in weaponry but nothing on amphibious warfare. Logistics posed a potential nightmare. The dispersal of trucks was haphazard, leaving them to individual commanders and ensuring confusion over transportation. The planes lacked sufficient fuel. Each fifty-gallon drum weighed four hundred pounds, and there was no moving or loading apparatus for them other than sheer manpower. The Cuban brigade had no bridging capabilities for transferring the equipment from the ships to the beach, no floodlights for the night-time operations, no supply distribution plan, and no maintenance materials other than hand tools. The troops had abundant ammunition and superb communications equipment, and they eventually secured a crane to unload supplies on the beach, but a single piece of machinery was incapable of handling 1,200 tons of goods in the time between a nocturnal landing and daylight. Without *any* opposition during the landing, the brigade's forces needed three days to process the supplies and equipment. "Their capability was marginal without resistance, but impossible with it."[25]

And yet, despite these critical flaws, the Joint Chiefs gave lukewarm approval to the plan and thus encouraged the president to believe it at least minimally acceptable.

Bissell, too, ignored the danger signs and urged the administration to act quickly in approving the invasion. In a March 11 White House meeting, he used a pointer and a map in presenting an articulate analysis of the proposed landing sites. The volunteers comprising the landing force had undergone difficult training for months and could not hold together beyond early April. The rainy season would hit Guatemala at that point and severely hamper operations, and that government wanted them out of the country. Moreover, the Castro regime was becoming stronger day by day. In a few months it would have operative fighter jets and Czech-trained pilots, along with ground forces fully adept at using Soviet weapons. If the brigade did not act soon, only American military force could overthrow Castro.[26]

Bissell advocated an all-out assault following a small-scale diversionary landing intended to pull Castro's defenses away from the target point. Pre-invasion air strikes would disable the Cuban air force, and the initial landing would go "virtually unopposed" by ground forces, leaving the paramilitary groups to take advantage of the "demoralizing shock" inflicted on Castro's forces to seize a beachhead. A slow buildup of manpower and matériel would lead to the establishment of a provisional government, which the United States intended to recognize after "a decent interval." Beneath Bissell's surface argument lay an implicit but driving force: the fear that if the White House terminated the program, the Cubans would publicly blast the United States as a phony defender of freedom and a coward in the face of Communism.

President Kennedy nonetheless remained hesitant, emphasizing that the Trinidad Plan exposed U.S. involvement. It was important, he insisted, to maintain the covert nature of the plan and thus the capacity to deny complicity. That concern in mind, he strongly objected to pre-landing air attacks because the invasion force did not possess an airstrip in Cuba and the White House could not claim the planes were indigenous in origin. More disturbing, the centerpiece of the Trinidad Plan was a "spectacular" assault reminiscent of D Day in World War II. "It looks too much like a military operation," he asserted. "And so you must change the place."[28]

In just four days, late in the morning of March 15, Bissell returned with a revised invasion plan intended to satisfy the president's concerns and calling for an alternative landing area previously under consideration—much farther west and on the Zapata Peninsula. Bissell had hurriedly made the changes, Lansdale later recalled, demonstrating his "almost high-strung" impatience with questions and now putting on a "sale job" in advocating a landing in the eastern sector of Zapata close to Cochinos Bay, or the Bay of Pigs. The new site, noted the Joint Chiefs, did not offer as much hope for military success as the Trinidad Plan, but their argument did not dissuade McNamara and other senior civilian advisers who focused on the political objections raised by the president. Bissell ignored the Joint Chiefs' weakly expressed preference for Trinidad because Zapata fitted the president's stipulations: a quiet night-time "infiltration of guerrillas in support of an internal revolution," and *not* "a small-scale World War II type of amphibious landing." The brigade would seize two airstrips capable of accommodating B-26s, allowing the White House to mask its role by claiming the air operations had originated in Cuba.[29]

The proposed landing spot at Zapata, Bissell explained, lay a hundred miles west of Trinidad at the Bay of Pigs and adjoining beaches, winding around the top of an easily defensible deepwater estuary on the southern coast of the island. The Bay of Pigs (named after pigs so aggressive that they attacked human beings) pierced the Cuban heartland, cutting twenty miles upward from the south and lapping ashore at a point just seventy-five miles southeast of Havana. On the eastern side of the bay's opening sat the town of Playa Girón, named after the most famous pirate of many who had sought sanctuary there, Gilberto Girón. A north-south highway connected Playa Larga at the top of the bay with Central Australia and its airport. Another highway ran along the east side of the bay, linking the two towns. Two other roads along with a pair of railways passed to and from Playa Girón and the Bay of Pigs. Zapata's swamps made it virtually impossible for Castro's motorized divisions to enter the area except through two narrow dirt causeways that paratroopers would close before the assault. Indeed, according to Bissell, the Zapata Peninsula had been the scene of guerrilla activities for more than a hundred years. The invasion forces would stage an "unspectacular" phased landing at night, off-loading until dawn before leaving and returning the following evening. They would encounter lighter opposition than at Trinidad and would acquire one or two airstrips capable of handling B-26s.[30] The White House thus had a rationale for denying involvement.

The Joint Chiefs had been reticent about expressing their doubts about the Trinidad Plan, but now that the president had done so they stepped to the front and welcomed the Zapata Plan as "the most feasible and the most likely to accomplish the objective." The remoteness of the region meant that Castro could not react quickly to the landing: He had no military forces of consequence nearby, and the swamps afforded a natural defense for the brigade by barring his use of armor except for tank fire. Lemnitzer argued strongly for Zapata, relying on the assertions of the CIA and his own staff in calling it "a guerrilla-type country" located so close to the seat of government that it would have a "psychological effect" on the local populace capable of inciting an insurrection. When Lemnitzer asked what the invasion force would do if the mission failed, Bissell confidently responded that the troops could escape through the swamps and into the mountains. The director of the Joint Staff, Army General Earle Wheeler, remained skeptical, warning that the plan had "less than a fair chance of success." But he saw no alternative since Trinidad lacked an airstrip large enough for B-26s. Air support was essential to the landing, he knew. Without studying the matter in detail, the Joint Chiefs within forty-eight hours accepted Bissell's claim that the area was suitable for guerrilla operations.[31]

Bissell, however, had not noted some of the difficulties in the landing area. Unlike at Trinidad, there were no docks, dangerous coral reefs ribbed the beaches, thick swamps blanketed the area above the landfall, and the water in some places was eight hundred feet deep and prohibited ships from anchoring.[32]

Marine General David Shoup was one of the few who voiced concern about Zapata's military features. The swamps bothered him, despite assurances that the Cuban invasion force could secure the area by setting out anti-tank mines and dropping parachutists to close access roads to the beachhead. He remained apprehensive about the distance the landing force would have to cover in getting its weapons ashore and the problems in maneuvering through the horrendous terrain. A large number of Cuban people would be there to help the brigade, Shoup was led to believe. But he had deep misgivings about the all-too-brief preparation program for a highly complex amphibious landing. "If this kind of an operation can be done with this kind of a force with this much training and knowledge about it, then we are wasting our time in our divisions, we ought to go on leave for three months out of four."[33]

Other negative assessments arose during a White House meeting, where Schlesinger repeated his warning that the planners had emphasized the military aspects of the operation without considering the political fallout.

The administration must not find itself in a situation similar to the U-2 crisis, in which the government clumsily changed its story to adopt a position transparently evident to the world as a lie. When the president left the room, Dulles cautioned his colleagues, "Don't forget that we have a disposal problem. If we have to take these men out of Guatemala, we will have to transfer them to the U.S., and we can't have them wandering around the country telling everyone what they have been doing." Schlesinger admitted to this problem but insisted that fear must not determine American policy.[34]

Bundy praised Bissell's attempt to make the landing "unspectacular and quiet, and plausibly Cuban," but recognized the necessity of controlling the air over Cuba. Castro had "a very sketchy" air force, Bundy told the president, "in very poor shape at the present" and "his Achilles' heel." Colonel Hawkins thought six to eight simultaneous assaults by B-26s bearing Cuban markings and piloted by Cubans would resolve the problem. This was still a "noisy enterprise," Bundy admitted. But if known Cuban rebels flew the planes out of Nicaragua "some little time" *before* the invasion and without revealing their origin, the two actions would appear to be separate and leave Castro with nothing substantive to take before the United Nations. Bissell and Hawkins had eased the State Department's political concerns and were "on the edge of a good answer."[35]

President Kennedy still had reservations. For political reasons, he opposed a dawn landing, wanting the ships out of the area by daylight to "reduce the noise level" and thereby leave the appearance of an indigenous guerrilla operation. At a March 16 meeting with the CIA, the president considered the two proposals: Trinidad, a daylight landing that would encounter opposition and required air support; and Zapata, a night-time landing expected to meet no resistance and hence needing no air cover. Bissell argued that the Zapata Plan marked an improvement over Trinidad in that the air drops of supplies and paratroopers would take place in the early dawn rather than the late afternoon, followed by a night landing with all ships withdrawn by morning's light. And if the brigade encountered stiff opposition, it could fade away into guerrilla status. Still not convinced, Kennedy approved the plan on a contingency basis, maintaining the right to cancel the operation as late as twenty-four hours before its scheduled beginning.[36]

Bissell was not straight with the president about either the chances of a popular uprising or escaping into the mountains. He had earlier argued that a small-scale infiltration would not have the "psychological effect" necessary to ignite a popular uprising and a wide revolt among Castro's military. Hence he had supported the brigade's all-out assault on Trinidad. But with that plan rejected by the president, Bissell had quietly shifted emphasis from instigating a rebellion to building a beach perimeter aimed at wearing down the Castro regime. Furthermore, he did not mention that the CIA had virtually abandoned guerrilla training five months earlier—*before* most of the Cubans arrived in Guatemala. As early as the autumn of 1960 Bissell realized that there was no chance to build an effective underground and that the invasion forces had to succeed on their own. But for some unexplained reason—perhaps his reliance on Castro's assassination or, failing that, a resort to U.S. military intervention in the face of failure—he did not tell the president that CIA operatives had failed to create an organized resistance on the island, meaning there was no chance for a popular insurrection because of the lack of a "communications and command and control net." Furthermore, even though Bissell informed the president that the chances of a retreat to the mountains and a switch to guerrilla warfare were poor in contrast to those of Trinidad, which was much closer to the Escambrays, he led him to believe Zapata a good possibility—despite its being eighty miles away, separated from the landing area by a nearly impenetrable maze of jungles and swamps, and reachable only by foot because of the lack of motorized transport. Robert Kennedy called this Bissell's "greatest mistake."[37]

Bissell and his strategists were woefully ignorant of Zapata's physical character and history. The Bay of Pigs rimmed the eastern side of the Zapata Peninsula, an isolated, swampy, barren, and deserted sector of the island that had long obstructed guerrilla warfare. Unconventional tactics were nearly impossible because of the thick marsh and lack of food sources in the rugged, mountainous terrain. Furthermore, the Zapata Swamp, more than a million miles of wilderness known as the "Great Swamp of the Caribbean," was thick in mangrove trees and infested with snakes, crocodiles, alligators, mosquitoes, huge flies, and sharp-shelled, toxic red land crabs that every spring (the expected invasion time) migrated out of the forests by the millions, carpeting the passageways and beaches in their rush to breed in the sea. To reach the mountains, the brigade would have to go through eighty miles of swamp and then around the city of Cienfuegos. Charcoal makers had dug numerous long and narrow channels through the marshy thicket for transporting their product to market, and Castro, to provide passage for his tanks, militia, and artillery, as well as to connect the inland sugar mills to the sea, had ordered the construction of three roads (Bissell had said two) through the swamp to supplement the two narrow-gauge railroads that were continually in disuse because of derailment. All these factors impeded an advance northward, undermined the chances for guerrilla action, and afforded no geographical refuge. And yet, in a critical error, one adviser asserted that Zapata "has traditionally been an area for guerrilla operations." Maximo Gomez, guerrilla chieftain during Cuba's war for independence of the 1890s, had refused to operate in that difficult setting, calling it a "geographical and military trap." And that was before the advent of helicopters (which Castro had) that made the area even more prohibitive because of their effectiveness against guerrillas.[38]

Given Bissell's faint hope for guerrilla tactics as a final resort, he displayed another mystifying piece of misjudgment by deciding against informing either the president or the Cubans of that alternative if they were unsuccessful in establishing a beachhead. This was "a bad mistake" and "unforgivable," Robert Kennedy later asserted. The CIA offered an explanation for never informing the brigade that the mountains provided a safety valve in the event of setbacks in the landing. Announcing a guerrilla option during the briefing, the American trainers on the scene feared, would weaken the Cubans' battlefield efforts. Rather than continue the fight, they might *choose* to fall back and become guerrillas. But the decision to keep this reserve plan secret raised false hopes among the Cuban forces that the rumors were true: In the event of failure on the beaches, American military forces would intervene. "We were never told about this [the guerrilla option]," complained Pepe San Román years afterward. "What we were told was, 'If you fail *we* [the Americans] will go in.' "[39]

What also becomes clear is that the Joint Chiefs made no actual decision for either Trinidad or Zapata and that they recommended the latter approach only after the president made his preference known. Bissell thought those military figures in attendance considered Zapata superior to Trinidad, but Burke insisted that he and his colleagues did not agree on either approach as better. The admiral admitted, however, that "inasmuch as the JCS did not disapprove this concept, it does imply approval." Gray concurred that the Joint Chiefs at no time resisted the Zapata Plan, leading the White House to believe they supported it.[40]

Furthermore, the Joint Chiefs did not consider Zapata militarily comparable to Trinidad, which called for pre-invasion air strikes along with tactical air cover both during and after D-Day. The Joint Chiefs spent nearly an hour stressing the critical need for air strikes prior to the landing and yet approved Zapata though knowing it lacked these measures. Only in the final days before the invasion did the strategists revise the Zapata Plan to include a D-2 (D-Day minus two) air strike in addition to those coming from Puerto Cabezas on D-1 and at dawn of D-Day.[41]

In fairness, the Joint Chiefs had neither a mandate nor sufficient time to consider the two plans. They had carefully reviewed the Trinidad Plan, but within rigid CIA guidelines authorizing only advice and help. Because of the secrecy involved, they studied it on a personal basis and without staff assistance. General Gray made the only complete analysis, which found Trinidad more suited for guerrilla operations. As for the Zapata Plan, they never received a copy because most of its components were the same as Trinidad's and the rush of time prevented further delay. Not until the invasion operation began did they learn Zapata's details. In Burke's words, "We had a hell of a short time to examine them." The Joint Chiefs therefore approved the Zapata Plan in an unorthodox, de facto manner: "Technically, no; morally, they did."[42]

Bissell insisted that those at the meeting concluded that even though Zapata would yield "less decisive results—and slower results," it carried "less initial risk" than Trinidad. "[W]e felt and hoped the Zapata Plan would be less risky but recognized its limitations—less chance of a build-up from friendly population." Opposition to the Zapata landing would be considerably smaller because of the rough terrain, although it would also be "more difficult for the guerrillas and volunteer recruits from the general public to get into the beachhead area to join up with the landing force."[43]

Ironically, the CIA's decision to upgrade its plan from infiltration to invasion became its worst enemy. It had earlier told the Joint Chiefs that this was *not* a military operation and blocked their involvement. But with the change to an amphibious landing, the magnitude of the operation went beyond the CIA's capacity and should have come under the planning, training, and execution of the Defense Department. Furthermore, even with the successful amphibious landings in World War II, none had taken place at night. Bissell later explained that preparation for an amphibious operation required moving the men to a jungle warfare training center, which would have worsened an already serious problem of discipline and morale in camp. Any attempt to keep such an operation covert would have been fruitless, if for no other reason than the large number of government agencies involved. A guerrilla operation could have been attributable to the Cubans, whereas an invasion made it impossible to deny U.S. involvement.[44]

President Kennedy confronted a monumental dilemma. Infiltration *might* conceal the American hand, but it lacked dramatic flair and was less likely to stir up a general uprising so vital to Castro's fall. Invasion offered a greater prospect for military success, but it left little hope for a popular uprising and greatly reduced the chances of plausible deniability. The result was a compromise based on a secret night-time landing that depended on three critical factors: the element of surprise, the expeditious offloading of men and supplies before daylight, and the rapid acquisition of a beachhead housing a provisional government deserving U.S. recognition and help. Compounding the problem, Admiral Burke complained, was that "amateurs" ran the entire operation.[45]

Regardless of the Joint Chiefs' doubts, there appeared no turning back in light of the certain political repercussions resulting from canceling a program that had come this far. They certainly knew that the quiet nature of a night-time invasion would undermine the chances of a popular insurrection—which the Joint Chiefs considered critical to success. Then why did they hold their collective tongue? No one within this tightly knit circle took the lead in protesting Zapata's military weaknesses, largely because Lemnitzer had accepted their advisory role rather than insisting on fulfilling their principal responsibility of making decisions on military matters. The CIA had succeeded in pushing the Joint Chiefs aside and taking control of all aspects of the program, and yet Bissell accused them of failing to make a careful evaluation of the operation. With scarcely a murmur of protest, they conceded military leadership to the CIA, whose expertise lay in covert action and *not* in battle preparation. Gray put his finger on an often fatal element that crept into this hurried decision-making process and left little time for careful reflection: "[A]s we became associated we became more interested in trying to make it go."[46]

In a dark premonition, Burke told the president that the odds for success were about 50 percent and that if no popular uprising occurred and the invasion failed, the forces had no way to evacuate. "Once they were landed they were there."[47]

III

President Kennedy had not yet given final approval, but the first step in the invasion process got under way on March 28 when the *Blagar* and the

Barbara J departed Key West, arriving at Puerto Cabezas on April 2. The two CIA case officers accompanying the infantry, Americans Grayston Lynch on the *Blagar* and William Robertson on the *Barbara J*, along with the ships' captains, were under orders to direct the landing operation in Cuba with the assistance of thirty-six small craft already in port.[48]

That same day the U.S. military command made a number of defense preparations relating to the coming assault. After reinforcing Guantanamo with a Marine Battalion Landing Team, it sent eighteen destroyer-type vessels to the area and ordered one jet fighter squadron to hover close to the naval base and another near Key West. Meanwhile the carrier *Essex*, carrying another jet squadron and accompanied by seven destroyers, would ostensibly conduct anti-submarine warfare operations southwest of Cuba in the Gulf of Mexico. Finally, the commander in chief of the North American Air Defense Command (CINCNORAD) took steps to protect Florida from retaliation.[49]

D-Day at first was April 5, but by late March the logistics of the operation made this date impossible to meet, and the president changed it to April 17. In the meantime the continued delay further sank morale among trainees, leading to anger and frustration. The previous January, 250 Cubans in Guatemala had mutinied, although most of them ultimately returned to the fold and the CIA escorted the others to prison camps deep in the jungle. Some men had trained in five different camps in less than a year and still did not know when or if the assault would begin. About twenty of them had been recently dispersed in Miami as a result of recalcitrant behavior—thus free to share information about the "secret" attack. A trainee in Panama complained that over one three-week period, "the only thing I did . . . was [clean] a small dam and the shooting range. After that we just didn't do anything, just sleep and eat, that's all." He then relocated to Florida, where the situation was no better. "There, the same history, sleep, eat, play cards and watch television." Complaints spread that the trainers were insufficient in number and rarely qualified. The makeshift base in New Orleans was a virtual swampland overrun with poisonous snakes. Demolition training took place on a narrow path connecting a makeshift theater with the mess hall, causing repeated interruptions as other trainees passed back and forth through the area. But the real problems were basic: lack of training materials for explosives, no suitable area for training, and no equipment for establishing such a place. Much of the paramilitary, intelligence, and psychological warfare training in Miami took place in safe houses, while in the

Washington area, CIA case officers taught a man in a hotel room how to make a parachute jump—which he later did in Cuba.[50]

The Guatemalan training sites became more publicized as the days wore on. The air base sat on a highly trafficked road and next to a railroad where passenger cars filled with Guatemalans often stopped on a siding and observed the training activities. Trainees did not grasp the critical importance of secrecy and freely discussed camp proceedings with inquiring locals and journalists. Whereas training remained clandestine in New Orleans, Miami, and Washington and on Vieques Island east of Puerto Rico, preparations in Guatemala became general knowledge both inside and outside the country. In a March news story entitled "The Big Buildup to Overthrow Castro," *U.S. News and World Report* announced an imminent invasion by hundreds of Cuban exiles.[51]

Poor security precautions and faulty communications also threatened the coming invasion. The "need to know" principle did not apply in this operation and led to a widespread dissemination of sensitive information by Cuban participants. Not separated from each other, they pooled their information and knew more than they should have known. Some CIA operatives worked under more than one case officer, leading to confusion and lack of unified control. Many of them knew each other and if arrested could expose the others. Well-trained operatives inexplicably carried identification documents that led to their arrest while visiting relatives under watch by the regime. Cubans in Miami, including Castro's spies, knew the operation's details and openly discussed the matter with friends. Censorship failed to block revealing information contained in trainees' letters to families. A Miami citizen overheard a CIA case officer briefing Cubans in a motel and relayed this information to the FBI. Screening of Cuban volunteers became almost nonexistent. Cover stories were poorly prepared, making it difficult to fool observers into believing that massive supplies went to "tourists" and "soldiers of fortune" in Guatemala. Compartmentalization of information at times denied knowledge to those who needed it. For example, those officials in charge of sending CIA officers to Cuba never had access to either the war room or the invasion plans. Another and more critical flaw: Resistance groups in Cuba did not learn the time of the invasion beforehand, further undercutting the chances of a mass uprising in support of the assault.[52]

In late March the powerful chair of the Senate Foreign Relations Committee, Democrat J. William Fulbright of Arkansas, sent the White House an extended memo warning that press stories and pictures showed the United States supporting an invasion by exiles secretly training in Florida, the Caribbean, or Guatemala. Would the United States let the venture fail in the "futile hope" of hiding its role, or resort to military force and thus undo the last three decades' effort to repair the damages of previous interventions? Assuming responsibility for restoring Cuban order would be "an endless can of worms" that violated a host of treaties and the OAS Charter renouncing a right to intervention. "[T]he Castro regime is a thorn in the flesh; but it is not a dagger in the heart." It admittedly hurt U.S. prestige and provided the Soviets a "base for agitation" throughout Latin America. But "to revert to the Teddy Roosevelt style of intervention in Cuba...would set us back another two generations."[53]

Fulbright's cautionary remarks did not slow the program, and the plan continued to unravel, leaving in its wake several alerts that the president repeatedly ignored, albeit with growing trepidation. "What do you think about this damned invasion?" asked Schlesinger one late March morning after an hour's discussion of a White Paper he was drafting to justify the intended destruction of Castro's regime. The president looked up from his desk at his adviser, seemingly born into his bow tie and straitlaced New England manner, and tersely replied, "I think about it as little as possible." The following day he sought the advice of Dean Acheson, the hard-nosed secretary of state during the tumultuous Truman years and still a leading Cold Warrior. "Do you know anything about this Cuba proposal?" "A Cuba proposal? I didn't know there was one." After Kennedy detailed the plan originating in the Eisenhower presidency, Acheson asked in disbelief, "Are you serious?" "I'm giving it serious thought," the president replied. "I don't know if I'm serious or just..." After pausing for a moment as they sat on a bench in the Rose Garden, he completed his thought. "I've been thinking about it." Kennedy had mentioned that the Cuban invasion force numbered fifteen hundred, which led Acheson to ask how many forces Castro could amass on the beaches that day. When told twenty-five thousand, he sighed and cuttingly remarked, "Well, it doesn't take Price-Waterhouse to figure out that fifteen hundred Cubans aren't as good as twenty-five thousand."[54]

Some observers had uncovered the invasion date. Two American journalists, Tad Szulc and Karl Meyer, independently compiled complete and accurate stories for national publication but postponed their release after direct White House appeals to wait until the invasion took place so as not to forewarn Castro and endanger the men. Yet Castro had surely learned the date from his chief ally in the Kremlin, Nikita Khrushchev. In a cable intercepted by the CIA in early April 1961, the Soviet embassy in Mexico City informed its home office in Moscow that the invasion would take place on April 17.[55]

As the clock ticked relentlessly toward D-Day, mixed reactions to the plan continued to bedevil the administration. Bowles warned Rusk that a covert interventionist operation would undermine the new president's public appeals for moral principle and improved Latin American relations. Bowles had shared the plan with John Kenneth Galbraith, the president's longtime friend and newly appointed ambassador to India, and he likewise cautioned against repeating the disasters stemming from the "adventurism" of the Truman and Eisenhower years. "The futile campaign to the Yalu ruined the Democrats in 1950," he warned President Kennedy. "Dulles got Guatemala at the price of losing all South America. The U-2 did not weigh the political cost of failure." Involvement in this coup attempt would undermine the "reputation you have already won for your conservative, thoughtful, non-belligerent stance."[56]

The president clearly felt the strain of decision and wanted a straw vote from his advisers on whether to go forward with the invasion. On April 4 the Joint Chiefs sent McNamara a detailed recommendation of the logistical operations needed to support the Zapata landing, and that same evening they met in the State Department with Kennedy and others to discuss the plan. Rusk opposed it, while McNamara favored the general idea but not all the specifics. The president preferred a series of infiltrations of 250 men each to leave the impression of a growing insurrection. Colonel Hawkins, however, feared that such contingents would not be large enough to threaten Castro and would only warn him and allow his forces to quash them one group at a time. Several present seemed inconclusive but raised no objections. Fulbright, invited to attend, repeated his opposition to an invasion based on information he had gleaned from newspapers. Mann and Adolf Berle, the chair of the State Department Task Force on Latin America, disagreed with Rusk and supported the invasion. Mann believed the plan hinged on a "1776 style" of uprising and control of the air, and he insisted this would probably be the last opportunity to overthrow Castro. Nitze, McNamara, and Mann voted for the plan, the latter declaring himself "finally pinned down" by the president. Berle acknowledged that the alternatives to doing nothing were risky, but if successful the rewards would be great. After this lengthy and indecisive statement, the president declared, "Well, Adolf, you haven't voted." Berle shot back, "I'd say, let her rip."[57]

Schlesinger continued to warn the president that an invasion came heavily freighted with political costs and urged him to approve a "quiet infiltration" followed by air drops. The CIA plan would work only if the landing took place by "a swift, surgical stroke," but the chances of this happening were so small that "I am against it." The United States could not hide its participation and would suffer a devastating blow to prestige in the event of failure. Castro would not collapse after a single assault, leading to a prolonged civil war in which the United States would likely become involved and might suffer "the humiliation of a defeat." There was no assurance of a popular uprising, so U.S. Marines might have to be dispatched. "Cuba will become our Hungary." And if we denied involvement, we would "invite a repetition of the U-2 episode, which made us look absurd before the world."[58]

Less than a week later, Schlesinger again warned the president that an invasion could inflict great political and diplomatic damage on the new American image of statesmanship. Few people thought Cuba a threat to American security, and most would condemn such action as "*calculated aggression against a small nation in defiance both of treaty obligations and of the international standards we have repeatedly asserted against the Communist world* [emphasis in original]." Many observers would consider the invasion "a reversion to economic imperialism of the pre–World War I, Platt-Amendment, big-stick, gunboat-diplomacy kind." If a protracted civil war developed, the Communists could label it a "David against Goliath" battle, making Castro "the defender of the colored races against white imperialism." The Soviets could emerge as "the patron and protector of nationalists, Negroes, new nations and peace," while the new administration would appear to be "a gang of capitalist imperialists maddened by the loss of profits and driven to aggression and war." The world would believe that the purpose of overthrowing Castro was "to make Cuba safe again for American capitalism."[59]

As invasion day approached, the president came under enormous pressure to act quickly because of the rapidly spreading public exposure of the imminent event. Bissell vigorously defended the plan at a White House meeting on April 6, pointing to proposals intended to deflect blame from the United States. To make it appear that the United States sought only to restrain Batista supporters, authorities could arrest Rolando Masferrer, a former Cuban senator who had violated America's Neutrality Act of 1939 by leading a private army; seize a B-25 plane that had operated against Castro; and confiscate a few small boats used by those trying to undermine his regime. Three days before the invasion, a pilot would defect in the midst of air strikes, and on D-2 guerrillas would land. Popular resistance to Castro would swell after the Cuban brigade landed, and to drive home this point a guerrilla uprising would erupt five days later in Pinar del Rio to the east. Bissell preferred a full-scale air assault on D-Day morning rather than the D-2 operation and limited strikes on invasion day. But political consider- ations dictated a more restrained approach. He cautioned that this alteration in plans put the major burden of destroying Castro's air force on the D-Day strikes. Even though Rusk now thought the Zapata Plan the best approach conceivable, President Kennedy repeated his political concerns and refused to approve until he had given the matter more thought. When he asked his advisers the latest date for calling off the invasion, they declared that his last chance was April 16. Bowles disagreed, making an argument in a memo- randum that could apply to any instance of foreign intervention. "A great deal of time and money has been spent and many individuals have been emotionally involved in its success. We should not, however, proceed with this adventure simply because we are wound up and cannot stop." The president nonetheless approved continued planning of all aspects of the operation; he again emphasized the importance of making it appear to be a Cuban program while sullenly acknowledging that "we would be accused."[60]

President Kennedy was correct in his fears. Despite his appeals, the *New York Times* on the next day, April 7, carried a front-page story by Tad Szulc headlined "Anti-Castro Units Trained to Fight at Florida Bases." Close to the end of the story appeared a smaller headline, "Invasion Reported Near." CBS likewise had uncovered "unmistakable signs" of an invasion plan in its "final stages." Castro "doesn't need agents over here," Kennedy disgustedly declared to his press secretary in the Oval Office. "All he has to do is read our papers."[61]

IV

In a pivotal White House meeting on April 12, Bissell thrust ahead, setting out the major points of Operation Zapata to the president, the secretary of state, the Joint Chiefs, and other NSC officials. On D-7, just two days earlier, the main invasion force had begun staging operations, with the last vessel departing for Cuba in the early morning of D-4, or April 13. The B-26 defections would begin on D-2 in tandem with limited air strikes, and

Cuban defectors would land in Miami and request asylum, declaring that they had just strafed Cuban aircraft on the ground as part of a burgeoning revolution. In the meantime a diversionary landing would take place at the mouth of the Mocambo River in Oriente Province east of Guantanamo on the night of D-3 to D-2. United States naval vessels would provide "un-obtrusive" protection of the landing vessels until they entered Cuban ter-ritorial waters. The main landing would take more time than originally planned, beginning in the night hours of D-1 and continuing to dawn on D-Day while under the protection of limited air strikes. After the invasion forces seized the airstrip, two B-26s and a liaison plane would land. The off-loading of supplies would resume on D-Day night and conclude by the breaking of light on D+1.[62]

President Kennedy again stressed the importance of no American in-volvement in the landing operation. More than a Cuban intervention was on his mind at the time. Pro-West forces in Laos were under siege from pro-Communist Pathet Lao guerrillas, and pressure had continued to build for stronger U.S. action in Vietnam. In response to a question at a White House press conference later that same day of April 12, he skirted the overthrow effort by asserting that "there will not be, under any conditions, an inter-vention in Cuba by the United States Armed Forces. This Government will do everything it possibly can . . . to make sure there are no Americans in-volved in any actions inside Cuba."[63]

United States involvement nonetheless remained highly possible. In a key observation, Bundy left the way open in the event of landing problems when he assured Rusk of no U.S. armed intervention "*unless quite new circumstances develop* [emphasis mine]." Lemnitzer indicated a greater readiness to act when he warned Atlantic commander Admiral Dennison that *premature* U.S. military intervention would abort the operation. In-tervention, the Joint Chiefs' chair cautioned, should take place only if Castro's forces threatened to destroy the landing party.[64] Clearly the deci-sion for military action belonged to the president as commander in chief. But if lives were at stake . . .

In an effort to draw the line in constantly shifting sand, U.S. military advisers drew up rules of engagement that prohibited offensive action but condoned defensive measures. American destroyers must remain in inter-national waters at least twenty miles outside the landing site. The rules applied to Soviet submarines as well. If a submarine commander refused to identify himself, Lemnitzer proclaimed, Americans were to "attack with all authorized means available." As the *Essex* and seven destroyers escorted the landing parties' vessels to Cuban waters, they could fire at Castro's planes if they approached with bomb bays open or launched an attack. But in the event of an engagement, the American ships were to abort the mission by taking the brigade to Vieques Island, where Camp Garcia provided refuge and housed a hospital manned by U.S. Army personnel.[65]

On April 13, at Puerto Cabezas, a man referred to as "Mr. Dick" joined Colonel Egan and other Americans at the last briefing of the doctors and the brigade's staff and battalion leaders just before the embarkation for Cuba. Mr. Dick had been there at least a couple of times before, clearly the highest person in charge. Under the steamy morning sun, they sat at two wooden tables before a blackboard to go over final details with the tall and angular man in glasses—Richard Bissell, as the Cubans suspected. After a second round of meetings in the afternoon, Pepe declared that Egan "assured us that we were going to have protection by sea, by air, and even from under the sea." The U.S. Navy, the brigade forces were convinced, would support the invasion. "Most of the Cubans were there," Pepe asserted, "because they knew the whole operation was going to be conducted by the Americans, not by me or anyone else. They did not trust me or anyone else. They just trusted the Americans. So they were going to fight because the United States was backing them." Bissell's presence guaranteed that Pepe and his comrades were not alone.[66]

The following day, just three days before D-Day, Colonel Hawkins completed the assignment from Bissell to inspect the brigade at Guatemala and Puerto Cabezas and submitted a highly optimistic assessment of the coming operation that was, according to Robert Kennedy, "the most instrumental paper" in convincing his brother to go ahead. And how welcome the news, especially since the president had earlier dispatched a special envoy to Nicaragua to dispel Cuban expectations of an American military intervention. Hawkins's credibility was unquestioned. After training at the Marine Corps School at Quantico in Virginia, he fought in World War II, escaping prison in the Philippines and engaging in guerrilla action before winning a Bronze Medal for the Okinawa assault and a Silver Star in the Korean War. He then became the chief paramilitary adviser on the Cuban Task Force when the operation changed from an infiltration to an amphibious invasion. The men in Guatemala, he reported, were highly motivated, well armed, and superbly trained; if they inflicted a single major blow to Castro's forces, the popular masses would abandon him and help the invaders. The brigade constituted "a truly formidable force." In a statement carrying considerable weight with the president, Hawkins warned that it would be a huge mistake to call off the invasion.[67]

Hawkins's assessment proved pivotal in encouraging others in the administration to concur. Dulles told the president at his desk that he "was certain our Guatemalan operation would succeed, and, Mr. President, the prospects for this plan are even better than they were for that one." McNamara and Rusk declared their support and, according to Robert Kennedy, so did the Joint Chiefs of Staff. Both Dulles and Bissell had impressive records and enthusiastically supported the invasion, asserted the attorney general. "What convinced me the most part," he continued, was that if the landing forces encountered insurmountable opposition, they could make their way through the swamps and into the mountains, where they could operate as guerrillas.[68]

Perhaps in the exuberance of the moment, Hawkins had unintentionally inflated the capabilities of the Cuban brigade. Its morale was decidedly high now that the operation was under way. But many of the men had just arrived in Guatemala and never wielded a weapon. Only 135 of them were soldiers, whereas the majority of the group were students—240 of them. The rest were a hodgepodge of doctors, lawyers, businessmen, peasants, and fishermen—some as young as sixteen, one as old as sixty-one. Although the CIA made every effort to exclude Batistianos, some of them crept into the boats at the last minute, ensuring an embarrassment for the United States if the invasion went awry and Castro publicly paraded either his captives or their bodies before the world. More than four decades afterward, Hawkins defended his positive evaluation by insisting that his only mandate in the inspection was to determine the Cubans' attitudes and capabilities; he was *not* to raise questions about whether to continue the operation. Bissell had made it clear that it would take place regardless of the findings.[69] Perhaps because of Hawkins's personal involvement in the training program, or simply because he so fervently *wanted* the operation to succeed that he had come to believe that it would, he found it easier to ignore realities and present a glowing picture to Washington.

As scheduled, another step in the staging operation began in the early evening of April 10, when a long truck convoy rolled out of the Guatemalan base with members of the 2506 Assault Brigade, en route to the port of departure at Puerto Cabezas. Each soldier carried an automatic weapon and a portable radio, providing defensive and communication capabilities if separated from the landing group. The trucks bounced along as their passengers sang the Cuban national anthem.[70]

A team of CIA and Pentagon officials from Washington arrived at Puerto Cabezas the following day to provide three days of briefing to the Cuban brigade commanders. On the final day, April 14, the advisers revealed the details of the invasion plan. Now, in a change of course, early morning air strikes on D-2 were to disable Castro's air force and, just before the pre-dawn landing, Underwater Demolition Teams would conduct a reconnaissance of the three beaches lying within forty miles of the main target point at the Bay of Pigs. Their objective: Jab lights into the sand as guidance into the best landing spots. In the meantime, paratroopers would jump far enough inland to seal off Castro's roads leading down to the sea. The decision for pre-invasion air strikes had overridden the State Department's opposition by incorporating a compromise between the Joint Chiefs, who feared that a less than all-out assault would warn Castro of an invasion without being strong enough to neutralize his air force, and the CIA, which advocated a major air attack on his planes *during* the invasion but not beforehand for political reasons. To hide the American hand and placate the State Department (and the president), Cuban pilots would hit Castro's airfields two days before the invasion, and then one would land in the United States and pronounce himself a defector. A transparent cover indeed—but one that might hold until U-2 reconnaissance planes photographed the damage and D-Day could begin with a dawn air strike intended to destroy whatever remained of Castro's air force.[71]

The rest of the plan was straightforward. The *Blagar* as command ship would supervise the landing on both Blue and Green beaches on the southern coast east of the Bay of Pigs. The *Barbara J* would disembark forces on Red Beach at the top of the bay and then patrol the eastern sector. The Blue Beach landing would consist of two battalions (one from the *Caribe*, the other from the *Rio Escondido*), along with tanks, trucks, and other vehicles. The *Blagar* would transport a third battalion from the *Atlántico* to Green Beach before returning to Blue Beach to direct the off-loading of supplies. The *Barbara J* would escort the *Houston* carrying two battalions for the landing at Red Beach. Then it would accompany the *Houston* back to Blue Beach for dropping off cargo before patrolling the waters ten miles east of Green Beach.[72]

By this time, according to the CIA, five hundred island guerrillas would have joined the brigade at its landing, and another five thousand would arrive within two days, helping it establish and hold a beachhead for the three days Castro needed to mount his defense. Castro had about twenty thousand land forces that included both regulars and militia: two regular forces of six thousand each, one in Santa Clara eighty miles away with tanks and artillery, the other ten hours away at Camp Libertad, a hundred miles distant near Havana. In the meantime, paratroopers would have closed his access to the sea at three locations: Horquitas close to Yaguaramas; Jocuma near the Covadonga Sugar Mill; and on the road connecting the Australia Sugar Mill and Playa Larga. At the briefing, Frank Bender (code name for Gerry Droller) of the CIA, who was the chief recruiter of the force—even though he was intensely disliked, had no knowledge of Latin America, and spoke no Spanish—assured them of U.S. help. The planes would destroy the enemy as it tried to reach the brigade. "We'll protect the invasion with an umbrella. The air will belong to us. Every five minutes there will be a plane over all the major roads of Cuba." Once the brigade took Playa Girón, its planes would destroy all the railroads and bridges "in order to isolate said areas from enemy operations." In a dramatic last-minute assurance, Bender announced to the trainees, "We will be there with you for the next step. But you will be so strong, you will be getting so many people to your side, that you won't want to wait for us. You will go straight ahead. You will put your hands out, turn left, and go straight into Havana." This pep talk drew shouts of acclamation, punctuated by more than a few teary eyes over the reality of at last taking action to bring down the hated Castro regime.[73]

The Cuban brigade left Nicaragua for Cuba via three merchant vessels and a U.S. Navy LSD (landing ship, dock), led by the *Blagar* and the *Barbara J.* The U.S. Navy escorted the ships as they took separate routes toward a rendezvous point forty miles off the Cuban coast. From there they moved on their own at night to a spot five thousand yards from the invasion area, unseen by Castro's forces. The LSD carried LCUs (landing craft, utility) and LCPs (landing craft, personnel), whose task was to transport troops, tanks, and trucks that Cuban crews took ashore. In the bellies of these huge vessels were jeeps, trucks, tanks, recoilless rifles, bazookas, mortars, and mines. Finally, the brigade brought enough arms and equipment to outfit thirty thousand Cuban dissidents expected to join the overthrow.[74]

While at sea, where a secret remained secret, the company leaders met at 9:00 A.M. on April 14 and three hours later revealed the mission's destination to the brigade—the Bay of Pigs. "In the swamp?" one asked incredulously. "We won't have any problems," a field officer replied before extolling the virtues of the area and assuring them of the acquisition of a beachhead followed by the arrival from Miami of members of the Cuban Revolutionary Council as a provisional government. "And then the Americans," he added. One repeated the first question with a smile. "Will we have to go into the swamp?" "No, not at all," the officer repeated. "We'll land on one of the three beaches that cover around forty kilometers of solid ground along the coast. I repeat: it's high, solid ground. It's the militia who will have to slog through the swamp if they want to get close to us, and it won't be easy for them, because our paratroopers will seize the two roads that run through the swamp from the nearest towns to the coast." To remove any doubts, he noted, "The U.S. chiefs say that everything will go so smoothly—and that we won't stop until we get to Havana. They expect a lot of people to join us."[75]

In a communications network so cumbersome that it impeded rapid exchanges of information and sometimes left the White House hours behind events, a Washington war room relayed messages from the Joint Chiefs to Admiral Dennison and the task force commander and then, finally, to the 2506 Assault Brigade. Even though "nobody ever knew who was doing what," according to Burke, the venture moved ahead. The State Department stood ready to recognize this landing force as a government; accompanying the brigade was the Cuban Revolutionary Council's representative, Cuban exile Captain Manuel Artime, a highly articulate doctor, poet, and psychiatrist whose father was a Communist. Artime commanded respect, for he had been an officer in Castro's army before breaking with him in November 1959 and organizing the Movement of Revolutionary Recovery. He then became the CIA's contact on the FRD (united exile front) and the Cuban connection between the agency's political and military actions. Once landed, the CIA intended to send lawyer José Miró Cardona, Castro's first prime minister in 1959 and now unanimously selected in Miami as chair of the Revolutionary Council, to head the provisional government.[76]

On that same Friday of April 14, the American airmen expecting to fly the combat missions out of Nicaragua were sorely disappointed. *Cuban* pilots would man the B-26s, already in formation and armed with five-hundred-pound bombs and rockets strapped under the wings. The C-54 and C-46 transports stood by in the grassy areas off the runway, laden with infantry, supplies, and parachutists as they awaited departure orders.[77]

D-Day loomed less than seventy-two hours away.

4

Politics

I was simply directed to reduce the scale and make
it "minimal." [President Kennedy] left it to me to
determine exactly what that meant, and I responded by
cutting the planned sixteen aircraft to eight.
—Richard Bissell, post–April 17, 1961

The final version of the Zapata Plan did not reach the Joint Chiefs until two
days before D-Day, making it too late to conduct their own study. Not that
it mattered. The CIA's revised plan had taken on a sense of urgency in light
of the approaching rainy season and the imminent arrival in Havana of two
Soviet destroyers and one hundred Cuban pilots trained in Czechoslovakia
to fly more than twenty Soviet MIG fighter jets not yet assembled in Cuba.
In a remarkable understatement, General Lemnitzer declared that the use of
MIGs "would have pretty well complicated the operation."[1]

I

The Joint Chiefs preferred a much stronger assault than entailed in the planned D-2 and D-1 strikes, but they had to accept the politically driven restraints and rely on the D-Day attack to finalize the destruction of Castro's air force. Each B-26 had a fuel capacity dictating a three-and-a-half-hour turnaround time. To reduce the dangers of visibility and fuel depletion, the planes would launch the first attacks at dawn of D-2 and then return to base for refueling before hitting the same targets again at dusk. The following day, D-1, or April 16, the planes would pound the same places again but expand the strikes to include infantry bases along with bridges and highways considered essential to Castro's defense network. The D-Day campaign would complete the operation with two more waves, totaling forty-eight sorties, and, by also knocking out Castro's microwave radio system, force his military leaders into either radio silence or open communications permitting intercepts of troop plans.[2]

The task appeared certain of success. Castro feared defections or sabotage and had concentrated his planes and tanks on a few strips in the open for easy surveillance, but in doing so left them vulnerable to bombing. His air strength in numbers was not impressive—sixteen to eighteen combat aircraft—but his planes easily outmatched the brigade's seventeen light B-26 bombers in air-to-air combat. Castro had five or six Lockheed T-33 jet trainers that, according to the CIA, were lightly armed and posed no threat; the same number of single-engine British Sea Furies, swift-moving prop fighters wielding rockets and cannons on the wings; and six B-26s of his own, fitted with machine guns on each wing and four in the rear. At minimum, the D-Day strikes would disable most of the planes that survived the D-2 and D-1 onslaughts, keeping them from the beachhead and facilitating the brigade's landing.[3]

But the administration's determination to conceal American culpability had drastically altered the air operation. It became evident that the D-2 phase had undergone a major change when on April 15 at two in the morning Nicaraguan time (three in Cuba), only nine of the seventeen Cuban-piloted B-26s departed Puerto Cabezas, eight bound for Cuba, one for Florida, and, most surprising to everyone there, eight remaining on the ground. Somehow, the reasoning went, the 50 percent reduction in squadron size would increase the chances of hiding America's involvement. The eight B-26s comprising the strike force were to hit the three targets at the same time, while the single plane, piloted by Captain Mario Zuniga, veered toward Florida. It bore a new coat of paint matching that of Castro's Rebel Air Force (FAR) B-26s, the Cuban government's identifying serial number 933, and phony battle damage inflicted on the engine cover just before takeoff. Thus the final card in the ruse: Zuniga's landing in Miami as a defector from Castro's air force. The United States could escape responsibility by proclaiming a revolution under way in Cuba.[4]

One of the American training pilots, Air National Guardsman Albert Persons from Birmingham, Alabama, could not understand why only eight planes participated in the D-2 operation. He and others concluded that the Washington representatives who arrived in Puerto Cabezas on the Thursday before the Saturday attacks had cut the number of aircraft. But why?[5]

The invasion had already appeared threatened when political concerns had earlier led to the decision to restrict the number of planes to sixteen from the original twenty-two. The two field officers heading the Zapata operation, Colonel Hawkins from the marines and Esterline from the CIA, had not considered the new number enough, and after Hawkins completed the planning for the attack, he concluded that the invasion could not work. Esterline concurred, and on the Sunday morning of April 9 he and Hawkins went to Bissell's Washington home to resign. The president's decision to shift the invasion from Trinidad to Zapata had already jeopardized the operation by eliminating the possibility of waging a guerrilla war from the Escambray Mountains; now, they insisted, sixteen B-26s were not sufficient to destroy Castro's air force. If any of his planes escaped the assault, they could sink the brigade's ships and scatter the ground forces into the Zapata Swamp. The White House must call off the invasion.[6]

Bissell insisted it was too late to cancel the operation but assured his two visitors that he would talk to the president about the air campaign. Hawkins and Esterline differed in their recollections of the meeting. Years afterward, Hawkins attested that Bissell had promised to "take immediate action with the president to use more aircraft and increase the power of the attack on the opposing air force." Esterline, however, recalled that Bissell promised "no more reductions on air strikes." In either case, their focus on the air assaults should have made it clear to Bissell that they were critical to success.[7]

But Hawkins and Esterline did not trust Bissell. Already convinced that he was self-centered and used everything and everybody for personal advantage, they believed he should have defended Trinidad as the invasion point along with a larger air strike contingent as critical to the operation.

They were now certain that Bissell had never defended the need for air operations and that the president, therefore, did not recognize the central importance of disabling Castro's air force. But they agreed to stay in their positions after Bissell questioned their loyalty and promised to emphasize the importance of the air assaults to the president. Esterline joined Hawkins in failing to grasp Bissell's determination to satisfy the president's political concerns and thereby keep the plan alive and concluded that he "was lying down and lying up for reasons that I don't yet totally understand."[8]

Not until 1996 did Hawkins and Esterline discover that two or three days prior to the D-2 strikes (thus *after* the assurances made at their April 9 meeting), Bissell *cut* the assault force by half, from sixteen to those eight that departed Nicaragua on D-2. President Kennedy, Bissell explained in his memoirs, wanted to "play down the magnitude of the invasion in the public eye" by imposing greater limitations on the number of planes used. "I was simply directed to reduce the scale and make it 'minimal.'" Without questioning the wisdom of this order, Bissell followed it. The president "left it to me to determine exactly what that meant, and I responded by cutting the planned sixteen aircraft to eight." Bissell defended his action by noting a revision in the April 12 CIA briefing memo sent to the president. Instead of a massive strike in coordination with the landings, the plan limited the scale of the bombings both before and on D-Day.[9]

Bissell never explained this decision to Hawkins and Esterline. Nor did he ever acknowledge this Sunday meeting in his memoirs—a meeting that proved pivotal in shaping the entire Cuba operation.[10]

By 9:30 A.M. on April 15, the first specks appeared in the distant eastern sky, marking the return of the D-2 attack force to its Nicaraguan base. Only five planes descended on the runway, four lightly damaged but the other one bearing a stream of holes in the fuselage and a large rip in the right wing panel. Two more planes eventually made it back, one first having to refuel at Britain's Grand Cayman Island and the other, with one engine hit, making an emergency landing at the U.S. Navy Base in Key West. Anti-aircraft artillery had struck the eighth plane over Havana, killing the pilot and navigator and sending it down in a fiery crash into the harbor. The ninth B-26 landed as planned in Miami, where Zuniga jumped out in his khaki pants, white T-shirt, and baseball cap, all with Cuban labels, puffing a Cuban cigarette while enthusiastically boasting that he and others had defected after strafing and bombing Castro's planes as part of a widespread insurrection.[11]

John F. Kennedy and Fidel Castro were bitter rivals throughout the president's shortened term in office. Kennedy, *Abbie Rowe, National Park Service/ John Fitzgerald Kennedy Library, Boston*; Castro, *Courtesy Library of Congress.*

Richard Bissell, CIA deputy director of plans and chief architect of the Bay of Pigs project, including both assassination and invasion. *Courtesy CIA*

Robert Maheu, a former FBI agent and now a private investigator, did contracted work for the CIA and served as "cut-out" in contacting the Mafia without leaving a trail of CIA involvement. *Courtesy Wide World Photos.*

Johnny Roselli acted as roving ambassador for the Mafia while maintaining thriving business enterprises in both Las Vegas and Los Angeles. He helped the CIA make contact with the underworld. *Courtesy Wide World Photos.*

Sam Giancana was the god-father of the Mafia's operation in Chicago known as "the Outfit." The CIA's hopes for Mafia assistance in assassinating Castro hinged on his cooperation in the project. *Courtesy Wide World Photos.*

Santo Trafficante was the godfather of the Mafia's southern operation in Florida who knew dissidents in Cuba interested in killing Castro and could serve as translator. *Courtesy Wide World Photos.*

Antonio Varona was integral to both CIA-Mafia plots to assassinate Castro, even though he distrusted agency figures because "they were Americans." *Courtesy Miami Herald.*

2506 Assault Brigade airstrip built by the United States at Retalhuleh, Guatemala. Camp Trax sat high in the mountains seen in the background. *Courtesy Antonio de la Cova.*

Senator John F. Kennedy and CIA director Allen Dulles prepare to meet the press at Hyannisport, Massachusetts, following Dulles's briefing of the president-elect. *Courtesy CIA.*

President John F. Kennedy and historian Arthur Schlesinger confer in the White House Oval Office. Schlesinger warned the president that involvement in the Bay of Pigs operation could undermine American credibility throughout the world. *Courtesy John F. Kennedy Library.*

President John F. Kennedy meets with National Security Affairs Adviser McGeorge Bundy in the White House Oval Office. Bundy served as liaison with the CIA, at one point early in the administration pushing for the establishment of an executive action capability in the agency. *Courtesy John F. Kennedy Library.*

President John F. Kennedy meets with members of the Joint Chiefs of Staff. From left to right: Air Force General Curtis LeMay, Admiral Arleigh Burke, Army General George Decker, Joint Chiefs Chair and Army General Lyman Lemnitzer, and Marine Corps Commandant General David Shoup. The Joint Chiefs virtually conceded military leadership in the Bay of Pigs operation to the CIA. *Courtesy John F. Kennedy Library.*

Parachute Battalion 1 before leaving camp at Camp Trax in Guatemala. *Courtesy Antonio de la Cova.*

Manuel Artime speaks to 2506 Assault Brigade at Camp Trax in Guatemala. *Courtesy Antonio de la Cova.*

Czech anti-aircraft gun used by Castro's forces. *Courtesy Antonio de la Cova.*

Sea Fury from Castro's Revolutionary Air Force. *Courtesy Antonio de la Cova.*

B-26 from Castro's Revolutionary Air Force. *Courtesy Antonio de la Cova.*

Lt. Rafael del Pino flew this T-33 jet as part of Castro's Revolutionary Air Force in defending against the Bay of Pigs invasion. At the last moment, Castro's engineers attached machine guns to his trainer jets' wings, making the craft highly effective against the Cuban brigade on the ground and its ships in the bay. *Courtesy Antonio de la Cova.*

Castro's air force sank the *Houston* on April 17, 1961, forcing the men to abandon the ship in shark-infested waters. *Courtesy Antonio de la Cova.*

Russian T-34 tank operated by Castro's forces. *Courtesy Antonio de la Cova.*

2506 Assault Brigade prisoners. *Courtesy Antonio de la Cova.*

2506 Assault Brigade weapons captured by Castro's forces. *Courtesy Antonio de la Cova.*

2506 Assault Brigade leader Pepe San Román in Havana prison. *Courtesy United Press International.*

2506 Assault Brigade prisoners berated by Fidel Castro at the Havana sports palace. *Courtesy Antonio de la Cova.*

President John F. Kennedy and Attorney General Robert F. Kennedy in discussion outside the White House Oval Office. *Courtesy John F. Kennedy Library.*

As a legendary veteran of both the OSS and the CIA, General Edward Lansdale headed the top-secret Mongoose program to eliminate Fidel Castro by any method deemed necessary. *Courtesy U.S. Air Force.*

President Kennedy meets in April 1962 with (left to right) Allen Dulles, former CIA director; Richard Bissell, former CIA deputy director of plans; and CIA director John McCone. *Courtesy CIA.*

Rolando Cubela (AMLASH), recruited by the CIA to lead a military coup against the Castro regime that hinged on the Maximum Leader's death, either in the course of the takeover or by outright assassination. *Courtesy Wide World Photos.*

President John F. Kennedy awards Allen Dulles the National Security Medal on November 28, 1961. *Courtesy John F. Kennedy Library.*

President John F. Kennedy awards Richard Bissell the National Security Medal on March 1, 1962. *Courtesy Wide World Photos.*

In a costly failure, the diversionary landing in Oriente Province to the east by 168 commandos on the *Santa Ana* did not take place because of poor leadership, the inability to find the landing site, and, most important, the presence of a substantial ground force commanded by Castro's brother Raúl. On the night of April 13 a reconnaissance team from the vessel discovered lights and, assuming Cuban troops were nearby, recommended delaying the landing until the next night. But on that second night the scouts heard jeeps and trucks. "They're waiting for us," declared a battalion officer whose superior believed him and refused to follow a CIA officer's insistence on going ahead with the landing. Raúl Castro had been there since early that month of April, in command of troops and an anti-aircraft battery consisting of half a dozen four-mouth machine guns. And he had spotted the *Santa Ana* waiting for nightfall. The ship withdrew, taking the sound equipment intended to simulate a great invasion and leaving Castro to concentrate his defenses at the Bay of Pigs.[12]

The brigade's spirits nonetheless ran high as initial reports asserted that the B-26s had severely damaged all three Cuban airfields. One pilot returning from Camp Libertad near Havana (the second delayed at Key West and the third shot down) reported that one bomb directly hit an air force ammunition center, destroying half of Castro's planes and setting off a string of explosions that continued for a half hour. At the airport near San Antonio de los Baños, two pilots (the third not yet returned from Grand Cayman) claimed to have demolished 80 percent of the enemy force, including at least one of three T-33s and three-fourths of the airfield along with the operations building. Smoke billowing upward from the bombings concealed the pummeled area, preventing an accurate damage assessment. And at Antonio Maceo Airport in Santiago de Cuba, according to two pilots, they destroyed two B-26s, disabled one T-33 and one C-47, and blew up fuel tanks, the anti-aircraft artillery nest, and the huge hangar. Rolling waves of fire enveloped the area, leaving every plane on the ramp in flames and the airfield no longer usable. Radio Swan had earlier lifted the spirits of the brigade by reporting a dispute with Castro and others in the prime minister's office, after which Che had been thrown out of the government and shot and wounded, and then following that account with the claim that the air raids had killed and wounded many Castro supporters and destroyed nearly all his military bases. Both stories later proved erroneous but at the moment meshed with the successful bombing assaults to make victory seem certain.[13]

Then came a shocking development: As the pilots prepared for that day's second wave of attacks, they learned that Washington had called them off along with those of the following day. Apparently the exuberant reports of overwhelming D-2 damage had convinced the White House that follow-up strikes were not necessary. Did that include the D-Day strikes as well? If so, Castro would have two days to recover and mount a defense. "There goes the whole fuckin' war!!!" shouted General Reid Doster of the Alabama Air National Guard, throwing his cap in disgust.[14]

The truth about the D-2 strikes did not come out until late in the morning of April 16, when follow-up intelligence reports and U-2 photos revealed a decidedly different story: The assault force had destroyed only five planes while temporarily disabling a few others. Most of Castro's planes survived for several reasons, including the possible failure to hit one runway and, doubtless because of the fear of U.S. attribution, the CIA's decision to ban the use of napalm except on tank farms without special permission. He still had two or three Sea Furies, a pair of B-26 bombers, and two to four T-33 jets—a force strong enough to place even greater importance onto the D-Day strikes.[15]

II

The Cuban crisis had meanwhile prompted an emergency meeting of the Political Committee of the UN General Assembly on the day of the April 15 attacks, spurred on by Castro's visit to two of the bombing sites and an angry demand for a UN investigation into U.S. "imperialist aggression." As members of the Fair Play for Cuba Committee demonstrated outside the UN building and New York's police on foot and horseback herded them behind wood barriers, those inside engaged in a series of fiery exchanges that threatened to expand the confrontation into more than a regional issue. Over the past few weeks, Cuban foreign minister Raúl Roa had repeatedly accused the United States of intentions to invade his homeland, and he now hotly charged the Kennedy administration with bombing Cuba as the first step. Especially striking in this greatly intensified Cold War atmosphere was the Soviet reaction. UN Ambassador Valerian Zorin ominously warned that "Cuba has many friends in the world who were ready to come to its aid, including the Soviet Union."[16]

In an incredible piece of either chicanery or sheer ineptitude, the White House had not alerted the U.S. ambassador to the United Nations, Adlai Stevenson, to American complicity in the air attack before he went on the world stage to deny the Cuban allegations. So in good faith he referred to President Kennedy's pledges at the April 12 press conference that U.S. armed forces would not "under any conditions" intervene in Cuba, that his administration would not permit U.S. citizens to take action against Cuba, and that no one could use the United States as a base against any foreign government. Defectors from the Cuban air force carried out the attacks, he proclaimed after receiving Rusk's assurances. One sought political asylum in Miami, Stevenson declared while displaying a wire service photo of the defector's plane.[17]

This phony defection story, hailed as ingenious by Hawkins along with Bissell and Barnes in the CIA, had a predictably brief life span. The first signs of trouble came when two more defections occurred: one the result of the CIA's decision to land another fraudulent defector in Key West in case the Miami hoax failed; the other a *real* defector who landed 340 miles north in Jacksonville. Soon after Zuniga's Miami arrival, two CIA officers in charge of the cover action "came bouncing into the office all laughter and joy and offered to have a couple of ceremonial drinks," according to Richard Drain, Esterline's operations chief for the Cuba Project. "I remember saying to them, 'well, I hope you are as happy about 5 o'clock this afternoon, as you are now ... because how long this holds up in Miami seemed to me very questionable indeed.'" Drain's prognosis proved correct. Reporters exposed the story as a sham, pointing to the differences between the plane in Jacksonville (the genuine defector) and those phonies in Miami and Key West. The so-called Cuban B-26 in Miami, they noted, wore a recent coat of paint, and its guns had not been fired. Especially devastating was Roa's public ridicule of Stevenson's picture presented as proof. The B-26 had a metal nose and hence was *American*, Roa sneered; Castro's B-26s bore Plexiglas fronts.[18]

Stevenson fumed with a potent mixture of fury and mortification. The White House had not kept him fully informed, allowing him to make statements discrediting his word in an international organization in which primary leverage rested on trust. Furthermore, the attack took place at a particularly inopportune time—two days before a regularly scheduled UN General Assembly debate over Cuba, thereby crushing any chance for improving relations. Schlesinger and others had briefed him a few days earlier in vague terms about some sort of Cuban operation, and Barnes had told him that Cuban exiles intended to invade their homeland in an effort to overthrow Castro. But no one mentioned either the air assault or the U.S. role in these events. Stevenson indignantly complained that he had received no warning, leaving him unprepared to defend the administration. His embarrassment heightened when the next day's newspapers all over the world carried the story on their front pages, including a picture of his triumphantly waving the B-26 photo as proof of U.S. innocence.[19]

The United States' Cuban policy threatened to convert its worst fears about Castro's political ideals into a self-fulfilling prophecy. For the first time, he publicly aligned his country with socialism at a location that today bears a bronze plaque commemorating the birthplace of its new direction. At the following day's state funerals of loyalists who perished in the air raids, he bitterly blamed Washington's leaders because they "cannot forgive us for achieving a Socialist revolution under their very noses." The crowd of ten thousand (mostly militia) defiantly shouted, "Fidel, Khrushchev, we are with you both!" The United States, Castro bombastically proclaimed, had committed an act worse than Japan's on December 7, 1941. "If the attack on Pearl Harbor is considered by the American people as a criminal, traitorous, cowardly act, then our people have a right to consider this act twice as criminal, twice as cunning, twice as traitorous, and a thousand times as cowardly." The White House denial of responsibility constituted the ultimate flight from reality. "Even Hollywood would not try to film such a story." Castro defiantly pronounced Cuba a socialist nation and inched it closer to the Soviet camp.[20]

While this matter raged in the UN, President Kennedy on that same day of April 16 approved the invasion. He waited until the last minute, finally deciding to go ahead after apparently regarding the disappointing news about the D-2 strikes as the last opportunity to act before Castro amassed his defenses and left direct U.S. military intervention as the only option for toppling his regime. Kennedy had other reasons as well. Failure to pursue the operation would make the Cuban brigade a potential embarrassment for the White House; embittered Cubans would publicly accuse the administration of betraying their trust and cowering before Communism; and Castro's fall would make the president look "tough" to Khrushchev, paying dividends not only in the hemisphere but around the globe in the hotly contested Cold War. According to Schlesinger, Kennedy felt certain that "he had successfully pared it down from a grandiose amphibious assault to a mass insurrection." He thought the brigade's forces had an "escape hatch" in the mountains, as the CIA repeatedly assured. Kennedy also admired their patriotic fervor, knew that success would encourage democracy's spread in the hemisphere, and believed in his own luck. But most of all, Schlesinger declared, Kennedy's newness in office—only seventy-seven days—made it impossible to determine which advisers to believe and trust. A formidable phalanx of power supported the plan—the Joint Chiefs and the CIA, along with the heads of the Defense and State departments. As Kennedy observed, "You always assumed that the military and intelligence people have some secret skill not available to ordinary mortals."[21]

Secretary of Defense McNamara's support weighed heavily in the final decision, but his reasoning demonstrated no grasp of the heavy odds against success and the enormous cost of failure. The United States, he argued, was at "the point of no return" and, in a statement remarkably similar to his later less than optimistic justifications for military escalation in Vietnam, he recommended going ahead despite only "a marginal probability of success." If the White House called off the operation, the Cuban forces would return to the United States and blast the administration as weak and hypocritical in its anti-Communist pronouncements. Besides, McNamara argued, if the Cuban brigade failed to take the beachhead, it could escape through the swamps and into the Escambray Mountains, where it would switch to guerrilla tactics and prove this was not a "total defeat." Finally, if Castro's units made it to the beaches and blocked passage to the mountains, the brigade could evacuate by sea. For some reason McNamara did not attempt to explain, he thought it easier for the Cuban invaders to make it through the swamps than for "Castro's units" to do the same. But couldn't Castro's militiamen, who knew the terrain, more expeditiously make the arduous passage?[22]

McNamara's remarks underlined the shaky nature of a project built on questionable premises and dubious assumptions. President Kennedy followed his defense secretary's logic, asserting that if the invasion failed to meet expectations, the press could not call it a disaster if the Cubans dissolved into the mountains. Flawed thinking and faulty presumptions did not stop here. The most rudimentary examination of a map shows the almost insurmountable hardships involved in escaping to the Escambray Mountains through a vast swampland. The CIA, however, had used a rough survey map of 1895 that somehow in its strategists' collective wisdom substantiated the argument for using the swamps as a guerrilla haven. Furthermore, the mountains were located on the east side of the Zapata

Swamp and just north of Trinidad—*eighty hard miles* from the Bay of Pigs. In the meantime, the Joint Chiefs argued that a mass insurrection provided the key to success, and yet the White House acknowledged that this was unlikely because of the communication and organizational difficulties inherent in a police state. First reports from the D-2 operation further contributed to the hopes built on sand. As McNamara attested, the president's advisers "assumed" that the raids had disabled most of Castro's planes and went ahead with the invasion, even though believing "the whole operation was marginal" *before* knowing that the D-2 assessment was a "major error." The Joint Chiefs likewise took the slippery slope, admitting to highly unfavorable odds but wanting "to give it a try."[23]

Blind faith in luck, a reliance on American ingenuity, and the felt need to do something, all dangerously catalyzed by an uncanny inability to recognize the unpleasant realities of a plan relentlessly churning toward a predictable implosion—these factors had combined with a growing obsession to get rid of Castro that thrust the administration into an operation pockmarked with warnings of failure.

III

Signs of impending trouble were many in number, but the most pivotal moments came when President Kennedy made two politically motivated decisions that posed greater dangers to the invasion. First, as noted earlier, he changed the target point from Trinidad to Zapata in an effort to retain the façade of plausible deniability. The Pentagon and others had emphasized the crucial nature of arousing popular support, and yet no one seemed to recognize that an after-dark landing in this largely uninhabited area offered little chance of igniting an insurrection. How, asked Esterline years afterward, could such an invasion inspire a popular uprising? Nobody was there "except alligators and ducks." Second, and more serious, the president late on April 16 *canceled* the D-Day strikes, using the same political reasoning that had dictated his changing the landing site to Zapata.[24]

How had the White House gotten itself into this position?

At 9:30 in the evening of April 16, McGeorge Bundy telephoned the CIA, stunning General Cabell with the president's directive to hold off the dawn strikes until the landing party seized an airstrip in Cuba from which to launch them. Dulles was in Puerto Rico at the time, purposely on a speaking engagement that supposedly gave him room to deny responsibility for the invasion but instead thrust Cabell into the middle of events that would shape the entire operation. In the continuing illogic of circular reasoning, Washington called off the D-Day assault until after the brigade established a beachhead, which its forces had little chance of accomplishing while unprotected from an attack above. Furthermore, the invasion force was already en route to Cuba, leaving no way to stop the operation short of causing another mutiny.[25] Castro's air force would thus gain free rein in the skies and full access to the enemy on the ground and at sea.

Political considerations prevailed over military realities in a decision that many observers both then and later have labeled the most damaging blow to the operation. According to the familiar story, the president and secretary of state were not aware of the signal importance of air support during an amphibious landing and told Bundy to halt the D-Day strikes. Kennedy's decision resulted from several considerations, including Soviet and Chinese warnings of retaliatory action in one of the world's hot spots (Berlin? Laos? Vietnam?), the initial optimistic reports of the D-2 strikes by now determined to be grossly wrong, his promise against direct U.S. intervention in Cuba, his advisers' assurances of a successful invasion without D-Day strikes, and, most important, his repeatedly expressed determination to hide the American hand. But he also did not want to put Stevenson into the position of lying to the UN—particularly after his humiliation over the alleged defection. The CIA cover story for the D-2 bombings had blown up in the administration's face, shattering its reputation for integrity and leading the president to believe Rusk and Bundy's argument that the only acceptable bombing site was the landing area—and even that under severe restrictions.[26]

Bundy invited Cabell to discuss the matter with Rusk, who "had the proxy of the President," by then off to his Virginia weekend retreat at Glen Ora. As for Bundy, he sarcastically declared that he was on the way to the UN in New York "to hold the hand of Ambassador Adlai Stevenson."[27]

Cabell was baffled by this turn of events. Why, he asked in his memoirs, hadn't the president consulted the CIA before making this drastic decision? He and his colleagues were close by and could have met with the president in moments. And why Bundy's rush? Stevenson confronted UN speeches; the brigade faced Castro's firepower.[28]

Cabell immediately notified Bissell, who together met with the secretary of state in his office within the hour, at 10:15 P.M. At the beginning of their conversation, Rusk took a phone call from someone not identified who,

Cabell and Bissell could tell, expressed deep concern over the canceled strikes. Bolstered by the knowledge that someone high in the Washington chain of command was equally alarmed, they tried to persuade Rusk to countermand the order. But he repeated Bundy's admonition—that the brigade must first secure a beachhead with a fully operational airstrip from which to initiate the strikes and make them appear indigenous in origin. The D-Day strikes were not crucial to the operation, argued Rusk; the ships "could unload and retire to the open sea before daylight." And "as for the troops ashore being unduly inconvenienced" by Castro's planes, he had learned while a colonel in the China-Burma-India theater of World War II "that air attacks could be more of a nuisance than a danger." Air protection, Rusk had earlier assured the president and the Joint Chiefs, was not essential to a guerrilla operation if the landing took place at night and in small craft. Rather than save Cuban lives on the beaches, Cabell and Bissell thought, the new policy sought to save American face in the UN. Rusk substantiated their suspicion when he triumphantly remarked that "military considerations had overruled the political when the D-2 air strike had been laid on. Now political considerations were taking over."[29]

Cabell and Bissell were flabbergasted. This was not a small-scale guerrilla infiltration; it was a major amphibious landing. A night-time operation of this magnitude guaranteed monstrous problems even when carried out by highly trained and experienced personnel. A slip in timing and the process could drag into daylight, fully exposing the brigade to Castro's planes. Cabell was particularly irritated by Rusk's claim to air war expertise. The secretary based his argument on *observations* in World War II, whereas Cabell had acquired his knowledge as a *participant* in that war, planning and executing two of the largest amphibious operations in history—at Normandy and in southern France. Failure to neutralize Castro's air force, Cabell and Bissell warned, would undermine the invasion and ensure a massive death toll while eliminating any hope of seizing the airstrip.[30]

Their argument did not dissuade the secretary, but it led to one change. In a move already worked out with the president as a suitable concession if necessary, Rusk authorized air cover in the beachhead area only. Cabell, not knowing of this prior arrangement, thought the secretary made this allowance based on his experiences in the early part of World War II, when the army accepted air force support of troops as its only combat mission. Rusk apparently saw a political distinction between bombing targets *away from* the battlefield and providing a protective shield *over* the battlefield.[31]

As if on impulse, Rusk abruptly telephoned the president in their presence and related their concern. After summarizing their argument, Rusk informed Kennedy of the modified air decision and went through the motions of securing his approval. Just as suddenly, Rusk cupped his hand over the phone and asked Cabell, "Do you wish to speak to the President?" Cabell pondered his reply, realizing that Rusk as the one in charge had rejected his plea and had then repeated the entire argument to the president before recommending that he turn it down. Would a continued protest endanger the newly won concession of beachhead protection? Would further delay increase the danger to the landing? Cabell considered himself a loyal servant and quickly dismissed the thought of opposing the commander in chief. Besides, he was certain that Kennedy would not budge because of his well-known political concerns and the sensitive situation with Stevenson and the UN.[32]

"No," Cabell finally replied to Rusk. How mind-shaking this was, Cabell recalled in his memoirs years afterward. "Does one say 'no' when invited to speak to the President?"[33] In one of those rare moments in history, Cabell had done just that.

The CIA staff stared in disbelief when Cabell and Bissell that same night reported the White House decision to cancel the air strikes. Hawkins slammed the desk with his hand, shouting, "Goddamn it, this is criminal negligence!" Esterline hotly agreed. "This is the goddamnest thing I have ever heard of." Cabell tried to calm them, arguing that their duty was to accept the decision. "I know that some of you have lived very close to this operation for a long time and feel very deeply about it, but when you get a change in the marching orders you have to react now and you have to take your orders and do what you are told."[34]

Hawkins refused to stand down and in tears called his commander, General Shoup, around 1:30 that morning. "General," Hawkins pleaded, "you've got to get ahold of the President because they have influenced him to call off the air strike. We're going to fail. You've got to help."

"Well," Shoup asked, "has he already made his decision?"

"Yes, they told us we're not going to do it."

"Christ knows that I can't do anything. Maybe if I'd had a chance beforehand..."[35]

Cabell had likewise made one last try, calling Major General David Gray from the Pentagon at one in the morning asking him to come down to the agency. "Now I want you to think up things that your people can do to help us." But they quickly realized the pointlessness of their discussion since the president had refused to authorize U.S. force. As Gray remarked to the officer escorting him into the hall after the meeting, "Surely Cabell realizes that this means this operation is doomed to failure."[36]

Cabell knew he had to act quickly to minimize the impact of this lethal threat to the mission. He must first stop the brigade's planes before they embarked for the airfield strikes and divert them to the beachhead as cover for the landing force. He had to warn the landing party to expedite operations because of the canceled assaults. And he must secure "outside help" in safeguarding the landing party—perhaps the U.S. Navy Task Force, which he knew had authorization to defend the landing party up to the moment it entered Cuban waters. He alerted the task force to stand ready while he sought approval to expand its use into protecting the landing itself.[37]

Cabell's efforts were only partly successful. He barely achieved the first objective. When the order stopping the D-Day strikes reached the Nicaraguan airstrip, the pilots were already in their cockpits and prepared for takeoff. He then notified the Cuban brigade of the canceled air strikes and, because the beachhead cover authorized by Rusk was light in number and heavy in restrictions, warned of freewheeling attacks from overhead. Four of the brigade's B-26s would hover over the landing site on D-Day, but only two at a time, all lacking rear gunnery and highly vulnerable to Castro's faster planes. The ships, Cabell emphasized to the commanders, *must* offload the brigade and materials before dawn. He was trying to win approval for additional air cover and for "early warning destroyers" to alert them of approaching enemy planes.[38]

Cabell telephoned Rusk about the new request for U.S. naval jet cover for the landing and, at 4:30 in the morning of D-Day, went to his apartment to seek approval.[39] Cabell must have recognized the futility of his proposal. Although the administration had sanctioned use of the navy task force only outside Cuban territorial waters, it had related that expedient to a D-Day strike plan that no longer was on the table. Use of navy jets under the original concept was politically acceptable because they were to help an alleged revolution against Castro already under way—spearheaded by a "Cuban" air attack and followed by an invasion comprised only of Cuban exiles. But the White House could not make a case for plausible deniability if American jets accompanied the Cuban B-26s covering the invasion.

This attempt was a touchy proposition in another way as well: It required extending the navy's protective CAP (combat air patrol) from twenty miles offshore down to three. Presented with this clearly unexpected request, Rusk said he preferred that Cabell speak with the president and asked the White House operator to place the call. In no time Kennedy picked up the phone. This time Cabell took the receiver, repeating his proposal to the president. Air cover was needed to the shoreline, he argued. If that was not acceptable, it should start at the three-mile limit. If neither proposal was satisfactory, the U.S. Navy fighters should be able to fly to the three-mile limit, at the least intimidating Castro's pilots even if not authorized to engage. Kennedy first spoke with Rusk before turning down all three requests. Cabell then sought authorization for using the U.S. Navy's early warning destroyers to notify the ships' commanders of approaching aircraft spotted on radar. The president approved this request but added a stipulation, again demonstrating the importance he attached to concealing the U.S. role. Not only must the destroyers remain in international waters, but he increased the distance to *thirty* miles off Cuba's coast instead of twenty.[40]

The invasion armada would stand alone, except for four B-26s circling overhead, two at a time and virtually incapable of air-to-air combat.

IV

Cabell and Bissell claimed they did everything possible to convince the president to authorize the D-Day strikes but that nothing could have altered his decision. "I don't think there's any point," Cabell remarked to critics insisting he should have tried harder. "I think I agree with that," Bissell replied. But he later called this a big mistake, saying they should have taken the matter to the president. What did they have to lose?[41]

Should Cabell have tried to stop the invasion? On the surface this seemed worth pursuing, and yet the president's eleventh-hour decision to cancel the air strikes made it too late to call off a massive enterprise already under way. The domestic and foreign humiliation, the impact on possible future ventures, the bitterness engendered among those Guatemalans and Nicaraguans working with the United States, the loss of massive amounts of matériel, the Cuban exiles' certain sense of betrayal—all factors dictated against terminating the operation. Cabell recalled a similar experience in Italy during World War II, when Americans were negotiating with representatives of Germany for a surrender and the Germans' biggest fear was mutiny. The Cuban situation was potentially more explosive in that it involved fresh and anxious patriots anticipating battle in a war just beginning as opposed to Germans already exhausted by a long war winding to an end.[42]

Rusk's story is considerably different. The administration, he explained, recognized air control as important to the invasion but nonetheless thought political considerations outweighed military needs. He opposed a D-Day strike after learning of the D-2 raids. In a statement having no basis in fact, he asserted that "neither the President nor I was clear that there was a D-2 air strike." They knew of the planned D-Day attack, but, Rusk declared, "I was caught by surprise with the first air strikes." He denied misleading Stevenson, insisting he kept the ambassador informed but "suddenly found out there were additional air strikes coming up. We didn't want him to have to lie to the UN." Furthermore, he continued, Cabell and Bissell "indicated that the air strikes would be important, not critical." When invited to call the president, "they indicated they didn't think the matter was that important." Rusk and the president therefore found no "overriding considerations" for D-Day strikes.[43]

Rusk's defense is not convincing, though it is understandable. Instead of relying on his wartime experience to determine his (and the president's) opposition to the D-Day strikes, he should have consulted the Joint Chiefs of Staff. But Cabell and Bissell bear a major part of the blame for not talking with the president even if they thought their cause hopeless. By not doing so, they left the impression that the D-Day assault was not critical and thereby encouraged Rusk to believe his appraisal correct. By no means did they consider the attacks *un*important to the invasion, as Rusk asserted. But, as Hawkins charged, they failed to make a strong case.[44]

Rusk and the president warrant criticism for reasons going beyond their failure to keep informed of all aspects of the operation. How could they have been unaware of the D-2 strikes? The secretary was not telling the truth. Several bits of evidence substantiate this charge, but let two instances suffice. On April 12, three days before the D-2 strikes, Rusk and the president attended a White House meeting, where the CIA presented a paper highlighting modifications in the Zapata Plan, including a reduction in scale of the *D-2 strikes*. Two days later, on April 14, President Kennedy instructed Bissell to cut the size of the *D-2 assault*.[45] Even if Kennedy never shared his April 14 decision with Rusk (which is highly doubtful), neither man could have been surprised by the D-2 strikes.

Faulty political reasoning lay behind canceling the D-Day strikes because the decision rested on a non-issue. What chance was there the world would believe American disclaimers about involvement in a D-Day bombing when the administration had already been caught in a lie about the D-2 raids? Other advisers recognized the stand as unrealistic. "I'm amazed," Bundy candidly conceded in retrospect, "that we thought there was a chance of deniability." Indeed, years afterward Rusk expressed the same doubts about plausible denial. "We were hoping for the maximum. In retrospect, however, this looks a little naïve." If you succeed, "all the problems solve themselves." But if you fail, "it's very nice if the United States is not involved."[46]

In a statement that is technically true but of dubious value, President Kennedy later asserted that CIA officials never spoke with him directly about the importance of the air strikes. He admitted that he should have sought the National Security Council's advice, and one can only ask again why neither he nor Rusk took the initiative in consulting either the Joint Chiefs—the nation's acknowledged military experts—or the CIA, the chief architect of the entire operation. Had he understood the essential role of the D-Day strikes, Kennedy asserted, he would have approved them. Had he talked with his advisers, one must add, he might have grasped their importance.[47]

After all these arguments and counterarguments, two questions remain: Why did such an intellectually talented president approve an invasion plan so obviously and egregiously flawed? And, just as mind-boggling, why did he further undercut that plan by reducing and then canceling the air strikes, particularly those on D-Day?

Both answers perhaps lay, at least in part, in the quiet but continuing White House interest in assassinating Castro.

While Bissell and Harvey crafted the executive action program, the initial attempt to assassinate Castro had fallen flat shortly after the packet of poisoned pills arrived in Cuba in early 1961. Orta "got scared" and "lost his nerve," according to Edwards. Maheu claimed that a communication mix-up occurred and the "go signal" never came. Orta, declared both Roselli and Maheu, developed "cold feet." Castro years afterward asserted that Orta had posed no danger because he no longer had access to the inner office once the regime became preoccupied with the imminent invasion. In actuality, Orta defected on the eve of the invasion in April after breaking with Castro the previous January (just before the pills arrived) over his Soviet alignment and had won asylum in the Mexican embassy.[48]

The botched poison plot should have signaled the nearly insurmountable difficulties involved in trying to kill Castro in a heavily guarded police state. Perhaps Ted Shackley, who was CIA station chief in Miami for three years beginning in 1962, offered the most astute observation on why any method of assassination had little chance for success: No Cuban male dared risk his life to become a martyr, for one of the major prizes in killing Castro was to remain alive afterward to enjoy the plaudits as hero and patriot. So close-quartered execution had no attraction because of the certainty of retribution. "Built into all their assassination outlines was action at a distance, an element that inevitably reduced any prospects of success."[49] And, one might add, a long-range killing by sniper fire did not assure fame; the action suggested no heroism, and identifying oneself as the assassin virtually guaranteed death before the wall.

Coincidence is a rare occurrence in history. So probably not by accident did the CIA make a special effort to inform the White House on April 13 that the Juan Orta poison plot had collapsed—just *one day* before the president directed Bissell to trim the size of the D-2 air strikes. Why else would Walter Elder, executive assistant to CIA deputy director Cabell, send Bundy, the president's national security adviser and link to the agency, a UPI news article detailing Orta's defection?[50] Perhaps in the midst of the controversy over the imminent invasion, the news would encourage presidential approval of the action by exposing a schism deep inside Castro's ruling circle. But it is likely that something else drove Cabell, through Elder, to contact Bundy at this critical time. Because it is all but certain that the CIA and the White House were allied in the assassination program, it follows that Orta's defection was *not* good news. The fundamental premise of the assassination plan had rested on direct access to Castro, and with Orta's departure went the critical first step of the invasion.

Bundy doubtless shared this news with the president, making it conceivable that he took this failed assassination attempt into consideration when terminating the D-2 strikes and yet approving the Bay of Pigs operation in the desperate hope it would still work. Kennedy's conversation with Senator Smathers shows that the CIA had counted on Castro's death at the time of the invasion, suggesting that it expected assassination to ignite a popular insurrection that would overcome the plan's imperfections. But even though the Orta effort failed, the president had to approve the invasion for the myriad reasons mentioned earlier. He then called off the D-Day strikes, somehow hoping to escape responsibility for the operation, but in doing so cut out another vital element in the plan and further diminished the chances for success.[51]

In another bitter twist in this story, it appears certain that Bissell had no knowledge of the failed poison plot and felt confident it would work. Besides, he believed, the president would *not* let the invasion fail, even if he had to send U.S. troops. Given these assumptions, argues the CIA's Sam Halpern, who worked on the overthrow program, Bissell had seen no need to take the phone that night in an effort to talk Kennedy into restoring the D-Day strikes.[52]

Hawkins did not know the deeper issues involved in these decisions and insisted that terminating the D-Day air assault ensured the plan's failure. In referring to his inspection of the training camps less than a week before the invasion, he declared, "Had I known before setting off for Central America that the President, in concert with Bissell, would at the last minute cut by half the number of aircraft to participate in the first strike, and then, when the troops were actually clearing the beaches, the President would suddenly and unexpectedly cancel the second air strike altogether, I would not have made the trip." Calling the episode "a disgraceful betrayal of the Cuban fighting men," Hawkins concluded that "Bissell deliberately kept us in the dark until the last minute, knowing that Esterline and I would be outraged by what had happened and might make another last-ditch effort to stop the operation as we had done a short while before." Neither Rusk nor the president understood "that you can't take a thin-skinned troop transport onto a hostile beach and drop anchor and start unloading troops with hostile fighters and bombers overhead."[53]

Also unaware of the assassination factor, Lemnitzer agreed with Hawkins's assessment, terming the canceled strikes a "surprise" and denying any role in the decision. He learned of the change in plans at two in the morning of April 17, when Generals Gray and Wheeler informed him the CIA had called, urging them to arrange air cover for the landing parties on D-Day. Lemnitzer favored the move but also grasped its political repercussions and told them, in a pointless recommendation, to talk with the State Department.[54]

The traditional story holds that neither the president nor his secretary of state grasped the importance of air cover to an amphibious operation, and that the CIA and Joint Chiefs failed to make this clear. Cabell and Bissell, the argument goes, should have driven home that point when they had the unique opportunity to speak directly to the president. This is not a convincing argument. Both Kennedy and Rusk had military backgrounds and surely recognized the necessity of air protection against enemy planes in an amphibious landing that stretched across forty miles of open beach. Common sense made this clear. As Dulles asserted from his *non*-military perspective, "You can't land naked vessels with ammunition and supplies on board in the face of any kind of hostile aviation that controls the air."[55] President Kennedy had to have known this but appealed to the defensible argument that he lacked military expertise and therefore had (without asking them) depended on the CIA and Joint Chiefs for guidance. Without Castro's assassination, he knew, the chances were not good for a general uprising. He also realized that U.S. involvement in D-Day air operations would make non-attribution impossible. The president therefore canceled the D-Day strikes in a futile effort to elude U.S. responsibility.

Political considerations had taken precedence over military necessities, helping to weaken an operation that, no longer reliant on Castro's death as a spur to a popular insurrection, had little chance for success except, perhaps, through direct U.S. military intervention. That was not going to happen. In a White House press conference sometime later, President Kennedy explained why he had *never* condoned U.S. air support during the invasion. "[I]f you are going to have United States air cover, you might as well have a complete United States commitment, which would have meant a full-fledged invasion by the United States. That was not the policy of the United States in April 1961."[56] Thus did he maintain the fiction that the Cuba project was *not* an American enterprise.

5

D-Day

There was a concert of the dying. —Cuban rebel,

April 17, 1961

Hold on. We're coming, we're coming with everything.

How long?

Three to four hours.

That's not enough time. You won't be here on time.

Farewell, friends. I am breaking this radio right now.

The Americans started crying. —Radio exchange at the

Bay of Pigs, April 17, 1961

The maritime armada looked formidable on the night of April 16 as it gathered at a spot forty miles off Cuba before relocating within three miles of its beaches. The command ships *Blagar* and *Barbara J,* both LCIs bought by the CIA from a private firm in Miami, were armed with .50-caliber machine guns and a pair of anti-aircraft 75-mm recoilless rifles (cannon referred to as "pom-poms"). The other vessels were fitted with .50-caliber machine guns mounted on revolving turrets on the bow, stern, port, and starboard sides. A U.S. Navy LSD transported three LCUs (purchased from the U.S. Navy) and four LCVPs, all packed with equipment and supplies, and seven chartered commercial freighters completed the pack, three of them to wait until after the initial landing to deliver additional ground and air force matériel. The vessels had been loaded at New Orleans before picking up the brigade's forces in Nicaragua and filing out of Puerto Cabezas on April 14, trying not to draw attention by taking separate routes to the initial rendezvous point.[1]

The 2506 Assault Brigade numbered 1,511 men, 177 in an airborne infantry company and the remainder in ground forces armed with Browning automatic rifles (BARs), recoilless rifles, machine guns, rocket launchers, mortars, and flamethrowers. Command ship *Blagar* carried arms for a thousand men; *Barbara J* transported the balance. Stored within the huge bellies of the transport vessels were five new M-41 tanks fitted with armor-piercing 76-mm guns superior to Castro's bigger Soviet tanks, a dozen heavy-duty trucks, a single aviation fuel tank truck, a bulldozer, a tractor crane, two big water trailers, and an assortment of smaller trucks and tractors. To record events on the beach, Colonel Frank Egan and a number of others on the vessels carried cameras given them in Guatemala.[2]

Five infantry battalions, a tank platoon, a heavy weapons detail, and an intelligence-reconnaissance team—all to overthrow Castro and free their homeland. On the *Blagar* was Cuban exile leader Manuel Artime, appointed "Delegate in the Invading Army" by the Cuban Revolutionary Council in New York, who at the proper time would declare a provisional government and immediately ask for U.S. recognition and aid. As the men boarded the ships, Nicaragua's president was there. General Luis Somoza, face powdered and in white suit and hat, holding an M-1, and surrounded by bodyguards wearing dark glasses and wielding submachine guns, shouted to the brigade, "Bring me some hairs from Fidel's beard!"[3]

I

After the ships had departed Nicaragua for Cuba, C-46 pilot Captain Edward Ferrer, from Havana and now contracted with the CIA, stared at them in the growing distance, visibly concerned about insufficient air cover for the invasion. The brigade had no fighter planes, he moaned, and the B-26s lacked tail guns, making them defenseless from the rear. One of the American advisers, Wade Gray from the Air National Guard in Birmingham, Alabama, patted him on the shoulder to reassure him. "I know. I know. But don't worry. We're gonna have Cuban pilots who don't speak Spanish and who have blond hair and blue eyes taking care of us, and an aircraft carrier which is loaded with the latest model fighters."

"We can't lose!"[4]

On the surface it appeared that way, for President Kennedy on D-Day had reluctantly approved additional naval air cover, only to unknowingly undermine that operation by attaching restrictions intended to avert a military confrontation, including a requirement that the planes remain outside Cuban waters. Burke insisted that the U.S. Navy had the right to move anywhere in international waters and could "just happen to be in the area." "Just don't get too close," the president warned. Burke stationed twenty-two warships well outside the Bay of Pigs, including a submarine, a dozen destroyers, the aircraft carrier *Essex* with jet fighters, and the helicopter carrier *Boxer* quartering two thousand marines. The two carriers were to remain at least fifty miles from Cuba; the planes could fly no closer than fifteen miles from shore; and no more than four planes could engage in the operation at one time. At the last moment, the president tacked on another stipulation: The warships, he told Burke, must stay at least twenty-five miles offshore.[5]

The rules of engagement were also highly restrictive. Americans could fight only if enemy aircraft strafed the ships or opened bomb bay doors in preparation for an attack. Under no conditions could an American pilot fire without provocation, nor could he engage in hot pursuit closer than fifteen miles from Cuba. "If unfriendly aircraft is shot down," the directive emphasized, "every effort shall be made to hide the fact that such action has occurred." The Joint Chiefs warned that the enemy gained a tactical advantage by having its offensive under way before the American planes could take action.[6] The rules remained in place.

Washington's war room buzzed with activity, sparkling with electronic maps and, with its people working around the clock and staying in constant contact with the CIA, leaving the misleading impression of efficiency. Messages clicked across the teletype, which General Gray forwarded to Admiral Dennison. Esterline and Hawkins, along with two officers from the air force and navy, ran the CIA Command Post pocketed near the Washington mall, in the deep recesses of the communications center in

Quarters Eye on Ohio Drive. These elaborate arrangements only at first concealed a critical weakness: Dennison's great difficulty in maintaining contact with the attack force—largely because he did not know the ships' communications circuits and had no other network connection.[7] The result was that the White House often fell behind in receiving news from the battle zone.

The biggest problems, however, lay in three basic premises of the battle plan: the D-Day strikes, now canceled; the military strength of the amphibious invasion, clearly suspect; and its expected impetus to a popular rebellion, a highly dubious proposition given Castro's police-state control, the choice of the lightly inhabited Zapata region for a nocturnal landing, the inability of CIA agents to establish a rapid communication and support system on the island, and the failed assassination plot. The call for direct American military participation refused to die. Without it, according to a State Department officer, Castro "would clobber the hell out of the invasion force." The Havana regime, long expecting an invasion and alerted by the D-2 assaults, had clamped down on security, bolstered air and ground defenses, housed a thousand Soviet-bloc people, including three hundred military advisers, and now, with the president's decision to call off the D-1 and D-Day strikes, controlled the skies. Furthermore, Operation Pluto bore a string of interconnected and potentially fatal flaws: The landing could not succeed without a popular insurrection, an insurrection would not take place without a successful landing, and neither could occur if Castro's planes were free to attack the brigade. As one observer poignantly noted, "We wouldn't put out any call for the people to rise until there was something solid for them to rise to."[8]

The brigade intended to invade Cuba at three beaches lying sixteen miles from each other on the Zapata Peninsula: Blue Beach in the middle, containing an airfield west of the small town of Playa Girón on the east coast of the Bay of Pigs; Red Beach on the left flank, located at the top of the bay and jutting twenty miles inland to a spot near Playa Larga; and Green Beach on the right, just twenty-one miles from Playa Girón. The three-pronged assault aimed at seizing an east-west beachhead forty miles in length and girded to the north by the huge Zapata Swamp. Control of Playa Larga would give the brigade its deepest point of penetration, putting it in the position to move toward Havana. This goal in mind, thirty airborne infantrymen would parachute from each of two C-46 planes just before daylight at Red Beach about ten miles from Playa Girón while four other transports dropped the remaining paratroopers at the junction of two roads at San Blas ten miles northeast of Blue Beach. Their objective: Seal off the coastal road in the east and the causeways cutting through the swamp from the upper interior, denying enemy access to the landing sites and opening the way for the advance north.[9]

Just before midnight preceding the landing, the operation began as two small underwater demolition teams in rubber rafts stealthily motored toward shore, each group—one of five Cubans, the other with three—led by an American and hence in violation of President Kennedy's directive against U.S. participation. With blackened faces and wearing black outfits and rubber sandals, the larger UDT team headed to Blue Beach, the other to Red Beach, their missions the same: Mark the best channels for the ships' approach with red and white lights visible only from the sea and turned on when the vessels came within a half mile of shore.[10]

The two Americans were vocal and highly visible. At Blue Beach was Grayston Lynch (known as Gray), a muscular, wide-bodied former member of the Special Forces in Laos who had twice been wounded in World War II, during the Normandy invasion and at the Battle of the Bulge, and again in the Korean War at Heartbreak Ridge. And at Red Beach was William "Rip" Robertson, called by the Cubans "the Alligator" because of his rough and scaly sun-dried skin. A flamboyant and irreverent battle-hardened marine in World War II, he had had paramilitary experience with the CIA in Korea and Guatemala and later became a close friend of Somoza. Both Americans were CIA case officers, Gray on the *Blagar* and Robertson on the *Barbara J.*[11]

As Gray's frogman team eased toward Blue Beach, the men gawked in disbelief at the tall lights beaming onto the beach from Playa Girón. It "was lit up like Coney Island," Gray sputtered. Didn't the CIA's home office assure them that no one inhabited the resort houses? Indeed, the agency had failed to note the construction workers and their families living in Playa Girón while building the new vacation mecca scheduled to open in less than a month—nearly two hundred buildings similar to motels in the United States. And of all things, they were having a party that had spilled onto the beach. No turning back now. The team drifted a short distance from the original landing site. From a thousand yards out, Gray scanned the beach with his binoculars, spotting six figures standing outside the buildings and peering toward the water. He quieted his boat's engine, trying to determine whether they had been seen. Everything remained still and black in the moonless night. A few moments later, the men on the beach went into a house and turned off the lights, prompting the frogmen to ease within five hundred yards of shore.[12]

But this silence proved only the eye of the storm. A hundred yards out the raft scraped a chain of jagged coral reefs, stalling the engine and forcing the men to slide into the water and lift the raft over the underwater obstruction before paddling toward the beach. As they cursed while hitting the water, Lynch bitterly recalled the CIA's insistence that the shadows in the water on the reconnaissance photos had been seaweed. What else could go wrong? The answer soon came when one of the marking lights suddenly turned on, bathing the entire raft and the men back on board with a bright blinking light. Gray beat the others scrambling to the light, covering it and grabbing for the switch, only to find it taped in the "off" position. A short had set it off. The blinking just as suddenly stopped, only to begin again a moment later, forcing Gray to angrily yank out every wire. But someone ashore had seen the light. Two men in a jeep, the militia head and a thirteen-year-old literacy teacher, had been examining the tourist area under construction and approached the water's edge, with the frogmen less than fifty yards from shore. Gray ordered his men to get out of the raft again and to hunch down behind it while he lay flat on its bottom, aiming his BAR toward shore. The jeep's driver trained its headlights directly onto the raft, thinking it a fishing boat and in need of directions for navigating through the dangerous reefs, but Gray could not have known this and reacted instinctively. In the first fighting at the Bay of Pigs, he and his men pumped round after round of fire from two BARs and four Thompson submachine guns into the jeep, demolishing everything except, ironically, its headlights while lightly wounding the young boy. They escaped, but the militia commander warned his superiors of an invasion.[13]

No time remained as Gray radioed the *Blagar* of their discovery and called for support fire and an immediate landing—*before* Castro's reinforcements arrived. The team of frogmen ran onto the beach, stabbing a blinking red light into the sand by the jeep's rumpled remains and another one about 150 yards east, along with a large white light to guide the path of entry. Gray and his five companions sought safety in a partially completed building just off the beach. At this point the entire town went dark, just before three trucks with lights off barreled onto the beach and discharged thirty militiamen. Before they could position themselves, the *Blagar* opened cannon and machine-gun fire, twice pummeling the entire beachhead in a ten-minute flurry that scattered the entire contingent into the woods and cleared the way for the landing. Enemy machine-gun fire injured one of the *Blagar*'s crew members, making him the first casualty of the invasion.[14]

Thus, contrary to President Kennedy's specific orders, an American was among the first to invade Cuba. There "wouldn't be a white face on the beach," Bissell had promised him. Indeed, Gray was not only the first to touch the sand but the first to engage in military action.[15] The Kennedy administration had lost all pretense to plausible deniability.

II

Not only was a rapid landing necessary because of the imminent arrival of Castro's main forces, but just before 1:00 A.M. the CIA station in Miami relayed a message from Washington, shocking Gray with news of the canceled D-Day strikes. And that was not all. The initial optimistic reports of the D-2 operation were wrong. "Castro still has operational aircraft," declared the notation on the yellow pad thrust into his hands. "Expect you will be under air attack at first light. Unload all men and supplies and take the ships to sea." [16]

The brigade commander at Blue Beach, Pepe San Román, learned of the coming air strikes just before hitting the shore and, after kneeling to kiss a handful of dirt as scattered militia fire whizzed over his head, ordered the hurried off-loading of troops and supplies. A few more local militiamen rushed onto the scene, briefly firing on the landing party before pulling back and alerting military installations throughout Cuba. Gray promised to stay until everything was ashore and won Pepe's hesitant approval of a decision to cancel the scheduled 7:00 A.M. landing at Green Beach and immediately divert the men and materials from the 3rd Battalion to Blue Beach. The *Blagar*, Gray added, must remain because its anti-aircraft guns posed the sole resistance against the imminent air assault. Pepe ignored the CIA's urgings to land everything now and delayed removing the heavy equipment until high tide around 7:00 A.M. To do otherwise would risk broken legs and drownings as the men jumped into the shallow water.[17]

Gray turned to watch the landing begin in the pale glow of the marker lights, suddenly realizing that he had failed to warn the brigade of the razor-edged reefs. Too late now, he watched in horror as the coral ripped the bottoms of two LCVPs that stubbornly kept coming despite taking on massive volumes of water.

One of them finally sank, leaving the troops to wade ashore in waist-high water that disabled their radios and cut off communication; the other managed to disembark all its troops before going to the bottom near the LCU *Atlántico*. Commanders frantically searched for another channel free from the coral reefs and wide enough for the three huge LCUs carting the tanks. Two ultimately made it ashore; the third, carrying a pair of M-41s, turned toward Red Beach when word came of the fighting there and the call for tanks. But the invasion at Blue Beach succeeded as the 4th Battalion made it ashore, the men yelling and cheering as they laid claim to the southern terminus of the road leading to the Bay of Pigs.[18]

Unknown to the brigade, however, Castro had learned at 3:15 in the morning that rebels were invading at Playa Girón and Playa Larga and that his militia forces were frantically trying to mount a resistance. But he had not yet managed to organize his defense units by the time of the attack: A mere five militia were at Larga, their only arms a machine gun with two hundred rounds and each man's Czech submachine gun with ninety rounds, while a half dozen charcoal makers and militia were at Girón, armed only with Czech M-52 semiautomatic rifles and a bare sixty rounds each. Not that the invasion was a surprise; like others, Castro was well aware of its imminence if not its location. Moscow had pinpointed the date; the D-2 strikes had sent a signal; he had spies in Miami and other places housing Cuban dissidents; and he could read the newspapers. After checking the report's veracity, he alerted all forces in the Zapata region while gathering more information from his microwave stations until they suddenly stopped working and left only a silence that suggested deep enemy encroachments. He could not be certain, however, for the area had neither radio stations nor telephone service to provide on-site news. The key to his defense, he knew, was an air assault before the invaders established a beachhead and declared a provisional government that sought U.S. recognition and help. Expecting to counter both an air and a ground attack, Castro ordered his planes to take off at dawn. Only a steady air and ground bombardment of the invasion force could hold on to the Bay of Pigs and keep the enemy on the eastern side of the swamp, where his tanks and militia could make the arduous advance and close in for the kill.[19]

Thus the Blue Beach landing continued without further incident until daylight broke at six. The off-loading did not go as quickly as needed, for two hundred men and more than a third of the brigade's heavy weapons were still on the ships as an enemy B-26 swooped in from the east, riddling one of the LCVPs unloading the mortar crews. The B-26 then headed toward Red Beach, only momentarily affording a lull in the action before two more planes circled in from the west. The troops unleashed several rounds of fire until realizing that one was a friendly B-26 escorting a C-46 for the parachute drop. "Cease fire!" shouted Gray, now back on board the *Blagar*. "We're shooting at our own planes!" Total confusion reigned, for the blue identification bands put on the wings and fuselage of the expedition's planes did not become decipherable until directly overhead. Two paratroopers sustained minor injuries but joined the others in the jumps.[20]

Shortly afterward, one of Castro's swift-moving Sea Furies burst onto the scene, followed by another one a few moments later. The first pilot went into a roll-and-dive maneuver while taking dead aim on an unarmed C-46 transport, but the *Blagar* blasted the plane into the sea before it could fire. The uneasy calm came to an end when the second Sea Fury appeared, circling the area in search of a target. Gray manned one of the *Blagar*'s .50-caliber machine guns and opened fire while inexplicably catching a glimpse of a radio operator standing nearby and holding a message. What now? The Sea Fury cut through the stream of tracers but hit nothing and swept up and away. Seizing the respite from the fighting, Gray quickly read the message thrust into his hands: "Castro's air force 100% destroyed. Do not fire on our planes. Remember they have blue bands on the wings and fuselage." Gray could not believe this and angrily scrawled a response: "If Castro's planes are 100% destroyed, then suggest you check Haiti, because somebody's air force is shooting the hell out of us." After cooling down, he crumpled both papers and threw them into the water. More messages rolled in, causing more confusion. "Never before have so many directed so few, with so many different directives," Gray acidly remarked.[21]

Action picked up again when out of the southeastern sky thundered two B-26s through the morning haze, one hot on the tail of the other and neither plane identifiable from below. Their loyalties became clear when a T-33 jet from Castro's air force stormed out of the sun to pepper the second B-26 in its unprotected rear, forcing the crippled plane to lower its landing gear and turn toward the Playa Girón airstrip. At the last instant, however, it pulled back upward, the captain realizing that the T-33 pilot had continued on its trailing path, not content to ground the B-26 but determined to destroy it. He cut loose another fiery outburst that tore into its rear and killed the navigator in the cockpit, sending the plane to the ground and into a roll and skid down the entire strip before it crashed to a stop in an explosive cloud of dust and oily black smoke. An hour later, the B-26 pilot stumbled out of the woods and onto the airstrip, having suffered only mild burns though knocked out and thrown free of the plane as it hit the ground. The brigade's thin air cover had not arrived, but it offered little hope of matching this withering assault.[22]

In the meantime, the 1st Battalion's parachutists seized San Blas and, with reinforcement from the 3rd Battalion and a heavy weapons group, set up outposts to close the two major roads into the beachhead, each stemming from San Blas, one to Covadonga, the other to Yaguaramas. Five C-46s and a C-54 had dropped 172 parachutists into the area at 7:30 A.M., not only an hour and a half past their scheduled dawn landing but without a sizable ammunition supply that missed the target. More than fifty paratroopers from the 1st Airborne Battalion meanwhile jumped into the area north of San Blas, likewise losing much of their ammunition in the drop and unable to communicate with the brigade because its radios were not working after their carriers had ducked underwater when enemy planes passed.[23]

By 8:25 A.M. the brigade had finished unloading its vehicles and tanks at Blue Beach, the success punctuated by the *Blagar*'s shooting down a silver-streaking T-33. The front end of the landing party steadily moved toward San Blas, reaching its destination an hour later and finding that the airborne troops had cleared the hospital region to the west. Pepe informed Gray that his forces had captured Playa Girón and the nearby airfield, along with 130 militia in the town. More encouraging news came when the civilian workers and the militia chief switched allegiances, with the latter choosing discretion over valor by swearing he had been "completely misinformed" and promising to cooperate with the invasion force.[24]

But the elation was short-lived, replaced by a sense of betrayal beginning to spread throughout the landing force. Where was the promised U.S. air support? The brigade came under a series of air attacks while moving north, leading the contract officer in charge of shipping to radio CIA headquarters for jet cover. If denied, he would order the freighters out to sea. United States planes were nearby, he knew, and had done nothing. One Cuban frogman reported a growing suspicion among the men that they were poorly armed intentionally and "sent in there to be slaughtered." The boats' engines had not worked, "the method of landing was silly, with those little boats," and the men running them had had only two days' training and could not do the job. Complaints spread throughout the ranks that lack of air support made it impossible to advance beyond the beach.[25]

Matters continued to deteriorate. About 3:00 P.M. local militia forces opened a blistering firestorm on the paratroopers at San Blas. With artillery and aircraft support, Castro's forces surrounded the outpost by late afternoon, leading Pepe to dispatch a tank and forces armed with mortars, recoilless rifles, and machine guns. The rescue force had little impact on the outcome. Those in the outpost retreated to a point south of San Blas, isolated from the others and unable to call for help because their portable radios were still out of commission. In the meantime eighty members of the airborne battalion reached the area above San Blas and stood ground with Castro's militia all D-Day night before retreating to the beach because they were out of food and water.[26] The road to Blue Beach lay open to Castro's forces.

III

Red Beach events were remarkably similar to those at Blue Beach. The *Barbara J* had escorted the *Houston* up the Bay of Pigs early in the morning of D-Day before disembarking an underwater demolition team to mark the landing site and preparing to cover the 2nd and 5th Infantry Battalions about to land. Additional protection came from three platoons manning heavy weapons, including a 4.2-inch mortar, a 40-mm recoilless rifle, and a 57-mm recoilless rifle along with a 3.5-inch bazooka. To slow the enemy advance, the 1st Airborne Battalion would drop paratroopers in two spots, at the northern end of the swamp and on the road above Playa Larga.[27]

Robertson led his three frogmen ashore a little after 1:15 A.M., marking one side of the beach while keeping a wary eye on thirty militia engaged in a drunken party nearby. But while creeping forty yards offshore to the other side of the beach, they came under small-arms fire. Robertson and his men drove the few militia away with a torrent of machine-gun fire, although the lengthy exchange made it impossible to implant the second marking light. But Robertson had a personal triumph in putting up a yellow luminous sign that read WELCOME LIBERATORS. COURTESY OF THE BARBARA J. Another delay ensued, caused by malfunctioning engines on the landing craft. By this time fifty militia had emerged from Playa Larga, followed twenty minutes later by a number of armed men jammed into a half-dozen trucks pulling out of a nearby construction site and roaring to the beachhead. The *Barbara J* raked the trucks, forcing everyone aboard to jump off and run. The brigade's forces claimed the town.[28]

As at Blue Beach, the first person hitting the beach was an American who engaged in a firefight. But involvement in Cuba was not new to Robertson. A month prior to the invasion, he had participated in a sabotage operation on a Cuban oil refinery.[29] Bissell had told the president the truth. There wasn't "*a* white face on the beach"; there were two.

The Red Beach landing struggled at the outset. Only 270 of the 399 men in the 2nd Battalion made it ashore because of enemy fire combined with mechanical and planning problems. Machine guns sprayed Robertson's reconnaissance boat, killing one of his men. Seven of nine landing craft developed engine trouble, leaving two boats carrying nine men in each to repeatedly make the twenty-minute run to the sand and, after another mishap, only one at the end. The boats were not the type needed, bitterly complained one officer. "They looked like speed boats for water skiing."[30]

None of the 5th Battalion's men had made it into the water. All 180 forces remained on the *Houston*, ordered *not* to land by their commander, Montero Duque. Like his men, he stood frozen in fear, pointing to engine troubles in the aluminum landing boats and preferring to await daylight. When Robertson hurriedly boarded the ship and hotly demanded an explanation, Duque just as hotly responded that his men lacked enough ammunition, that his landing craft were not reliable, and that Castro might have artillery. "Look, mister," shouted Robertson in disgust, "it's your war and your country, not mine. If you're too scared to land and fight, then stay here and rot." Duque did not budge. Nor did his men.[31]

Thus the invasion brigade at Red Beach posed no real threat to Castro's legions. Small in manpower, it carried only two days' worth of supplies that included four 81-mm mortars, four light machine guns, and four 57-mm recoilless rifles, along with rocket launchers, grenades, and BARs. Furthermore, Castro had been aware of their landing beforehand. Close to the beach sat an abandoned radio station with the switches on and the apparatus still warm. The brigade angrily destroyed the entire network, though knowing it was too late. Contrary to intelligence reports, Castro's communication system extended to the beaches around the Bay of Pigs. The CIA had been wrong again.[32]

As daylight broke, Castro's air assault at Red Beach began with a flurry. A B-26 machine-gunned the *Barbara J*, disabling two engines and coming close to sinking it with another burst before retaliatory fire downed the plane on its third pass. Another B-26 swept by several times, its bombs missing both vessels, but a Sea Fury followed, strafing and firing rockets that hit the *Houston* close to its waterline and killed two while wounding five. The worst news was yet to come, however, for a T-33 zoomed onto the scene, this time surprisingly firing *rockets* that barely missed the *Barbara J* but twice struck the *Houston*. The *Barbara J*, however, had suffered a split seam from the rockets' percussion and took on more water, and the *Houston* lost its steerage and started to sink. Fire broke out on the *Houston*, raging out of control below and threatening to kill everyone aboard. The crew could neither put out the fire nor escape. The ship's fire hoses had been torn apart by the enemy's machine guns, and one of its only two lifeboats had rotted from disuse. As another Sea Fury resumed the attack, the captain frantically struggled to maneuver the burning hulk toward shore while gas seeped into the water and surrounded both ships in what could become a deadly ring of fire. About a hundred yards out, many of the more than two hundred men jumped overboard in life jackets; up to twenty of them were killed in the water by the strafing, while another ten or more either drowned or fell victim to sharks. The *Houston* ran aground on the western side of the bay as its survivors frantically scampered onto Red Beach, only to confront a storm of militia fire that scattered them into the swamp. Duque and his men had made it to shore—though not by choice.[33]

At this point, the focus shifted back to Blue Beach, where, three hours later, a Sea Fury closed in to three hundred feet and fired four rockets at the *Rio Escondido*. Three missed, but one hit its bridge near two hundred barrels of aviation gasoline on deck, setting the ship afire. The missile also shredded the fire hoses, making it impossible to put out the gasoline-fed flames rapidly licking toward twenty tons of explosives below. Ignoring the danger, rescue crews from the *Blagar* saved everyone aboard just before the *Rio* became engulfed in one-hundred-foot-high flames and exploded in a mammoth fireball that took the shape of a mushroom seen sixteen miles away at Red Beach. "Gray!" radioed Rip. "What the hell was that?" Told that the *Rio Escondido* had exploded, Rip replied in shock, "My God, Gray! For a moment, I thought Fidel had the A-bomb!"[34]

The *Rio Escondido* sank close to Playa Girón, taking down ten days' supply of ammunition and the communication van along with other goods. The brigade's forces at Blue Beach had little ammunition and could not communicate with their expected air cover.[35]

The men who made it to Red Beach fared no better. They inched northward for four miles, but Castro's forces swarmed into the area, preventing them from reaching the southern end of the road they were to block.

Fighting continued all day, with a dozen tanks arriving in midafternoon and artillery shelling the area in an unbroken barrage. Militia forces likewise steadily pounded the landing site, suffering numerous casualties and extensive tank damage but depleting the brigade's ammunition and forcing its withdrawal to Blue Beach.[36]

Events at Red Beach north and east of the Bay of Pigs ended just as badly for the brigade as those above Blue Beach. Fourteen miles north of Playa Larga, paratroopers seized the road to Central Australia, but they could not hold it for long because their heavy equipment missed the mark during the drop and disappeared in the swamps. One other group got lost in the marsh, and still another missed the drop zone. A contingent of brigade forces occupied Playa Larga until they ran out of ammunition and had to retreat in the face of a wall of fire from enemy tanks, rifles, mortars, bazookas, and automatic weapons. To the east, the brigade put up stands at San Blas, in an area close to Covadonga northeast of the Zapata Swamp above Blue Beach, and on the road below Yaguarmas east of Covadonga. But it had to withdraw in a battle providing what one young student termed his "baptism of fire." When the tank commanders finally called off the assault, "we heard the yelling of the wounded," he recalled in horror. "There was a concert of the dying."[37]

The roads to Red Beach as well as Blue Beach lay open to Castro's steadily advancing forces.

The CIA had no choice but to follow the original plan—though belatedly—by ordering all remaining ships out to sea to await dark, then return and unload. Pepe, either unaware of this arrangement or choosing to ignore it, angrily rebuked the *Blagar*'s U.S. commander for making "that withdrawal against my orders to hold his position and fight." Military principles made it clear that "the commander of the support forces takes orders from the commander of the supported forces." The U.S. commander crisply replied, "A higher authority has ordered the contrary." Gray too was reluctant to withdraw until he read the last part of the message declaring that the "Navy will provide cover at 12-mile limit." American help at last? The three slowly trudging LCUs went first, followed by the freighters *Atlántico* and *Caribe* and then the *Barbara J* and the *Blagar,* but not without incident. The convoy encountered another B-26 attack in which the *Blagar*'s guns hit the plane's fuel tanks as the pilot unleashed a second round of rockets, causing it to explode in a swirling ball of fire, and a Sea Fury inflicted additional damage on the *Barbara J* before return fire chased it off.

Farther out to sea the *Blagar*'s captain saw two U.S. destroyers and radioed for help. The commander of five destroyers in the vicinity, Captain Robert Crutchfield, sent a crushing reply: "My heart is with you, but I cannot help you. My orders are not to become engaged in any way."[38]

Problems continued to plague the convoy's departure. The boarding of *Rio Escondido*'s badly shaken survivors onto the *Blagar* had demoralized its sixty crew members, leading two of them to join the new arrivals in arming themselves and refusing to return to the landing site. But the captain's forces quickly subdued the mutineers and convinced the others of their responsibilities to the twelve hundred comrades stranded on the beach. The two freighters carrying the ammunition, the *Atlántico* and the *Caribe*, ignored the *Blagar*'s directive to meet at the rendezvous point and continued south, the first making it more than a hundred miles before deciding to turn around, and the second more than two hundred miles, at which point a U.S. destroyer fired a shot across its bow and forced a reverse course. The two ships' late return further undermined the invasion operation. The *Atlántico* did not get back until the late afternoon of April 18, and the *Caribe* failed to appear until after the battle was over.[39]

As for the assured navy support at dawn, the jets had not appeared, but word arrived that they were still "on the way."[40]

By the close of D-Day, both beachheads were on the verge of collapse. Many forces at Red Beach were nearly out of ammunition and had to turn back south. During the night, four C-54s and two C-46s tried to replenish supplies. Five drops at Blue Beach were successful, but one arms cache at Red Beach drifted so far out in the water that the landing party could save only part of the load.[41]

The air cover operations had also gone badly. Brigade B-26s launched thirteen close-support strikes on D-Day and four more that night, but they were not effective. Nearly panicked over the deadly effectiveness of the T-33s, the CIA realized how badly the D-2 strikes had failed and asked Washington to authorize a pre-dawn bombing assault on Cuban airfields while Castro's jets were on the ground. Surprisingly, the request won approval, leading Cabell to believe that the nation's leaders were "a thoroughly-scared bunch."[42]

But everything went wrong with this rapidly assembled, jury-rigged operation. Six B-26s were to hit San Antonio de los Baños on D-Day night, but two aborted on takeoff and the others could not find their targets through the low clouds and dense fog. By early dawn of April 18, three more planes headed for the target, but one failed at takeoff, and the other two again could not locate the bombing points through the scud and lingering haze.[43]

Castro's forces won the first day's air campaign but at a heavy expense that again points to the debilitating impact of the president's decision to call off the D-Day strikes. Rebel B-26s sank one of his gunboats and hit several hundred of his ground forces at Red Beach, and anti-aircraft fire brought down two Sea Furies and two B-26s. But his T-33s proved devastating, downing four B-26s and forcing the remainder to seek refuge in Nicaragua or other friendly airfields. Bissell and other CIA strategists had erroneously assumed that the so-called T-Bird was merely a lightly armed training plane, but they were wrong, dead wrong. Castro's engineers (or perhaps the Soviet-bloc technicians in Cuba) had recently fitted the jets with rockets under their wings along with a pair of .50-caliber machine guns—each capable of firing seventeen hundred rounds per minute. The T-33 shot out of the sun with such blazing speed that the only warning of its presence was the sound of rockets already whistling toward their target. The outcome could have been worse. Had Castro's planes launched concerted attacks rather than sporadic assaults by one or two planes at a time, they could have inflicted even more damage while not exposing themselves to as much concentrated fire.[44]

And, as for the CIA's predicted outpouring of popular support for the invasion, nothing of the sort took place. The landing spot, of course, was less densely inhabited than that of Trinidad, which made the pool of potential assistance inherently thin. The CIA had failed to establish a tight network of communication with the guerrillas in the mountains, who were not aware of the timing of the invasion and were a prohibitive distance from the beachhead. Castro had clamped down on dissidents days before the invasion, putting a hundred thousand in prison and further diminishing the sources of indigenous help. The five hundred guerrillas the CIA assured were nearby to help the brigade never showed. Castro telephoned his forces at the Covadonga Sugar Mill about fifteen miles north of Blue Beach, inspiring them and others to resist the invasion. Operation Peter Pan had meanwhile taken priority among many families, with the first five hundred children removed from the embattled area by the end of March, and the balance of a total of more than fourteen thousand in a mass exodus that lasted until October 1962. The result was that only a small number of citizens and militia helped the brigade by transporting supplies, nursing the wounded, providing food and water, and joining the fight. Whether too frightened to break with Castro or simply loyal to the regime, most Cubans stayed out of the battle, leaving the brigade alone on the beaches.[45]

In an appropriate epitaph to that one day in April, Pepe radioed Gray on the *Blagar*, pleading for reinforcements. "Gray, the enemy tanks are already into our position in Girón. Right here very close to us. You can hear the guns. I am ordering the retreat."

"Hold on," Gray responded in ignoring the administration's restrictions. "We're coming, we're coming with everything."

"How long?"

"Three to four hours."

"That's not enough time. You won't be here on time. Farewell, friends. I am breaking this radio right now."

According to a sailor on the scene, "The Americans started crying."[46]

6

Requiem

I will not be evacuated. We will fight to the end here if we have to. —2506 Assault Brigade Commander Pepe San Román, April 18, 1961

Goddamnit, Mr. President, we are involved, and there is no way to hide it. We are involved! —Admiral Arleigh Burke, April 18, 1961

Do you people realize how desperate the situation is? Do you back us up or quit? All we want is low jet cover and jet close support. Enemy has this support. I need it badly or cannot survive. Please don't desert us. —2506 Assault Brigade Commander Pepe San Román, April 18, 1961

[They had a] good plan, poorly executed. —Fidel Castro, June 15, 1961

The morning after the invasion opened in ominous fashion for the brigade. At 4:00 A.M. Blue Beach underwent heavy artillery shelling near San Blas that thundered on throughout the day. In the meantime a brigade commander deepened the growing despair by erroneously reporting that four Russian MIG-15s had joined Castro's T-33s and a dozen tanks in the assault. Those on the ground often mistook the identity of jets, resulting in several alleged MIG sightings. But this fear was not entirely unfounded. If not yet in the air, nearly two dozen MIGs sat on Castro's airfields, still uncrated or not fully assembled while awaiting the imminent return of his pilots training in Czechoslovakia.[1]

Within three hours the brigade's forces fell back to a spot north of San Blas. Rebel planes, Pepe insisted, could have destroyed Castro's artillery and tanks, but only a single B-26 appeared that night, its machine guns and napalm (recently authorized) incapable of driving back the enemy. The brigade suffered few casualties but ran dangerously low on ammunition. When the CIA informed Pepe that evacuation would begin after dark, he defiantly shot back, "I will not be evacuated. We will fight to the end here if we have to."[2]

I

Like the ground forces, the airborne battalion had little success in its first pitched firefight a little after midnight of D-Day. Paratroopers scurried back down to San Blas by midafternoon, where Castro's heavy artillery pounded them nonstop into the following day. A rebel B-26 came to their aid, strafing the artillery emplacements and dropping napalm that enveloped Castro's forces in flames and allowed the brigade to advance northward with the tanks. But Castro sensed the imminent collapse of the invasion and rushed down from Havana to the battlefront, accompanied by a photographer to record his victory while he sat with his head protruding out of a tank. Renewed artillery fire drove the brigade forces back to the beach. Seeing a ship offshore, they swam to it and abandoned the area.[3]

Red Beach likewise came under heavy fire in the early morning of April 18, beginning with a tank bombardment at 3:00 A.M. that, combined with militia and plane fire at dawn, forced the brigade into a retreat east to Blue Beach. Low on ammunition and hit hard with twenty casualties, the men rested two hours before reloading and heading back to Red Beach, determined to close the road that had allowed the tanks into the landing site. Again they became mired down in a deadly assault just west of Blue Beach. By late afternoon friendly B-26s disabled a large number of tanks, trucks, and buses. But in the early evening enemy tanks and troops were again rolling west in three spaced columns, all bearing down on Blue Beach.[4]

The CIA stretched the rules of engagement by sending a half-dozen B-26s, two of them piloted by Americans and all under cover of U.S. Navy Combat Air Patrol planes, to help the brigade at Red Beach. When the Cuban pilots appeared exhausted from the previous day's action, two contracted American civilian pilots volunteered for the mission, rallying several Cuban crews to join them. The B-26s departed Puerto Cabezas in midafternoon, bound for the battlefront. North of Blue Beach they spotted a seven-mile-long convoy of tanks, trucks, and militiamen approaching Playa Larga, then held by the brigade. Two of the planes peeled off in an attack, one hitting the lead vehicle with a rocket and the other destroying the last truck at the end of the line. The convoy immobilized, all six B-26s repeatedly battered the chaotic mass with bombs, rockets, machine guns, and napalm, destroying seven tanks and twenty troop-filled trucks while inflicting eighteen hundred casualties and leaving two miles of smoke and fire churning upward.[5]

But the bad news continued to outweigh the good, leading the White House to discuss evacuation. As early as D-Day afternoon, Lemnitzer and Burke had pondered the use of destroyers to save those on the beach and by nightfall authorized cover from four B-26s previously assigned to Laos. The following day, four more B-26s became available, along with four T-33s and a few C-130s to deliver ammunition. Everything was ready for the drops that night, but the go-ahead order never came.[6]

The politics of plausible deniability continued to dog the operation, hindering the evacuation effort as well as the military offensive. The on-site commander on board the *Essex*, Rear Admiral John Clark, later insisted that the brigade's removal could have succeeded with ample protection. "If we'd been allowed to use counterforce we could have taken them all out." But under orders not to engage, the unprotected American rescue vessels had to remain at least three miles offshore to stay out of artillery range.[7]

U.S.-Soviet relations sharply deteriorated during the crisis. Shortly before nine in the morning of April 18, the State Department received a telegram from its Moscow embassy, reporting that Khrushchev had accused the United States of underwriting the invasion. "I approach you, Mr. President, with an urgent call to put an end to aggression against the Republic of Cuba," the premier wrote. Otherwise, he warned, the Soviet Union would help the Cuban government repel the armed attack. President Kennedy denied any plans for a military intervention in Cuba, asserting that surely the Soviet Union did not intend to fabricate a pretext for inflaming other areas in the world: "What your government believes is its own business; what it does in the world is the world's business."[8]

Desperation dominated the Washington command. "Real big mess," Burke disgustedly declared at an emergency cabinet meeting at noon. No one knew what to do. Just before the meeting, Bundy maneuvered around the president's directives against U.S. military involvement by re-commending White House authorization of "neutrally-painted U.S. planes" to destroy Castro's air force "and then let the battle go its way." Nothing came of this proposal. The Joint Chiefs, Burke complained, had been "kept ignorant" and told only "partial truths." Those responsible for the operation were "in a real bad hole because they had the hell cut out of them." Bissell, according to General Wheeler, "could hardly talk coherently at the outset." In contrast to his earlier almost boyish exuberance in presenting the CIA plan, he "was tremendously upset" and came without a map or anything in hand while trying to explain the dire situation. The president revealed his concern by facial expressions and body language, wanting to take decisive action but clearly handcuffed by his self-imposed rules of plausible deni-ability. The disaster had resulted primarily from a pair of Castro's T-33 trainer jets, which graphically exposed the perils of an amphibious landing without air support. "Perhaps," the president remarked almost wistfully, "we ought to put in the navy air off the carrier which was lying offshore."[9]

As a consensus immediately developed for naval action, the president left for the Oval Office, followed by his brother, Rusk, McNamara, Dulles, Lemnitzer, and Burke. There, Robert Kennedy hotly told the admiral that the president looked to him for counsel. But Burke stammered that "it is late!" After ten minutes this meeting broke up, and they returned to the cabinet room. President Kennedy had made his decision: He would *not* send navy planes.[10]

After the meeting adjourned, the president called Burke twice within a half hour for advice. In doing so, Burke noted, Kennedy complained that the others in the room "weren't helpful" and bypassed normal channels by putting him in charge. "That is a helluva thing."[11]

Mixed signals bedeviled the decision-making process. Burke directed Admirals Dennison and Clark to send unmarked naval planes to gather firsthand information on the embattled beachhead. An hour later, Burke changed his mind, telling them to prepare the unmarked planes for combat and a number of unmarked boats for evacuating survivors. No one contemplated U.S. military intervention, he insisted, even though events appeared to be moving in that direction. "We are operating almost entirely in the dark," he said, and "may be in desperate straits."[12]

From the *Essex* in the late afternoon, Clark passed on the words of those involved in the landing operation to describe the grim situation. Pepe declared that his Blue Beach forces "must have jet air support in next few hours or will be wiped out. Under heavy attack by MIG jets and heavy tanks." Moments later he claimed to be under assault by MIG-15s and T-33s. "Request jet support or cannot hold. Situation critical."

Soon another plea for help: "Have no ammo left for tanks and very little left for troops. Enemy just launched heavy land attack supported by tanks. Cannot hold for long."

Finally: "Under heavy attack supported by 12 tanks. Need air support immediately. Red Beach wiped out. Request air strikes immediately."[13]

No response from Washington.

The White House intended to do virtually nothing. Dennison ordered six unmarked F3H jets from the *Essex* to make preparations for entering the target area by dawn for possible combat with what he feared would be four MIGs. There was no way to hide the American role, he told the Joint Chiefs. Burke pulled the president out of a formal function, urging him to authorize navy fighters to protect the landing of ammunition and supplies to the beleaguered forces.

"We just can't become involved," insisted Kennedy.

"Goddamnit, Mr. President, we are involved, and there is no way to hide it. We are involved!"[14]

The president would not budge.[15]

How about two unmarked and unarmed navy fighters to fly over the Bay of Pigs and perhaps intimidate Castro's pilots to leave? Again, the president refused.[16]

At 5:12 P.M. firsthand reports indicated that Red Beach had been "wiped out." A dozen enemy tanks accompanied by trucks and other vehicles were moving unhindered in that direction. All along the road near La Seiba were burned-out brigade tanks and trucks with no troops in sight. No one detected any combat, either in the air or on the ground.[17]

Shortly before midnight Pepe sent another frantic message from Blue Beach. "Do you people realize how desperate the situation is? Do you back us up or quit? All we want is low jet cover and jet close support. Enemy has this support. I need it badly or cannot survive. Please don't desert us. Am out of tank and bazooka ammo. Tanks will hit me at dawn. I will not be evacuated. Will fight to the end if we have to. Need medical supplies urgently."[18]

No help arrived.

II

Early in the morning of the third day, April 19, Castro's columns resumed artillery fire on the besieged troops hunkered in at San Blas above Blue Beach. Pepe ordered a counterattack but had little ammunition and soon ordered a withdrawal.[19]

Around 3:30 in Washington that same morning, Bissell secured the president's approval to put Blue Beach under one hour's protective cover by navy CAP beginning at 6:30 A.M. Acting in less than ten minutes, the Joint Chiefs saddled the pilots of six unmarked jets from the *Essex* with the virtually impossible task of defending the transports and B-26s en route to the area *without hitting ground targets or seeking combat.* "We had permission to be there," declared an unidentified person at the Naval War College years afterward, "but not to engage." To conceal the American role if shot down, the pilots would carry no identification papers and, despite flying over shark-filled waters, ditch *only at sea* if necessary. Robertson would meanwhile land on the beach to confer with Pepe about possible evacuation proceedings. If evacuation proved necessary, it would take place in unmarked boats manned by crews in dungarees in a transparent effort to hide their identification. Two destroyers were to hover offshore while reconnaissance planes assessed the situation.[20]

Burke dutifully followed the president's orders in keeping U.S. involvement "to as low a level as possible." It was frustrating. "God knows this operation is as difficult as possible and we are trying to do all we can without much info and without having been in on all initial stages. I too am irked and tired and I realize many of these suggestions are more difficult." The

Joint Chiefs stayed within the rules of engagement by authorizing only early warning vessels, except that, in accordance with the president's recent directive, they now had to stay *thirty* miles off Cuba rather than twenty.[21]

The cover operation got under way before dawn on April 19, when six B-26s departed Puerto Cabezas, two at a time and a half hour apart to spread out their arrivals over the beachhead. With exhausted Cuban pilots and utter desperation on the ground, the CIA authorized Alabama Air National Guardsmen to fly two of the planes. The B-26s arrived as scheduled but soon found themselves alone and fully exposed to two of Castro's T-33s. As the pilots radioed for their promised jet support, the enemy planes closed in, shooting down both American-piloted B-26s from behind, one into the sea and the other into a crash-landing near a sugar mill above Playa Larga. Before the first B-26 went down in flames, the two Americans aboard parachuted into the water but were captured and executed by Castro's forces. The other two Americans survived the forced landing, only to die in a fiery exchange with enemy militia. The remaining B-26s returned to Puerto Cabezas that morning, one hit forty times while making a strike north of San Blas and, with one engine dead, flying barely a hundred feet above water before landing safely on the airstrip.[22]

The navy jets arrived at the battle scene just as the last B-26s limped away, *a full hour* after the T-33s began their assault and themselves had left.[23]

Castro's news voice, Prensa Latina, denied the executions of the two Americans shot down at sea, insisting that they died in the crash. But the photo of their bodies sent to Latin American news outlets showed the men in inflated life jackets and no boots, indicating they were alive when hitting the water. Most conclusive, each American had a bullet hole in his forehead. Castro's propaganda merchants scrambled to cover their mistake by releasing a second photo, this one with only a single change: The Americans were in *de*flated life jackets but retained the telltale mark of execution. Taking advantage of these gaffes, the CIA circulated *both* pictures throughout Latin America.[24]

The White House still held on to the fig leaf of innocence. Robert Kennedy assured his brother on April 19 that "[no] U.S. citizen participated in the April 17 invasion." And, as part of the concerted cover up, he declared in January 1963 that no Americans died at the Bay of Pigs. Neither assertion was true. Two Americans had been the first to hit the beach on the first day of the invasion; four Americans had died on the third and last day.[25]

What caused this disaster? Curiously, the navy log for this period disappeared, making it impossible to say with certainty. The commander of the *Essex*, Captain S. S. "Pete" Searcy, claimed he followed orders in destroying all papers relating to these events. "This is a big damn cover-up," he muttered to himself at the time and declared later in an interview. Gray made a private inquiry and found Esterline responsible for an egregious error: In setting the time for the rendezvous, he had failed to take into account the one-hour time difference between Puerto Cabezas and the beachhead, meaning that the B-26s never had a chance to meet with the six unmarked jets from the *Essex*. Virtually defenseless, the brigade's planes met Castro's T-33s instead.[26]

But Gray's allegation cannot be correct. Both Esterline and Hawkins have categorically denied the charge, pointing out that no one on the Cuba Task Force, Esterline included, had the authority to write and send such a cable. Such an operation came under the authority of the CIA air staff led by Colonel Stanley Beerli of the U.S. Air Force, who reported directly to Bissell as head of the entire program. It stands to reason that *Bissell* set the rendezvous time. *He* was the one who won the president's approval of the proposal at 3:30 in the morning and *within ten minutes* notified the Joint Chiefs (who had no decision-making power in this CIA-run operation) to prepare the jets. Bissell doubtless called for the 6:30 rendezvous so that they arrived shortly after daylight in Cuba; but he did not remember that Nicaragua was in a different time zone.[27]

"No hits, no runs—all errors," acidly remarked an American pilot on learning the mission's fate.[28]

In a somber Washington meeting that same morning, General Gray briefed the Joint Chiefs on the hopeless situation. Pepe had exclaimed in disgust: "Have you quit? Aren't you going to support me any more?" Believing no assistance imminent, he asserted over the radio: "Regardless of whether you help or not, I will fight on regardless." What Pepe did not know was that some goods were in the air and on the way. But less than an hour later, the *Essex* intercepted brigade exchanges indicating that his forces had watched helplessly as most of the air drops missed the target area and fell into the sea.[29]

Lemnitzer sensed a total collapse of the beachhead and remarked to the president that the time had come for the landing party to follow the plan by switching to guerrilla operations. But Bissell astounded the general by asserting that the landing forces did not have guerrilla training. How could this be? The plan Lemnitzer saw had included that option. He did not realize that guerrilla tactics had sometime earlier lost nearly all interest, resulting in an almost exclusive focus on conventional training. Two alternatives remained: U.S. military intervention or full-scale evacuation, the first drawing little support, the second considered an admission to defeat.[30]

By noon of April 19 the brigade forces at Blue Beach had huddled in a small resort, isolated by a roadblock above the beaches and soon to confront a large enemy convoy. CIA officers in Nicaragua informed their home office in Washington that the situation was "completely out of our hands."[31]

In the operation's waning moments, Pepe repeatedly begged for assistance. At 11:18 A.M. of April 19: "We are out of ammo and fighting on the beach. Please send help. We cannot hold."

Thirteen minutes later, another message: "Out of ammunition. Men fighting in water. If no help given Blue Beach lost."

"In water. Out of ammo. Enemy closing in. Help must arrive in next hour."

"When your help will be here and with what?"

"Why your help has not come?"

And, finally, "Am destroying all equipment and communications. Tanks are in sight. I have nothing to fight with. Am taking to woods. I cannot repeat cannot wait for you."

Silence punctuated his final transmission.[32]

The entire beachhead had collapsed, and the remainder of the Cuban brigade, out of ammunition and supplies, saw no signs of a rescue operation and had to surrender.

At 2:17 P.M. the brigade's ship commander, Captain Sven Ryberg on the *Blagar*, somberly pronounced a requiem befitting those three days and nights at the Bay of Pigs: "Blue Beach was lost and no troops were on Blue Beach. Men fled into woods."[33]

Evacuation vessels were en route to the beachhead but turned around when news arrived of the operation's collapse. Castro's forces held the beach, making evacuation impossible. The two American destroyers left the area under heavy shore battery fire, returning full speed to the brigade's ships farther out to sea.[34]

By five that evening, a scant twenty forces remained on Blue Beach, no officers among them and the exhausted survivors armed only with rifles. Five of them found a small boat at water's edge and rowed with their hands into the bay. Eight others soon secured another boat, but an enemy plane swooped over, killing them while missing the five. After drifting toward the keys, they were picked up by a destroyer four days later.[35]

The evacuation proved only minimally successful. At 8:42 P.M. the Joint Chiefs arranged for a destroyer to remain off the beach during the night and just outside the range of shore guns in the event evacuees appeared. To stay beyond artillery fire, other destroyers searched for stragglers by cruising along the beaches two miles offshore at night and five miles out during the day. Although it was a difficult arrangement, two Americans worked with Cuban frogmen over the next few days in picking up twenty-six bedraggled and starving survivors in the keys west of the Bay of Pigs; they found no one on the east side.[36]

Nothing remained of the amphibious encounter, according to one report, except Castro, who was "waiting on the beach." In less than three days, his forces had crushed the brigade, killing 114 of the 1,511-man force and capturing 1,179, including Pepe and Artime, and had seized enormous piles of brigade weaponry. Survival in the swamps had come at heavy costs— several days of choking down insects and the raw meat of lizards, crocodiles, snakes, and chickens; drinking the reptiles' blood and human urine—all with the certainty of death magnified by Castro's helicopters constantly thumping loudly overhead, his militias swarming all around while randomly firing their machine guns into the bush, the sense of despair as artillery shelled the area. But the brigade had not gone down easily. In the air war from April 15–19, the Cuban rebels flew thirty-six missions, inflicting some damage but losing eight planes and fourteen pilots, including the four Americans among the eight killed. Castro's doctors estimated that his forces suffered 3,650 casualties, including 1,250 deaths in battle and another 400 from wounds and insufficient medical care. Castro assumed both mythical and international status as his country became a self-proclaimed socialist headquarters in the hemisphere and a Cold War friend of the Soviet Union. The blood shed at the Bay of Pigs solidified his rule and marked Cuba's move into the Communist camp.[37]

III

Who bore responsibility for this debacle? The president? The CIA? The Joint Chiefs of Staff? Or Castro? As in most events that shape history, everyone involved shares some degree of accountability.

Many participants vented their anger on President Kennedy. One of the American pilots, Albert Persons, criticized him for switching the invasion from Trinidad to Zapata and then refusing to take decisive military action. Persons exonerated the CIA by asserting that the Cuban invasion "was allowed to fail." The fiasco stemmed from "timidity, indecisiveness and poor judgment at the highest, policy-making levels of government—which is at the White House, in the White House staff and the President's cabinet." After changing the invasion site and ordering a night-time landing, Kennedy reduced the scale of the D-2 raids, canceled the D-1 and D-Day strikes, and sent the brigade ashore without adequate air protection. Captain Edward Ferrer of the rebel air force concurred, expressing the commonly held views of his Cuban colleagues that President Kennedy's decision to call off the D-Day strikes "doomed the invasion to failure." Esterline had earlier given this same gloomy assessment, and Hawkins added another dimension to this explanation by claiming that the State Department "crippled and destroyed" the operation by convincing the president to terminate the air strikes.[38]

Brigade commanders likewise attributed the failed expedition to President Kennedy's decision to call off the D-Day strikes. "Without air support," Pepe moaned, "we were sure of going to our death." They had received assurances that the planes would destroy all of Castro's defense capabilities. But that did not happen. Another Cuban leader noted that the planes were to take out the airfields and the tanks. "That was the initial plan, so why didn't they tell us we couldn't carry on with the invasion because the air strikes were stopped?" U.S. jets could have helped. "We could have arranged to take all the insignia off." Without air defenses, "it's just like sending a bunch of human beings to get killed."[39]

A consensus quickly developed that the lack of air support proved pivotal to the failure. Lynch asserted that the men could have made it ashore despite the enemy's B-26s and Sea Furies, if they had had air protection against the T-33s. General Thomas White, air force chief of staff, thought the D-Day strikes critical to the plan and argued that, without them, the D-2 raids served only to warn Castro of the invasion. It was "difficult to say what an air strike on D-Day at dawn would have done, but it might very well have made the difference." Burke had counted on the air force to disable Castro's planes, and Hawkins insisted that "the real key was control of the air." In a perplexing change of form, Bissell, who had put up only token resistance to both reducing the D-2 strikes and canceling the D-Day raids, joined military figures in considering the air war a decisive factor. Instead of more than forty sorties before the invasion, the number catapulted down to eight and became "the operation's death sentence." And yet neither the CIA nor the Joint Chiefs told the president that air cover was essential to success. This did not mean that air cover would have guaranteed victory, he added, but without it, the operation "didn't have a chance."[40]

The CIA in-house study of October 1961 likewise attributed a great part of Castro's success to the canceled D-Day strikes. The president made this decision without conferring with military leaders who could have explained the vital relationship of air strikes to an amphibious operation. But the CIA also bore responsibility. When Cabell and Bissell turned down the opportunity to discuss the matter with the president, they led the secretary of state to conclude that he was correct in thinking the air assault nonessential to the landing.[41]

Another aspect of the air campaign proved vital to Castro's victory. Despite ample warning of the landing, he was unable to marshal his defenses beforehand and was particularly vulnerable in the crucial first hours. Indeed, at the time of the invasion, his on-the-spot ground forces *totaled* no more than a dozen, and this number included militia. Not for seventy-two hours afterward—as the CIA had calculated—did he amass enough soldiers and heavy weaponry to match that of the brigade. And even then he had to rely on personal communications with his forces in issuing orders because of the destruction of his radio network. One cannot be certain that the president's decision to cancel the D-1 and D-Day strikes spared Castro's air force from destruction. But it is irrefutable that the air assaults Castro launched during the brigade's attempt to land bought the time needed for his ground units to reach the battle scene.[42]

Lack of respect for the enemy also hurt the brigade's operation, for Castro surprised the Kennedy administration by mounting a strong defense both in the air and on the ground. Bissell admitted to underestimating Castro's air strength and his organizational and inspirational skills. The T-33s, in particular, were armed and deadly and commanded by pilots of unexpected ability. In a statement suggesting either naïveté or sheer arrogance, General White declared that he and others in the air force had never considered the possibility of Castro's specialists converting the T-33s into combat planes. American strategists also miscalculated the strength and abilities of Castro's ground defense. "We hadn't known that the militia could run tanks," conceded Lynch. Bissell admitted to poor planning based on faulty assumptions about Castro's fighting abilities. "We would never have adopted the Zapata Plan if we had known that he had coordinated forces that would close in and fight as they did."[43]

A factor commonly overlooked was the fierce determination of Castro and his followers to resist the invasion. Castro viciously denounced the brigade forces as "mercenaries" and referred to the victory as the "Battle of Girón," thereby branding his enemies as traitors to the revolution and extolling the outcome as what a travel map now calls "the first defeat of imperialism in America." Each antagonist in the domestic struggle considered itself the true progenitor of the revolution, resulting in a vendetta-like internecine struggle that had to play out on the battlefield. In a costly mistake, Bissell and others grossly underestimated the tenacity of those Cuban people remaining loyal to Castro.[44]

The most incisive critique of the invasion effort came from its target, Fidel Castro. Shortly afterward, Ernest Halperin of the Massachusetts Institute of Technology met with Castro in Havana. "So," Halperin asked, "why do you think the invasion failed?" "Lack of air cover," Castro replied without hesitation. Furthermore, he continued on another occasion, the rebel planes dropped their airborne battalions too close to the beaches, allowing his tanks and artillery to use the causeways to Playa Girón and Playa Larga. He was amazed that the paratroopers did not engage his men until eight in the morning of the assault and that the brigade commanders were not aware of the special passages used by his men to enter the Zapata region. He was surprised that the battalion that evacuated the sinking *Houston* did not rendezvous with the forces fighting at Playa Larga. Zapata was a superb choice in military terms, particularly if the invaders had cut off the causeways and held the beachhead long enough to build a base for planes and ships and to announce a provisional government that requested outside assistance. "I could, in the invaders' position, have held the place, and at this particular place it would have been almost impossible for us to flank them." They had a "good plan, poorly executed."[45]

From the Kennedy administration's perspective, the main story at the Bay of Pigs was missed opportunities. The CIA knew that Castro's planes could not fly in the dark, which meant that its original plan had been sound: Have the merchant vessels leave the beaches before dawn and return that night to finish off-loading. But they lingered into the daylight hours, making them ready targets for the air assault. The Playa Girón airport was usable despite the CIA's disclaimers. Pepe attested that the CIA had erroneous information that the airstrip was unfinished—including U-2 photographs showing it still under construction. His men thus carried gasoline-powered saws to remove the trees by the highway and allow the big-winged B-26s and C-46s to land. "When we got there," he declared, "we found that the airport had been completed, even to the last detail of its control tower." Had they known this, the brigade could have occupied the airstrip, dispatched C-54s to bring in supplies at night, and sent B-26s to provide cover and air support for the landing. In addition, the shorter distance between the takeoff point and the beaches would have removed the need for extra gasoline and en-abled the brigade to restore the tail guns to the B-26s.[46]

In defense of the White House, it remained surprisingly uninformed of events because of the CIA's operational failures, poor intelligence, com-munication breakdowns caused by damaged or destroyed signal equipment, and the absence of an American on the scene to provide firsthand reports. The Joint Chiefs emphasized from the beginning that a popular insurrection was crucial to the plan and received repeated CIA assurances of its hap-pening as a result of the invasion. But the CIA had been unable to build a communication network with the island's dissidents, Castro clapped thousands of them in prison a week prior to the invasion, and the assassi-nation plan failed. Furthermore, the strategists underestimated the fighting capacity of Castro's forces, overestimated the number of defections from his army and militia forces once the landing began, and erroneously counted on massive support once ashore and implanted on the beach. As for the guerrillas in the Escambray Mountains, they were starving because the peasants had refused them food and they were unable to live off the land. And once President Kennedy had publicly promised no U.S. intervention, hardly anyone was willing to risk death at "the Wall" by firing squad. His decision to move the landing site from Trinidad to Zapata meant that instead of having a nearby mountainous refuge, the brigade confronted a much greater distance to the Escambrays and a huge and deadly swamp in between. Information after the landing continued to be incomplete. Not until the morning of April 19—after the rebel defeat—did the president learn that the brigade had lost the beachhead and was fighting in the water. Robert Kennedy insisted that his brother had declared on D-Day that "he'd rather be called an aggressor than a bum" and was ready "to go as far as necessary to assure success." Indeed, "he used to walk around on that White House lawn thinking he'd like to do something if he knew what was going on."[47]

President Kennedy acted on a number of false assumptions. He thought he had approved a quiet, night-time landing; that the brigade could escape into the mountains and take up guerrilla tactics; that it had expected no direct American help; that a popular uprising would occur; that Castro's growing military strength made this a now-or-never operation; that the infiltration would be clandestine and a success. But the new president did not know whom to trust for advice, his administration had had no time to fully assess the plan, and it had not yet made preparations for crisis planning. The landing process stretched into daylight; the mountains were too far from the coast to provide sanctuary; the brigade had not received adequate guerrilla training and counted on U.S. military support; no rebellion took place; Castro's forces were militarily capable; and the landing operation was too large to be a secret and too small to win.[48]

Still, the fact remains that President Kennedy approved the plan. In retrospect, he should have trusted his instincts and called it off even though fresh in office and dealing with experts. His political concerns were senseless in that the operation could never remain quiet in an open, democratic society. Instead of listening to Schlesinger and Fulbright, the president went with Rusk, McNamara, and other advisers in believing it would be a low-key, successful operation without seriously considering the possibility that it might not work. Hope overcame doubt and encouraged a program that was in a state of implosion before it began.[49]

The chief fault lay with the president and his advisers for believing they could hide the American hand and therefore allowing political considerations to interfere with a military operation. In this instance, the priorities became reversed and undermined the entire operation. The president never grasped either the interconnected importance of the D-2, D-1, and D-Day strikes to the invasion or the desperate plight of the brigade under storm on the beach. As the plan's architect, Bissell gave in too readily to the president's politically driven restrictions on both Zapata and the D-2 operation. He and Cabell then failed to exhaust every effort at convincing Kennedy that the D-1 and D-Day assaults were vital to success, particularly in view of the limited impact of the D-2 strikes. Baffling still is their decision to decline Rusk's invitation to appeal directly to the president about restoring the D-Day attacks. Or did both the president and Bissell count too heavily on Castro's assassination as bellwether to the invasion?

Not surprisingly, the White House blamed both the CIA and the Joint Chiefs of Staff for failing to emphasize the military importance of the D-Day strikes. President Kennedy asserted that neither group of advisers approached him directly about the crucial role of air support in an amphibious landing or asked him to extend naval air cover over the supply convoy moving to Blue Beach. Bundy maintained that no one had warned of the lethal potential of the T-33s, a lapse in judgment that contributed to the decision against launching a D-Day strike. "I suggest," he asserted, "that one reason for the later decision not to launch an air strike on the morning of D-Day was that this capability of the Castro air force was never put forward as significant." If anyone had warned "that calling off or modifying the air strikes would cause the operation to fail—or even damage it severely—the President would have reversed any such decision as that on Sunday." The president declared that had he understood the critical nature of the D-Day strikes, he would have approved them. Rusk likewise later agreed that the strikes should have taken place, but he thought their advocates did not make a strong case.[50]

One cannot be sure that a heart-to-heart conversation with the president would have made a difference; but it is certain that the lack of such a conversation allowed events to continue their course.

Hard questions remain: First and primary, how did so many of the brightest minds in Washington become so irrationally involved in a venture that appeared certain to fail because of self-imposed restraints and inept planning—moreover, a venture against Castro's Cuba, a country that posed no danger to national security? Wouldn't even a successful invasion have led to a prolonged military occupation of an alienated populace, guaranteeing more costs in prestige and credibility than any possible political or military gains? How could even civilian leaders fail to recognize that huge transport ships needed air protection from enemy planes while engaged in the long and slow process of off-loading men, matériel, vehicles, and heavy weaponry onto a beachhead, whether at night or in the daytime? What led them to believe the entire landing operation could take place before dawn? Or that they could safely retreat at daybreak and return unscathed the following evening? Why didn't the nation's military experts speak out about the defects in the plan? What led Washington to think the brigade could launch a surprise landing, given all the publicity about its preparations in Guatemala, the widespread knowledge of the invasion among news correspondents and others, and the gift of warning provided by the D-2 attacks?

The Cold War mindset had gripped the Kennedy administration, driving it into approving a fatally flawed plan to remove Castro as an alleged Communist and a potential threat to U.S. and hemispheric safety. A sense of alarm propelled the operation, heightened by the surety of more Soviet military aid and the imminent arrival of Czech-trained Cuban pilots expecting to fly the Soviet MIGs already on the island though not yet ready for use. Such a hurried atmosphere resulted in careless policymaking, faulty execution of a poorly conceived plan, a mindless faith in luck and ingenuity, and a nonsensical political fear of attribution that undermined an already weak military operation.

But another, more personal consideration looms just as important in explaining the failure. The Kennedy brothers' animosity toward Castro had blinded them to the dangers of this ill-conceived action. Losing their hold on reality, they supported a Cuban intervention that demonstrated the uncontrollable course of events once a nation thrusts itself into another nation's domestic affairs and, worse, does so without an exit strategy. How can the intervening nation withdraw short of losing prestige, causing further internal turmoil, and leaving a legacy of ill will within the invaded state and perhaps among its neighbors? The forceful imposition of one culture onto another, particularly when the focus is on regime change, has rarely if ever satisfied all parties involved. The Cuba story provides a classic example of how building a national policy on a personal obsession grounded in self-righteousness can lead to disastrous results.

7

Inquisition

I think we were closer to success than you realize.

—Allen Dulles, April 26, 1961

[Plausible denial was] a pathetic illusion.

—Lyman Kirkpatrick, October 1961

After an emotional meeting with friends and relatives of those who died at the Bay of Pigs, President Kennedy moaned to Richard Nixon that this marked "the worst experience of my life." He later told the press, "There's an old saying that victory has a hundred fathers and defeat is an orphan." But the president publicly assumed full blame for the debacle, declaring in no uncertain terms, "I am the responsible officer of the government." Privately, however, he castigated the Joint Chiefs as "[t]hose sons-of-bitches with all the fruit salad [who] just sat there nodding, saying it would work," and "those CIA bastards" whose office I would like "to splinter" into "a thousand pieces and scatter . . . to the winds." His most valued advisers had opened him to ridicule. Less profile and more courage, critics sarcastically demanded in alluding to his Pulitzer Prize–winning work, *Profiles in Courage*. Not only did the Bay of Pigs fiasco expose him to the charge of imperialism; worse, it showed he wasn't even good at it. "All my life I've known better than to depend on the experts. How could I have been so stupid?" So strongly did he feel that he turned primarily to his closest confidants for advice and directed his brother Robert to impose strict controls on the agency.[1]

In the immediate aftermath of the failed invasion, President Kennedy appointed a special commission to determine the reasons for the outcome, and within six months the CIA's inspector general launched an internal investigation having the same objective. The two teams reached strikingly similar conclusions that did nothing to dissuade the administration from its continued resolve to overthrow Castro.

I

President Kennedy quickly regained his hard-line Cold War composure and joined his brother in a virtual vendetta against Castro. To restore U.S. prestige, they would have to take a firm stand, not only in Cuba but also in Berlin, Vietnam, and other trouble spots. Cuba, though, was the centerpiece. Castro's removal became the top priority on the administration's agenda, for it would help to determine the course of the Cold War, refurbish the stature needed by the White House to pursue its ambitious domestic program, and, no less important, satisfy the Kennedys' growing obsession with eliminating their Cuban adversary. On the day following the collapsed invasion, President Kennedy told the American Society of Newspaper Editors that "our restraint is not inexhaustible" and shortly afterward pledged support to the hemisphere's republics while exhorting them into action. "Should it ever appear that the inter-American doctrine of non-interference merely conceals or excuses a policy of nonaction—if the nations of this Hemisphere should fail to meet their commitments against outside Communist penetration—then I want it clearly understood that this Government will not hesitate in meeting its primary obligations which are the security of our Nation!"[2]

Western Europeans were baffled by the president's preoccupation with Castro and feared an outright U.S. invasion of Cuba. Schlesinger had just returned from the Continent and noted deep "shock and disillusion" over the "Cuban debacle" among news correspondents, journalists, political leaders, editors, publishers, and diplomats. How could the United States be "so incompetent, irresponsible and stupid"? The new administration had promised a reasoned approach to the Cold War and yet had continued John Foster Dulles's "self-righteous" and "trigger happy" policies. "Kennedy has lost his magic," said one contemporary. Others asked, "Why was Cuba such a threat to you? Why couldn't you live with Cuba, as the USSR lives with Turkey and Finland?"[3]

Some Europeans wondered whether that one day in April signaled the beginning of a foreign policy built on forceful intervention. "If Cuba were just an accident, all right," remarked an editor of the London *Observer*. "But everything since Cuba suggests that the Kennedy who launched that invasion was the *real* Kennedy" and that he appeared obsessed with guerrilla warfare and paramilitary operations. A number of Europeans declared, "It's not Cuba that worries me; it's the aftermath." A victim of bad advice, many lamented. Nothing, Schlesinger asserted, would do more to restore faith in the administration than "a visible shake-up and subordination of CIA."[4]

The president's greatest concern was that the Soviet Union would take advantage of the situation to convert Cuba into a missile base. His brother feared that Cuba would become "Mr. Khrushchev's arsenal" within two years and called for manufacturing a pretext for taking decisive action. "If it was reported" that Castro's planes had attacked Guantanamo, the United States could call this "an act of war" and take appropriate countermeasures. The time had come for a showdown. "If we don't want Russia to set up missile bases in Cuba, we had better decide now what we are willing to do to stop it."[5]

The White House pulsated with a potent mixture of shock, embarrassment, and anger in the Bay of Pigs aftermath. The cabinet gathered before noon on April 20 in what Chester Bowles from the State Department termed "as grim as any meeting" he ever attended. The president appeared "shattered," sullenly watching the meeting deteriorate into an "almost savage" affair. The invasion plan had had little chance for success, Labor Secretary Arthur Goldberg sharply asserted in a sentiment that few had been bold enough to voice *before* April 17; the White House should never have approved the operation without having American troops ready for action. The angriest remarks came from the attorney general and, uncharacteristically, the director of the Bureau of the Budget, David Bell. After forty-five minutes of rambling and bitter discussions, the president abruptly stood and bolted into his office. Surely his thoughts turned on how mutely compliant his colleagues had been during the halcyon days before the invasion. Anyone can be courageous after the fact. Why hadn't his advisers, all charter members of what *New York Times* journalist and writer David Halberstam later dubbed "the best and the brightest," expressed misgivings *before* the disaster?[6]

Bowles, Johnson, and McNamara joined Robert Kennedy in following the president out of the room, determined to pursue the matter in the Oval Office. The tension did not abate in the new confines. Robert Kennedy repeatedly criticized the State Department for failing the White House, and when Bowles refuted the charges, the attorney general lashed into him. Bowles knew his argument carried little weight when matched against that of the president's brother. He also realized that his standing within the administration suffered daily because of his tardy switch from Stevenson to Kennedy in the race for the Democratic presidential nomination. What bothered Bowles was that Johnson's and Robert Kennedy's lack of foreign policy experience made them susceptible to simple "military-CIA-paramilitary type answers" presented in "specific logistical terms which can be added, subtracted, multiplied, or divided." The president remained in "acute shock" during that tense half-hour conference, but he was "almost frantic" in demanding action.[7]

The president increasingly leaned toward removing Castro by U.S. military force. The critics appeared correct—partial intervention could never work and, in fact, was a formula for failure. The Cuban exiles were not capable of defeating the regime's forces, which meant that *Americans* must do the job. Either go in with full force, or don't go in at all. Kennedy posed hard questions. How many American forces were required? What was the timetable for success? How many casualties could we expect, both Cuban and American? Did we have enough military forces to deal with problems elsewhere while focusing on Cuba? To find answers, he wanted the Defense Department to draft an invasion plan. Although McNamara emphasized that military action was not "probable," he could do little to downplay the importance of the president's directive.[8]

The following day McNamara told the Joint Chiefs of Staff and the secretaries of the services what the president wanted. First, the military must "accept appropriate responsibility" for the Bay of Pigs and "avoid back-biting." We can learn a number of lessons from this episode, McNamara insisted. Most notably, the military alone must handle military operations, and the government should never begin a program without expecting to complete it or to accept the consequences of failure. These thoughts in mind, the president wanted the Joint Chiefs to draw up a plan to invade

Cuba, although McNamara again termed that action "unlikely." But by casting part of the blame onto the Joint Chiefs, the defense secretary had angered them, making them more determined to run the next venture. If the CIA had "lost its nerve," Lemnitzer testily remarked, the Joint Chiefs would gladly take over the job.[9]

Thirty-five officials attended an embittered Saturday morning meeting of the National Security Council, where Robert Kennedy slammed anyone objecting to immediate and decisive action. Bowles repeatedly warned against pitting the United States against an island and mobilizing world sympathy for Castro in a "David and Goliath struggle." His argument swayed no one. The "fire eaters," Bowles asserted, "brutally and abruptly" dismissed caution while others remained silent, only their facial expressions revealing deep concern about taking rash action. The president's advisers were not accustomed to failure and their "pride and confidence had been deeply wounded." Most alarming was the absence of "moral integrity" among "tired, frustrated, and personally humiliated" advisers.[10]

Momentum continued to swell in favor of an invasion. Secretary of the Army Elvis Stahr proposed the establishment of a "Freedom Brigade" in the U.S. Army composed of volunteer Cuban nationals trained in Special Forces tactics who would infiltrate Cuba preceding a U.S. invasion. Not only would this action drum up popular support, but it would facilitate an exit strategy. American forces would "get in and get out quickly," leaving military occupation to the Freedom Brigade as protector of a U.S.-recognized government.[11]

Anger and frustration had led to demands for a quick and sure resolution of the Castro problem, and that dictated a direct path to the objective rather than one dependent on Cuban exiles acting within the slower, uncertain, and indirect nature of covert operations. Not surprisingly, American soldiers and firepower emerged in the discussions as the sole guarantors of success.

II

As the talks turned more toward a military solution, President Kennedy telephoned New York and invited General Maxwell Taylor, then president of the Lincoln Center for the Performing Arts, to the White House the next morning to discuss the Cuban issue. Taylor had opposed Eisenhower's policy of massive retaliation and soon became one of the few generals President Kennedy admired. In the Oval Office on April 22, the president expressed grave concern about the "ghastly disaster" at the Bay of Pigs and asked Taylor to head an investigation into what went wrong and why. Gazing around the room at Vice President Johnson, Bundy, and others, Taylor "sensed an air . . . of a command post that had been overrun by the enemy. There were the same glazed eyes, subdued voices, and slow speech that I remembered observing in commanders routed at the Battle of the Bulge or recovering from the shock of their first action. In this instance, the latter was a more accurate analogy because this new administration had, indeed, engaged in its first bloody action and was learning the sting of defeat."[12]

That same day, Kennedy wrote a letter authorizing Taylor "to take a close look at all our practices and programs in the areas of military and paramilitary, guerrilla and anti-guerrilla activity which fall short of outright war." The mandate's broad language surprised the general; he was "to chart a path toward the future" that permitted his committee to "roam the whole field of intelligence and everything else."[13]

President Kennedy asked Taylor to work with Robert Kennedy, Burke, and Dulles in analyzing recent Cuban events as a basis for improving America's short-of-war strategy. For two hours that same afternoon, the Taylor Committee (or Cuba Study Group) held the first of several meetings over the next month with CIA, State, and Defense Department personnel, inquiring into matters affecting national security but with a special eye on Cuba. The committee decided against recording the hearings, causing some participants (usually not identified by name in the records) to claim they could not remember more than a few of the statements attributed to them.[14]

In this frenetic atmosphere, the assassination option quietly burbled upward again. The plan had gone underground on invasion eve, only to resurface when the Bay of Pigs failure graphically demonstrated the importance of a popular uprising. Wouldn't Castro's death have incited an insurrection? But was the CIA-Mafia assassination plan dead or merely dormant? CIA security chief Sheffield Edwards tied the beginnings of the operation to the Bay of Pigs effort and its termination to the unsuccessful invasion. Hardly a reliable source, he claimed that after April 17, 1961, "The plan, as I recall, petered out." But Jim O'Connell confirmed only the first part of his superior's assertion, agreeing that the assassination plan came to a standstill with the Bay of Pigs but claiming there was "something going on" afterward. O'Connell concurred with agency colleague William Harvey that soon after the invasion, assassination again became a "going operation."[15]

The key questions about the CIA-Mafia assassination plan: How much did Robert Kennedy (and hence his brother the president) know, and when did he know it? As shown earlier, Bissell claimed that Dulles told the president-elect of *only* the invasion plan before his inauguration, and when pushed on whether President Kennedy had been made aware of the assassination project, Bissell asserted, "I think he might have been, but I have no knowledge of my own." Dulles bore the responsibility of telling the president but, more appropriately, *after* he had taken office. "I assumed that he [Dulles] had at least intimated that some such thing was underway." He believed that "at some stage" Dulles would have advised both Presidents Eisenhower and Kennedy, but in vague language to protect them by providing plausible deniability.[16]

Another indication of President Kennedy's awareness of assassination discussions came when Edwards claimed that Bissell briefed the Taylor Committee *and* the attorney general on the CIA's use of the Mafia, albeit *without mentioning assassination*. Bissell agreed with the assertion, insisting he said nothing about assassination to the Taylor Committee because no one raised the issue. Confirmation came from Taylor and Burke, who asserted that neither Bissell nor Dulles mentioned the subject in the briefing. But Bissell admitted to telling the attorney general in "circumlocutious" language that "signaled" the CIA's intention to kill Castro. "We were trying to use elements of the underworld against Castro." When asked whether his reference to the underworld meant killing Castro, he responded, "I think that is a way of using these people against him."[17]

Edwards and Bissell frequently disagreed over several aspects of the CIA-Mafia story, but they concurred in this crucial instance: that Robert Kennedy (and hence the president) knew about the collaboration and its purpose. The two CIA figures' history of contradictory testimonies makes anything they said suspect, but their agreement on this sensitive point ironically suggests that they were telling the truth on a matter having profound implications. After the Bay of Pigs, the Kennedys focused even more on bringing down the Havana regime—and by immediate action. Even without a specific reference to assassination by either Dulles in January 1961 or Bissell five months later in May, the two agency figures had spoken in language clear enough to make the president and his brother aware of the

CIA-Mafia effort to kill Castro. Besides, the Kennedys were patently familiar with Giancana's mob actions because of their work on the congressional committee headed by Senator John McClellan that exposed organized crime in the 1950s; certainly they realized that the Mafia's involvement in Castro's removal meant assassination.

The administration nonetheless denied knowledge of an assassination effort, either before or after the Bay of Pigs operation. Years later, Rusk claimed to remember no talk of assassinating Castro, though admitting that everyone knew the Cuban chieftain and others could die in the landing attempt. "But we did not link to that a pinpointed, personal attack on Castro." In a questionable argument used by General Gordon Gray in the Eisenhower presidency, Rusk insisted that promoting a coup was "by no means the same thing as a political assassination." They were "pretty different." The Taylor Committee did not question the CIA about covert actions in Cuba *unrelated* to the Bay of Pigs operation (confirming Bissell's claim). "We didn't look at anything that was not directly pertinent," Taylor declared, "but we didn't go looking for any extraneous matters." He knew nothing about an alleged CIA contact with the Mafia to kill Castro. He also had no discussions with the president or any other administration official about assassination plans after the Bay of Pigs, and he had not heard of any CIA authorization for such an operation.[18]

But stronger evidence supports the contrary argument. Given the president's and attorney general's obsession with Castro, it is inconceivable that assassination did not cross their minds. The CIA was directly answerable to the president and would not have undertaken such a venture without his approval. The executive action program was still in its early stages of development, and even though it had no relation to the Mafia plan, its primary target was Castro. Both Kennedys knew about the CIA's collaboration with the Mafia and did nothing to discourage the idea. The CIA's internal inquiry of 1967 concluded that the CIA-Mafia plan to assassinate Castro did not come to a halt with the Bay of Pigs invasion, and Richard Helms, the CIA director who ordered the investigation, alluded to extreme measures when attesting that after the Bay of Pigs failure, the administration heightened its efforts to remove Castro. "The principal driving force was the Attorney General, Robert Kennedy. There isn't any question about this." The humiliation "whetted the appetite of the Administration to get rid of this regime by some other device." In a thinly veiled reference to assassination, Helms did not recall "any plans that were approved or that were viable specifically directed at eliminating Castro, but that there were con-versations about it, I haven't the slightest doubt."[19]

Furthermore, Rusk's and Taylor's responses echo each other, again suggesting the tactics of plausible deniability. It is indisputable that the CIA and the White House regarded Castro's assassination as a vital ingredient in the attempt to incite a popular insurrection and topple the regime. As noted earlier, Bissell as main strategist expressed his reliance on assassination as a critical part of the plan, and Schlesinger admitted to this years afterward. Yet Rusk maintained the fiction that no one mentioned assassination and that, by extrapolation, such a measure could not have been part of an overthrow effort. Taylor was just as evasive, emphatically (and truthfully) denying any committee pursuance of covert matters that he categorized as having no relation to the invasion. Like Rusk, Taylor claimed to have heard no mention of assassination, while emphasizing that the matter lay outside the committee's purview because it "was not exactly pertinent" or was "extraneous." It is curious, though, that Taylor now defined the investigation's parameters so narrowly after earlier declaring his committee's mandate so broad that it could "roam the whole field of intelligence and everything else."[20] Rusk's and Taylor's carefully structured wording and bland refusal to see any connection between assassination and invasion both strongly suggested calculated attempts to cloud the facts.

Thus at the time of the Taylor inquiry, the White House had not strayed from its objective of managing a regime change in Cuba. Rather, the options had narrowed to a military invasion, perhaps preceded (again) by Castro's assassination as impetus to a rebellion.

III

A cardinal principle in decision making is to construct the worst-case scenario in preparing for unforeseen problems. What becomes clear from the Taylor investigation is that two presidential administrations operated under the *best-case* scenario and, in so doing, virtually invited surprises and ultimate failure. How could policymakers handle unexpected problems without exploring all possible outcomes and conducting war games beforehand? General Gray confirmed this flawed premise by asserting that the covert plan rested "on the assumption of the most optimistic thing that could happen."[21]

The initial lapse by both the Eisenhower and Kennedy administrations lay in failing to put together a cohesive plan in writing that rested on an intricate relationship between political and military means and objectives. When Taylor asked for the "concept" behind the plan, Gray admitted that the planners had no overarching design holding the plan together. Burke agreed. "We made our mistake in not drawing up what we thought the concept was and presenting it to the State Department and CIA." Gray never got the information needed because "we were holding it so tight." "How is it possible," Taylor asked, "to keep from tying the hands of our military men by these political considerations?" By involving all departments at the beginning of the planning process, Gray responded. He had helped to draw up a paper to this effect, which the Joint Chiefs approved and forwarded to the defense secretary. But nothing came of this effort, probably because of the pause between presidential administrations. Instead of a coordinated effort, the CIA formulated the concepts, the Joint Chiefs evaluated them, and the State Department became involved only later on an informal basis. After President Kennedy approved the operation on a contingency basis, the Joint Chiefs finished the planning—on the eve of the invasion and hence too late to make changes.[22]

The Taylor inquiry revealed that the Joint Chiefs thought the Trinidad Plan had greater potential for success than the Zapata Plan, even if the odds were not encouraging. Had Trinidad been the target, Gray insisted, the invasion brigade would have had more time to establish a beachhead because Castro needed at least two days to mount an effective defense, the first to bring his forces together and the second for travel to the landing site. Furthermore, Trinidad was more populated than Zapata and offered a greater opportunity for attracting indigenous help. "The key to the plan was popular uprisings all over the island—which would pin down the militia in other areas." Still, the chances at Trinidad were never higher than 40 percent. General Decker remarked on another occasion that under certain critical conditions, the Trinidad Plan had a "reasonable chance of initial success." But rebel planes must destroy Castro's air force before the invasion. The landing must be a surprise. And it must take place at a site far enough east to pose problems for Castro's moving troops out of Havana and yet close enough to the mountains to provide a guerrilla haven.[23]

Rusk blamed the Joint Chiefs for making it appear that either Trinidad or Zapata was acceptable. They first approved the Trinidad Plan, which was a larger and "more spectacular operation." But the president objected, arguing that his administration could not plausibly deny responsibility for a

Trinidad invasion. Not only did Zapata meet the political needs of a quiet landing, but its airstrip at Playa Girón could accommodate B-26s and thereby promote the myth of an internal uprising. If the Joint Chiefs preferred Trinidad, Rusk declared, "[t]hey didn't put their view in writing and that didn't come through."[24]

Zapata was nonetheless a sound choice, insisted the Joint Chiefs. It would have worked "if the plan had been brought to fruition," remarked Shoup. Dulles took offense at the general's implicit criticism of the CIA. "Do you realize how many military men we had on this Task Force? Some of your best officers. We took a great deal of responsibility, but we called on the Defense Department and I looked to them for military judgments. I didn't look to our people for military judgments." Shoup did not shrink from the rebuke, blaming the practitioners more than the planners. "I spent a lot of sleepless hours over this because . . . there was no plan for helping these men if there was something unforeseen, an act of God or something, that prevented a successful landing. In my opinion there would be no way to save them. There was no way to guarantee its success, but if the plan was executed, as planned, I believe it would have been successful." General Decker concurred. "If we had thought the plan would fail, we certainly would have advised the President."[25]

Lemnitzer vehemently denied McNamara's earlier assertion that the Joint Chiefs had preferred Zapata over Trinidad. "I just don't understand how he got that impression." The general offered to produce his notes showing that they had twice found none of the three alternative plans "as feasible and likely to accomplish the objectives as the present paramilitary plan. I don't see how you can say it any clearer than that."[26]

Shoup reiterated a central truth from the beginning: that the mission hinged on a popular insurrection. "I don't think any military man would ever think that this force could overthrow Castro without support. They could never expect anything but annihilation." Without popular backing, Castro's thousands easily crushed the rebels' hundreds who hit the beach. Rusk thought a popular uprising highly likely and "utterly essential" to causing domestic chaos and "ousting Castro." With no organized opposition on the beach, the "highly-trained" invasion force would have confronted the militia units "and beat the hell out of them." This "bloody nose" would have stirred up massive popular support and brought victory.[27]

It slowly became obvious that a popular uprising had never been possible. Dulles suddenly backpedaled in defending the CIA, surprisingly asserting that he and others had never expected a spontaneous popular revolt. In doing so, the CIA director ignored what he had said earlier along with the distribution of thousands of propaganda leaflets calling for an uprising and the huge piles of military equipment on board the landing vessels that would arm thirty thousand expected recruits. The first step, he now insisted, was the "shock plan" of the landing, followed by "longer range" uprisings. Trinidad promised "more of a shock treatment which might have brought the Cuban people around to our side." The Zapata Plan diminished that chance, for the area was remote and sparsely populated, and the purpose of the night-time landing was to *reduce* popular attention while quietly securing a beachhead. Gray agreed. They "did not anticipate immediate uprisings—but uprisings on a slower basis." Cabell concurred even more hazily, asserting that "we meant joining-up of forces and not necessarily civilian uprisings." Lemnitzer attested that the Joint Chiefs had no information affirming the likelihood of an insurrection, and yet the CIA thought the chances good. "I remember Dick Bissell, evaluating this for the President, indicated there was sabotage, bombings and there were also various groups that were asking or begging for arms." Intelligence analysts, Lemnitzer charged, had underestimated Castro's hold on his people. In a further attempt to deflect blame, Cabell later explained that the CIA expected "only an *opportunity to foment uprisings* [emphasis in original] from the beachhead. No success at the beach; no opportunity to foment uprisings."[28]

The Joint Chiefs still did not realize that the possibility of a popular uprising never existed. The CIA failed to establish a communications network with Cuban dissidents, most of whom Castro jailed before the invasion in a strong-arm move that effectively eliminated the pool of supporters. The president's decision to move the landing site to Zapata doused the potential spark needed to ignite a rebellion. And, of course, the assassination plot had failed. The sixty Cuban Volunteer Air Force returnees agreed that the chances for popular support of the invasion were virtually nonexistent, remarking that 80 percent of Cubans would never join an uprising until they knew it was winning.[29] And yet, they might have noted, they could not win without an uprising. Castro's defensive tactics closed the door on insurrection. By rounding up thousands of suspected traitors beforehand, he cut the heart out of a potential rebellion and, combined with the air attacks and spirited popular and military support, saved his regime.

IV

Several advisers still defended the Zapata Plan, insisting that the swamps had not ruled out guerrilla tactics. When Robert Kennedy asked Burke how a few hundred men expected to hold a large beach against thousands of enemy forces, the admiral declared that "they would slip through and become guerrillas." Shoup later concurred, noting that the swamps were not supposed to be a problem. Dulles chimed in on this point, arguing that Castro "would not have been able to concentrate all his troops on one spot." Gray also defended the Zapata Plan, declaring that mid-April marked the beginning of the rainy season and the terrain "should not have been too bad." Bissell too emphasized that the Zapata landings were at night and in secluded areas, reducing the chances of confronting police or militia. "We thought that if this force were to land without a big show, the operation could then take on the guise of a rebel infiltration."[30]

Other advisers, however, now spoke out in recognizing that the swamps were not the brigade's ally. General Wheeler admitted that the Joint Chiefs had accepted the CIA's claim to Zapata's suitability for guerrilla operations without launching their own study. Bundy did not recall any lengthy discussions of the relative merits of Zapata and Trinidad regarding potential guerrilla operations. In an area blanketed by swamps, he found it impractical to believe that the landing force could transform into guerrillas capable of surviving until the local populace rallied behind Castro's overthrow.[31]

Some administration members nevertheless remained under the illusion that the guerrilla option provided a safety valve. If no popular uprising took place, Rusk asserted, the Cuban brigade could melt into the swamps, which were "stated to be the home of guerrillas." When a panel member asked whether anyone pointed out that Cuban guerrillas had not used the Zapata area in this century, Rusk blandly responded, "I don't recall." Lemnitzer later asserted that his staff and the CIA considered Zapata good guerrilla territory, despite the swamps. In fact, he added, Zapata was comparable to Vietnam in that American soldiers were "having the devil's own time chasing the guerrillas through the swamps." Castro would have similar problems in going after the Cuban soldiers turned guerrillas. But, the committee member insisted, the avenues of escape from the beachhead were much smaller than in Vietnam, meaning that the invasion forces would have had great difficulty reaching the towns and villages in Cuba. Furthermore, the landing parties had had no guerrilla training. Lemnitzer shook his head in rejecting that assertion. "I don't agree with that because they were trained as guerrillas for nine months." But only until early November 1960, the committee member correctly noted. And even then, a mere three hundred of the five hundred in the brigade at the time underwent such training.[32]

The Joint Chiefs' chair was not aware of this reality, insisting that he and his colleagues thought the landing force had no intention of remaining on the beach and could easily switch to guerrilla tactics. "Every bit of information that we were able to gather from the CIA was that the guerrilla aspects were always considered as a main element of the plan." "General," the questioner asserted, "if you look at that area and talk with anybody who has been there, you couldn't possibly become guerrillas in that damn place." But Lemnitzer was still not dissuaded. "I don't see why not." The committee member pushed the issue. "Where are you going to get the water and the food? It's not like Vietnam." It was possible, Lemnitzer stubbornly insisted, "that these fellows would establish themselves as guerrillas in the Escambray Mountains or in the swamps and they would receive air drops."[33]

Lemnitzer's argument made no sense. Like McNamara and others in the administration, he failed to recognize both the treacherous conditions of the swamps and how far the Escambray Mountains were from the beachhead. He did not take into account Castro's use of helicopters in finding and killing his enemy. Lemnitzer also continued to believe the guerrillas could live off the land and the populace. But this reasoning rested on wishful thinking rather than hard facts. Neither the swamps nor the mountains provided a feasible headquarters for conducting guerrilla operations once Zapata became the landing site.

Burke came to his colleague's faltering defense, emphasizing again the importance of popular assistance. "Guerrillas couldn't sustain themselves in any of these areas until they got support from the populace. Supplies would have to be carried in to them until they received support from the populace."

The questioner lamented, "The President had the same impression that you did—that if worst came to worst, this group could become guerrillas, but as we've gotten into it, it's become obvious that this possibility never really existed."

Lemnitzer finally saw the truth. "Then we were badly misinformed."[34]

When asked if the Joint Chiefs bore responsibility for the outcome, Shoup replied, "That's not my understanding." Lest there be doubt, he added, "I don't feel that I or the other Joint Chiefs had any responsibility for the success of this plan."[35]

Burke blamed the CIA. The Joint Chiefs' task was to "comment on the plan"; the CIA was responsible for "the actual conduct of the operation."

Dulles retorted, "But that was done by military personnel."

"But not under our command structure," Burke shot back.

One of the committee members appeared bewildered. "The President had the right to look to the Joint Chiefs for advice during the planning or execution phase if they thought they had something important to offer."

"That's true," Shoup admitted, but "limited by [our] knowledge of all aspects of the plan."

Committee member: "And in the absence of hearing from the Chiefs [the president] had a right to assume that everything was going satisfactorily."

"Yes," Shoup allowed, again emphasizing "to the limit of our knowledge. I want to tell you this right now. Had I as an individual heard that they were going to call off the air strikes I'd have asked that the commander in chief be informed. I'd have called him myself because it was absolutely essential to success. The D-2 affair was only a half effort."

The committee member clarified the point by asking, "Do you feel that you had absolute and complete knowledge about this operation?"

"Absolutely not," the general stated for the third time.

But the committee member declared it the Joint Chiefs' duty to know all details of a military operation. "Did you understand that the President and his advisors were looking to you for your military evaluation of this plan?" When Shoup stated that the only request made to the Joint Chiefs was to determine which of the three alternatives they thought best, the committee member further pressed the issue. "[D]id you understand that during that period of time that the President was looking to you, the JCS, for the military evaluation of the operation?"

Again, an evasive response: "I would have to presume that in accordance with his title as commander in chief he would be thinking about the military part."

A further probe: "But you understand that he wanted to get your advice and ideas also?"

And still another feint: "That was never stated."

The committee member had driven home his argument. "There was a general impression that the Joint Chiefs of Staff had approved this operation. I don't think there is any doubt but what they went ahead thinking that you and the other Joint Chiefs had approved the plan, but you now say that you didn't have full knowledge and information in order to evaluate the plan. That in itself is of some significance for the future."[36]

In one of the final meetings of the Taylor hearings, a committee member asked Burke whether the Joint Chiefs had fulfilled their responsibility to President Kennedy. "This is a most difficult question," the admiral replied. According to the restrictive guidelines set by the CIA, "yes, they did discharge their responsibility; but morally, they did not." Clearly uncomfortable with the question, Burke continued. "In looking back on it now, I regret . . . that I did not insist on things that I felt uneasy about. I felt uneasy about being briefed instead of having something in writing so that I could wrestle with it." In a remorseful remark that rang hollow in the stilled room, he asserted, "I should have insisted."[37]

The Joint Chiefs warrant severe criticism for not strongly stating their reservations about the Zapata Plan; in failing to do so, they erroneously suggested to the president a preference for it over Trinidad. Burke should have learned the problems in this type of approach early in the administration. At one point, the president expressed appreciation for his support of a proposition discussed in a meeting. When Burke appeared puzzled and said he did not support it, Kennedy said, "You certainly do; you were in this meeting, weren't you?" "Yes, sir, I was." "But you let that go by and you didn't say anything?" "Mr. President, I was not asked to express an opinion on that." "Well, when you sit there and let it go by without saying anything, I think that you approve it." Indeed, Taylor told the president that by the Joint Chiefs' going along with the Zapata Plan, they left the impression of having approved it. But they had expressed a preference for Trinidad from the beginning, a point never made clear to senior civilian advisers. The Joint Chiefs examined the Zapata Plan on a "piecemeal" basis and within a "limited context" and therefore made no proper analysis of the operation. Thus they "participated and acquiesced in the Zapata Plan but never gave it formal approval."[38]

Taylor's committee concluded that the Joint Chiefs should have made their views known. Because they remained quiet, they never became part of the Zapata Plan's developmental process and neither participated in decision making nor had a military commander on the scene to supervise the operation. Early in the planning stage, Lemnitzer did not speak out when the CIA broadened its domain to take control over the invasion's crucial military components. Shoup was more blunt—if only after six years had passed. For the CIA to develop an invasion force "without the know-how and all the experience and backing of a military force just astounded me." At first it wanted to send "a canoe full of people in there and then it just kept growing like Topsy." The Joint Chiefs knew "damn well" that the plan could not succeed without air cover, but they were asked only to support a plan already in place.[39] The Joint Chiefs quietly accepted a secondary role of evaluation and review rather than demanding leadership in their field of expertise—military operations. Although detecting several military weaknesses in the plan, they failed the president by not expressing their misgivings.

No one accepted blame for the failure at the Bay of Pigs. The Joint Chiefs insisted that the CIA misled them. The CIA countered that the military failed to execute a sound plan. The White House held both parties responsible, asserting that they did not provide the proper advice. So much easier to use military force.

V

The long train of testimonies revealed the prevailing sentiment: that the fatal flaw in the operation was the administration's excessive concern about plausible deniability. In an argument later echoed by military leaders in Vietnam, one adviser after another lamented that political concerns prevented them from winning. For a plan of this magnitude to succeed, Lemnitzer declared, it must be all-out military in nature and never restricted by political demands for secrecy. He did not believe it possible for armed forces to conduct covert actions. "I think it's a contradiction in terms." Shoup likewise saw no way to keep this type of operation covert. Indeed, Bundy declared, "I doubt very much whether large-scale operations of this sort can or should be 'covert.'" This "obsession with secrecy" undermined the chances for success by limiting the involvement of those advisory groups who should have helped in the planning. Rusk agreed with this assessment, declaring that plausible deniability never had a chance to work. The CIA inspector general's October study also cited the inherent conflict between political and military needs. "The Agency was driving forward without knowing precisely where it was going." The plan and CIA involvement had become public knowledge by November 1960, making plausible denial "a pathetic illusion."[40]

Surprisingly, Bissell years afterward joined his colleagues in expressing doubt about the feasibility of plausible deniability. The truth about America's involvement was so widely talked about in the weeks before the operation that it became impossible to deny the U.S. role. If the administration had realized that the public would hold it responsible despite all denials, it could have authorized volunteer American pilots and more sophisticated weaponry without deploying more than a few American volunteers on the ground. But everyone believed "the fig leaf was still in place" and opposed stronger measures. The "deep reluctance of Rusk to drop the fig leaf if the operation was going to be done at all, the President's own reluctance to drop the fig leaf, these, I think, in the final weeks did contribute to the ultimate failure of the operation."[41]

The Taylor Committee appeared to grasp the danger of a political-military conflict in planning such operations when it made a number of recommendations, two applying specifically to Cuba. First, overt paramilitary activities must come under Defense Department purview, leaving the CIA responsible for covert operations and the State Department to handle political matters. Future paramilitary operations must therefore focus not only on military and covert actions but also on the interplay of political, economic, ideological, and intelligence considerations. Second, and more striking, the United States must not abandon the effort at regime change in Cuba. It must pursue a strong program of "political, military, economic and propaganda action against Castro."[42]

One question emerges from these admissions to overemphasizing the importance of plausible deniability: If so many advisers recognized the pitfalls in allowing political considerations to interfere with a military mission, why did no one speak out? Perhaps they were like Cabell, who did not want to appear disloyal to the president. Or perchance they hesitated to take the risk, remaining silent and thus being part of the hoped-for victory by not objecting, while leaving themselves a way out of culpability in the event of failure by not having spoken for the plan. And yet those advisers who chose to comply with a flawed policy rather than express honest differences did the president and the nation a great disservice.

Most revealing, neither the Taylor inquiry nor the CIA internal study uncovered major opposition to continuing the effort to unseat Castro; indeed, most advisers felt confident that the Zapata Plan would have worked had the administration resorted to force. "I think we were closer to success than you realize," declared Dulles. One of the staunchest critics of the operation, CIA Inspector General Lyman Kirkpatrick, later pointed to U-2 photos showing that Castro had moved his tanks at Camp Libertad bumper to bumper and relocated all planes not destroyed by the D-2 strikes into two airfields. Further air strikes could have destroyed the tanks and the planes, including the jets "that made the difference." Berle later expressed displeasure with the president's decision against U.S. military force. Bissell insisted that CIA intelligence proved "essentially accurate," virtually assuring an "initial success." Ironically, given his failure two times to make this case to the president, he insisted that the operation would have worked had the D-Day strikes taken place. The president's "political compromises" aimed at achieving plausible deniability, which came at the expense of "maximum effectiveness." The United States "should not support an operation such as this involving the use of force without having also made the decision to use whatever force is needed to achieve success."[43]

Not surprisingly, less than a week after McNamara's request, the Joint Chiefs submitted a detailed plan for overthrowing Castro by military force. The timetable was clear: eighteen days from initial preparations to first assault. After reinforcing Guantanamo and evacuating dependents, D-Day would begin with a coordinated air and marine assault on the Havana area in western Cuba, accompanied by a blockade if required. Within a week American forces would control the capital city, and in less than a month and a half organized resistance would collapse, permitting a withdrawal no more than ninety days after the invasion. The army expected 16 percent ground casualties based on a thirty-day military operation that included four days of intense fighting, followed by cleanup operations.[44]

According to Wheeler, the plan guaranteed a "quick overthrow of the Castro government." The assault must be "swift, sharp, and overwhelming," aimed at achieving "world-wide surprise" and presenting a "fait accompli." In a recommendation mindful of Robert Kennedy's earlier suggestion, the Joint Chiefs called for the "creation of an incident" to justify U.S. military action.[45]

The CIA added immediacy to the plan by informing the National Security Council that since the previous September $100 million of military goods had arrived in Cuba, including tanks, helicopters, assault weapons, anti-aircraft artillery, military vehicles, and infantry weapons and ammunition. Soviet and Czech technicians were on the scene, helping to assemble the weapons and teaching the Cubans how to use them. Cuban pilots were continuing to train inside Czechoslovakia, in preparation for flying Soviet MIGs already in Cuba when operational.[46]

On April 29, less than two weeks after the Bay of Pigs invasion and while the Taylor inquiry continued, President Kennedy gave contingent approval to a new invasion plan, this one based on direct U.S. military involvement. About sixty thousand troops, not counting air and naval personnel, would spearhead an assault aimed at seizing the island in an upgraded timetable of eight days. Guerrillas would operate for some time afterward in the Escambray Mountains and Oriente Province. McNamara emphasized again, however, that this contingency plan did not make military action "probable." But if truthful, his was a naïve assertion. This rigid mindset in place, the Taylor team bolstered the plan by inferring that military measures were appropriate in promoting regime change and that, in its own broad words that bear repeating, the administration must pursue "political, military, economic and propaganda action against Castro."[47] If assassination was not specifically part of the plan, it fitted the liberal guidelines of the new interventionist approach, with its wider scope.

The sheer momentum of such a juggernaut, particularly with the Joint Chiefs' smarting over charges of inaction during the Bay of Pigs buildup, provided added impetus to the military solution. The president, severely chastened and humiliated by his first Cold War defeat, feverishly worked with his brother in pushing the program. And the CIA, also under fire, chafed at the opportunity to set matters right. The call for a military invasion under these strained circumstances threatened to take on a life of its own, leaving little room for opposition and no restrictions on methods.

Two Democratic senators sensed a coming military action and warned President Kennedy against taking that route. What the United States had to do, his friend Mike Mansfield insisted, was "to face up to the fact that we have made a mistake." An angry reaction would only "intensify the mistake" by solidifying Castro's hold on Cuba. If the United States pursued economic reforms through the Alliance for Progress, massive unrest would drop, diminishing the chances of Castroism spreading in Latin America. Claiborne Pell, like Mansfield, warned Rusk against the use of force, also emphasizing the Alliance for Progress and arguing that the Cuban people would ultimately overthrow Castro.[48] But their remarks did not push the White House off its military course.

In the president's defense, he did not want to move prematurely and resisted enormous pressure for quick and decisive action. A special task force on Cuba insisted that U.S. military intervention offered the only way to overthrow Castro. The National Security Council did not push for immediate military action but wanted it left as an option. The president rejected an air force recommendation for "rather heavy and perhaps indiscriminate bombardment." He also opposed a naval blockade though approving air surveillance every two or three days. Rusk argued that the United States must bring down Castro before all South America became Communist, and Schlesinger too climbed aboard this crest of emotion, warning of Cuba's becoming a "Soviet outpost in the hemisphere." The president did not follow Stahr's recommendation to form a Cuban Freedom Brigade, but he approved the induction of Cuban volunteers into the American army for Special Forces training. Pleased with the warm reaction to their proposal, the Joint Chiefs directed Admiral Dennison to submit a detailed plan for a surprise army, navy, and air force attack on Cuba.[49]

Regime change in Cuba thus became the central focus of the Kennedy administration, demonstrating that the Bay of Pigs experience had not deterred interventionism but made it the heart of future policies targeting Castro as well as other undesirable foreign leaders. Just as the Joint Chiefs considered their specialty—military action—the sole solution to the Cuban problem, so did the CIA argue that its area of expertise—paramilitary operations—offered the best remedy. The military response threatened to become the key to resolving growing problems in Vietnam, while the CIA's covert approach to the Bay of Pigs operation became a virtual reference point for similar actions in Africa, Latin America, the Middle East, and Southeast Asia. Shoup agreed that the failure had increased the emphasis on counterinsurgency preparation and noted the president's letter of commendation on the education of marines in guerrilla warfare. Not everyone approved. Colonel Hawkins lamented more than thirty years afterward that Washington's leaders "continue to harbor unrealistically overblown ideas about what can be accomplished by covert, deniable means."[50]

The outcome at the Bay of Pigs had not undermined the drive for regime change; rather, its proponents now insisted that a renewed effort would succeed if *Americans* played the central role in an operation that had graduated from a quiet night-time landing to an all-out military invasion.

Epilogue

[Richard Bissell] leaves an enduring legacy. —President
John F. Kennedy, March 1, 1962

To the Kennedy White House, the Bay of Pigs operation appeared more a setback than a defeat in that it only temporarily shelved the attempt to overthrow Castro. Military intervention remained the priority to policy-makers demanding a rapid solution; covert action appealed to those seeking to undermine his stature as critical to encouraging domestic unrest. Still others considered assassination essential to igniting a popular insurrection as prelude to invasion. And, finally, some wanted to combine all the above.

In the meantime the Cold War churned upward in intensity as Khrushchev seemed determined to test whether Kennedy's unwillingness to take strong action in Cuba had revealed a personal weakness worth exploiting. The two leaders met at a summit conference in Vienna in June 1961, where Khrushchev attempted to cow the young president with hard demands that the United States pull out of Berlin by the end of the year or face decisive Soviet action. The result was a dramatic American military buildup, threats and counterthreats of war, and in August the Soviet erection of a concrete and barbed-wire wall separating East and West Berlin that symbolized the great chasm between the two chief antagonists in the Cold

War. The Americans refused to withdraw from West Berlin, reminding old-timers of the late 1940s showdown when the city became a virtual hostage of the Soviets because it sat a hundred miles inside their sector of East Germany, connected to the outside world only by access roads and air corridors. As was the case less than two decades earlier, the crisis passed without incident but left a legacy of heightened international tension.

In the fall of 1961 the Kennedy administration, still stinging from the Bay of Pigs, resumed its attempt to eliminate Castro by creating a top-secret program code-named Operation Mongoose, run by Robert Kennedy, and by completing the preparation of Project ZR/RIFLE, or executive action, before linking it to a revived CIA-Mafia assassination effort. As a forerunner to Mongoose, White House adviser Richard Goodwin had convinced the president to appoint his brother to head a "command operation" for Cuba. At an early November White House meeting, President Kennedy approved the continued preparation of a plan for removing Castro—Mongoose—that ran parallel to the executive action program. Among those at the meeting were Robert Kennedy, Cabell, Bissell, and King, who were all familiar with the CIA-Mafia collaboration, and Bundy, who had initially encouraged Bissell to establish an executive action capability. The attorney general readily assumed the task of toppling Castro, promising "to stir things up" in Cuba. He could not guarantee Castro's fall, "but we have nothing to lose."[1]

President Kennedy appointed Air Force General Edward Lansdale as Mongoose's chief of operations to coordinate the overthrow. Lansdale was gruff and outspoken, not averse to playing outside the rules, and highly unpopular with the State Department, among other government agencies, for his brash behavior, but he had won the president's confidence in the early days of the administration with his James Bond image and his first-hand report on Vietnam that helped shape policy. He was well qualified for this new covert task, having specialized in psychological warfare in the Office of Strategic Services in World War II and as a CIA operative in the Philippines and Vietnam during the 1950s. Indeed, Lansdale had been the prototype for a character in two best-selling novels of the 1950s, *The Quiet American*, by British writer Graham Greene, and Eugene Burdick and William Lederer's *The Ugly American* (both made into movies). Lansdale and his colleagues would answer to the newly organized supervisory committee, an expansion of the NSC 5412 Special Group into the Special Group (Augmented), or SGA, that included Bundy and U. Alexis Johnson from the State Department, Roswell Gilpatrick from Defense, the new CIA director as of that month of November, Republican John McCone (Dulles had recently retired), and General Lemnitzer from the Special Group, now augmented by Taylor and the attorney general.[2]

Mongoose quickly ballooned into a large enterprise. In addition to the core group of advisers, William Harvey from the CIA, already well known as a problem solver, would continue his groundwork on the executive action program while taking on this new central role in the Mongoose operation. He would work under Lansdale's direction as head of more than two hundred members of Task Force W (the letter standing for William Walker, the American filibusterer executed in Honduras in 1860) at the same time he was putting the finishing touches on ZR/RIFLE. Another four hundred people from the CIA's home office and Miami station (code-named JMWAVE) were primarily responsible for implementing the overthrow.[3]

Controversy lingers over the methods considered in the Mongoose operation, but Lansdale asserted that the options were wide open and for that reason did *not* exclude assassination. Mongoose members carefully avoided the term but never ruled out the method. At the first meeting with the SGA in the Old Executive Office Building adjacent to the White House, Lansdale immediately sensed the urgency to succeed by any means thought necessary. He knew he was acting for the president and was to report at least once a week to his brother. Lansdale was no stranger to decisive covert action and later suggested the naïveté of his superiors by almost glibly remarking that the Bay of Pigs failure had had a "traumatic" effect on the White House, making assassination "a taboo subject" that its policymakers dreamed about at night but refused to think about during the day. McNamara later admitted that the White House was "hysterical" about Castro after the Bay of Pigs, but said, "I don't believe we contemplated assassination."[4]

Yet McNamara's words do not ring true, since the president still smarted from the Bay of Pigs humiliation and clearly pondered Castro's assassination. Kennedy had earlier discussed the subject with his friend Senator George Smathers, who sharply disapproved of such action; he now raised it again with journalist Tad Szulc of the *New York Times*, who had just returned from Cuba after talking with Castro about the invasion. In the Oval Office on November 9, with Goodwin there, the president casually inquired about the conversation in Havana but then suddenly leaned forward in his rocking chair and asked, "What would you think if I ordered Castro to be assassinated?" A horrible idea, Szulc replied without hesitation. An assassination would not guarantee a change in the Cuban government, and the United States must not take part in murder. "I agree with you completely," the president responded, much as he had to Smathers. "My brother and I believe," he said, that "for moral reasons" the United States could not approve assassination.[5]

But the president's disclaimer fails to stand up, given his implicit approval of both executive action and (with his brother) the CIA-Mafia plan. To hide his interest in assassination, Kennedy smiled and admitted to "testing" Szulc, saying, "I'm glad you feel the same way." Szulc thought the president under "terrific pressure from advisers (think he said intelligence people, but not positive) to okay a Castro murder" and believed him when he asserted that it was "the kind of thing I'm never going to do." Days afterward, according to Goodwin, the president remarked, "We can't get into that kind of thing, or we would all be targets." Goodwin was not aware of either assassination plan and likewise thought the president sincere.[6]

Despite President Kennedy's professed opposition to assassination, he did nothing to discourage its proponents. He surely knew what his brother had learned: that the CIA-Mafia effort remained intact but in a dormant state, awaiting some signal to begin anew. That in mind, it is likely he tried to cover himself by renouncing the subject to Szulc. In a further attempt to publicly distance himself from an assassination policy, President Kennedy proclaimed at the University of Washington, "We cannot, as a free nation, compete with our adversaries in tactics of terror, assassination, false promises, counterfeit mobs and crises."[7]

The Mongoose committee soon exasperated the president by its inability to ensure a fast and favorable result. In a late November meeting in the Oval Office, he told Lansdale and McCone that he wanted a specific plan within two weeks. Robert Kennedy agreed, emphasizing the need for "immediate dynamic action." McCone cautioned against anything "reckless," expressing concern that the administration seemed in "shock" after the Bay of Pigs. But President Kennedy refused to wait. He again brought up the subject, once more blasting Bissell and the CIA for failing to see that the landing area was not suitable for guerrilla operations and the Joint Chiefs for spending less than a half hour examining the operation before recommending White House approval. The next day, Kennedy approved the Mongoose operation, clearly expecting a quick remedy.[8]

Thus under intense pressure from the White House, the Mongoose team searched for a solution to the Castro problem. In late January 1962 the president insisted that "the final chapter on Cuba has not been written" and that "it's got to be done and will be done." The next day several committee members met in the office of the attorney general, who emphasized that Cuba was the administration's "top priority" and that "all else is secondary" with "no time, money, effort or manpower... to be spared." Lest there be doubt, he emphasized, "Nothing [was] to stand in [the] way of getting this done... no excuses."[9]

Robert Kennedy thus led an operation that increasingly narrowed its choices to assassination. According to Marshall Carter, the CIA's new deputy director, the attorney general acted as "a sort of rat terrier type who was picking all the time on everybody,... a typical movie DA who never lets up on the witness." He was the president's "alter ego," his "hatchet man." Confirmation of his central role came from the CIA's station chief in Miami, Ted Shackley, who declared that in the spring of 1962 he received directives from Harvey to do whatever was necessary to bring about a regime change in Cuba. The CIA had transferred Shackley from Berlin shortly after the Bay of Pigs to wage what Bissell called a "secret war" against Castro. The attorney general, Shackley soon concluded, personified an "attack dog" leading the White House effort. The "driving force" was a "personal vendetta" by the president and his brother, who had been humiliated by the invasion and wanted Castro out, "whether by palace revolt, military coup, popular uprising, or assassination."[10]

Richard Helms, now director of the CIA's Office of Special Operations (covert action), argued that the administration's urgency in getting rid of Castro after the Bay of Pigs debacle led advisers to believe that assassination had implicit approval. "I remember vividly [that the pressure to overthrow Castro] was very intense" and that "there were no limitations put on the means." The attorney general set the tone, clarifying "what I understood was desired." The "atmosphere of the day," the very "temper of the times," signaled a desire to get rid of Castro, and "if he had been gotten rid of by this means [assassination] that this would have been acceptable to certain individuals." There was a "flat-out effort ordered by the White House, the President, Bobby Kennedy who was after all his man, his right hand in these matters, to unseat the Castro government, to do everything possible to get rid of it by whatever device could be found." Helms's orders, he said, were to dispose of Castro, and "nobody... ever said to me, any personal attack on that man is ruled out." And nothing could appear on paper. "I can't imagine anybody wanting something in writing saying I have just charged Mr. Jones to go out and shoot Mr. Smith." Helms emphasized that "it was the policy at the time to get rid of Castro, and if killing him was one of the things that was to be done in this connection, that was within what was expected."[11]

Chances grew for assassination in early 1962, when Harvey received instructions to take over the CIA-Mafia project and now, with executive action and Task Force W, held three leadership positions that focused on eliminating Castro. Ironically, just as the president publicly renounced assassination the previous November, the executive action program secretly neared completion and Bissell asked Harvey to resurrect the Mafia operation and consider the "application of the ZR/RIFLE program to Cuba." Harvey regarded ZR/RIFLE and the Mafia project as one and the same. Bissell concurred, asserting that "the contact with the syndicate which had Castro as its target...folded into the ZR/RIFLE project.... And they became one."[12]

Harvey asserted that his assignment came from the top. Assassination fell "perfectly within the province of an intelligence service" and "on proper orders from the proper highest authority." Approval "must come from the Chief Executive" or "the President," Harvey insisted, although he never knew the specifics of the authority granted. "I was completely convinced during this entire period, that this operation had the full authority of every pertinent echelon of CIA and had full authority of the White House, either from the President or from someone authorized and known to be authorized to speak for the President." This meant "[a]pproval in principle" from the CIA director and "presumably from the White House." Did he believe President Kennedy knew? "Yes, quite frankly I did."[13]

In April 1962, Harvey contacted Roselli, and they revived the poison scheme by implementing Varona's proposal made during the Venetian Causeway talks of the fall of 1960. Varona had remained actively involved in the overthrow, recently visiting the State Department on two occasions— in late February and late March 1962, the second meeting with Bundy present—to call for another invasion attempt supported by American military force. Just three weeks later, in April, Roselli convinced O'Connell to approve giving Varona CIA poison pills in exchange for $50,000 in cash and $10,000 worth of communications apparatus for his speedboats. Varona agreed to forward the pills to a chef in a restaurant often patronized by Castro—a coffee shop in the Hotel Havana Libre—who could slip the poison into his food. But this plan fizzled like the first one, this time when, according to Castro years afterward, the would-be assassin was unable to put the poison into a chocolate milkshake after finding the small glass vial, containing the pills frozen to the ice in the freezer.[14]

The Kennedy administration had imposed an economic embargo on Cuba in February 1962 in an effort to stir up resistance to the regime, but its real hopes lay in the use of U.S. troops. Admiral Dennison sent the Joint Chiefs a carefully constructed invasion plan that attempted to correct the deficiencies of the Bay of Pigs operation by mandating air assaults intended to eliminate the Cuban air force and severely damage Castro's ground forces as the prelude to a second invasion attempt. Roger Hilsman, a hard-nosed White House adviser who had recently advocated an escalated military involvement in Vietnam, warned "that unless a popular uprising in Cuba is promptly supported by overt U.S. military action, it would probably lead to another Hungary." If the White House did not "bite the bullet,...I am afraid we may be heading for a fiasco that could be worse for us than the ill-fated operation of last year." Lansdale had compiled a kaleidoscopic list of thirty-two "tasks" for Mongoose, but he focused on the Joint Chiefs' call for military intervention, asking them and the State Department to devise "pretexts" for doing so. He wanted a proposal by March 13, and they promptly sent McNamara a cascade of recommendations code-named Northwoods and aimed at provoking war with Cuba.[15]

In a White House meeting three days later, President Kennedy gave "tacit authorization" to Mongoose's objective of overthrowing the Castro regime but again put no limitations on means and thereby left the way open for any measure deemed viable. Robert Kennedy had repeatedly called for war by pretext, perhaps leading Lansdale to seek "pretexts" for American military intervention. And at an April 11 meeting SGA members urged preparation for "necessary military action" and specifically referred to one suggestion in the Northwoods scheme in asking McCone to look into the prospect of "manufacturing MIG type planes" to fabricate a justification. The Joint Chiefs' proposal "on pretext or provocative actions," noted the SGA, was "a very thoughtful and useful document." Lemnitzer complained that the "civilian hierarchy was crippled not only by inexperience, but also by arrogance arising from failure to recognize its own limitations. The problem," he asserted, "was simply that the civilians would not accept military judgments." Then came April 17, 1961. "The Bay of Pigs fiasco broke the dike," according to one contemporary report.[16]

In this pressurized atmosphere, Goodwin remembered that in a large August 1962 meeting of the SGA and other advisers, McNamara raised the subject of assassination "out of the blue in the middle of a discussion of other subjects" dealing with Cuba. "The only way to get rid of Castro," the defense secretary asserted, was "to kill him." That was "the only real solution." At long last, Harvey must have thought with satisfaction, the ultimate solution had emerged from the shadows. "Oh, you mean Executive Action," he declared in wedding McNamara's proposal with the assassination program that Bissell had asked Harvey to develop at White House bidding. Yes, responded McNamara in implicitly acknowledging an awareness of that capability. "I mean it, Dick," he said, turning to Goodwin, who had never heard the term *executive action* before but instantly realized it meant assassination. "It's the only way. I really mean it."[17]

Fire lay behind the smoke and excitement generated at the SGA meeting, for even though McCone upbraided McNamara for his indiscretion both before his colleagues and in a personal confrontation afterward, he was throughout this sensitive period quietly supporting the recruitment of a Cuban defector as a potential assassin—Rolando Cubela Secades (code-named AMLASH by the CIA). A medical doctor and at one time a major and hence among the highest-ranking officers in Castro's army, Cubela had a history of unstable behavior that did not quash the CIA's interest in his disenchantment with the Communist leanings of the new regime and his open talk about eliminating his onetime idolized leader. Most important, he had a record as an assassin and, as a trusted associate of Fidel, his brother Raúl, and Che Guevara, was close enough to Castro to heighten the chances of success. Jumping at the opportunity, McCone had approved instructions to the CIA station in Miami (where Shackley considered assassination one of his weapons) two months *before* the August SGA meeting to explore Cubela's possibilities.[18]

II

But every aspect of the movement toward Castro's assassination came to an abrupt halt in mid-October, when the Kennedy administration discovered that the Soviets were constructing missile sites in Cuba with the intention of attaching nuclear warheads capable of striking Washington, D.C. The result was a threatened nuclear confrontation that shifted the White House concern from Castro. Various theories arose then and afterward about why Khrushchev had embarked on this reckless course. Pressure the United

States out of Berlin? Bargain for the U.S. withdrawal of missiles from Turkey and Italy? Achieve nuclear parity by intimidating the United States? Spread socialist doctrine throughout the Caribbean? Or protect Cuba from a U.S. invasion and gain stature in Latin America and the world?

All these factors played into the premier's design, which rested on his assumption of presidential weakness demonstrated at the Bay of Pigs. But given the invasion attempt, Castro's appeal to Moscow for help, and his fear of imminent U.S. military action, it appears more convincing to believe Khrushchev's assertion that his central purpose was to establish a strategic balance with the United States while protecting an ally. The president, or so Khrushchev believed, would once again do nothing.[19]

Khrushchev's suspicions of U.S. military action in Cuba were justified, for, as shown, Admiral Dennison had recently submitted a lengthy invasion plan to the Joint Chiefs of Staff. The Soviet premier was aware of its general features, thanks to his intelligence corps. Just hours after the Joint Chiefs received the proposal, the KGB notified the Kremlin that "military specialists of the USA had revised an operational plan against Cuba, which, according to this information, is supported by President Kennedy."[20]

The story of how the two superpowers narrowly averted a nuclear confrontation is familiar to most readers, but not so well known is the visceral White House anger with Castro. In exchange for the Soviets' removing the missiles, the United States promised not to invade Cuba. But why were the missiles there in the first place? Castro had *welcomed* them. The Kennedy administration, asserted Helms years afterward, "certainly would like to have punished Castro for the Cuban missile crisis." It was so livid over his actions that in the heat of the crisis the attorney general spent valuable time informing the SGA of the president's demand to eliminate his arch-enemy. We need "massive activity," Robert Kennedy declared while repeating his brother's displeasure with the Mongoose program. Indeed, the White House shut down the Mongoose operation after the missile crisis had passed later that month, but *not* as part of an often alleged general effort to defuse the international atmosphere. "Nothing was moving forward," the attorney general hotly complained to Lansdale. An embittered discussion followed, resulting in the SGA's call for "new and more dynamic approaches" from Lansdale. "We'll have to do something drastic about Cuba," the president told Bundy and McCone in the immediate aftermath of the Soviet war scare.[21]

The following December (1962) the Kennedy administration adopted a highly unusual approach to Cuba: a two-headed policy of assassination and accommodation, both aimed at eliminating Castro and intimately linked with another objective—ridding the island of Soviet troops still there after the missile crisis. The assassination option had resumed almost immediately after the missile settlement, whereas the interest in a rapprochement grew soon after a late December 1962 agreement to release the Bay of Pigs captives for a huge ransom in food and drugs. Bundy recommended that the president establish a quiet communication with Castro, and the result was a "compromise" between "hard" and "soft" lines. The White House sought to reduce Castro's power, either by attracting Cuba from Sino-Soviet influence or by replacing him with someone sympathetic with this purpose. It demanded that all Soviet troops leave Cuba, even permitting Castro to remain in power if that was the only way to get them out. The threat was more imagined than real, for no Soviet combat forces were in Cuba, although nearly seven thousand military advisers and technicians were possibly still on the island. But U.S. prestige rested heavily on a total withdrawal, leading the White House to favor Castro's removal as the major means of ending the Soviet presence.[22]

The idea of assassination seemed impossible for the Kennedys to let go, undermining the oft-argued claim that the president seriously sought an accommodation with Castro. The administration consistently maintained its staunch anti-Castro policy in the aftermath of the Bay of Pigs, working toward a military invasion with American forces while intending to precede it with assassination. Sam Halpern in the CIA insisted that the story that "the Kennedys wanted to be friends with Castro . . . is sheer, utter nonsense." An unusual policy indeed: at one and the same time, the White House attempting to befriend him while trying to kill him.[23]

For nearly a year, however, the administration's determination to eliminate Castro floundered until, in the fall of 1963, the CIA out of desperation reestablished contact with Cubela—shortly after the White House had approved another military coup, this one in South Vietnam that initially stalled and left Diem in power. President Kennedy had directed State and Defense Department advisers to plan another invasion by Cuban exiles, but this time followed by direct U.S. military involvement. The Cubela story that had begun more than a year and a half earlier melded into this new project.[24]

To replace Task Force W from the now defunct Mongoose program, the administration had set up in the spring of 1962 the Special Affairs Staff (SAS), headed by Harvard Law School graduate Desmond FitzGerald, a close friend of the Kennedys in the CIA's Plans Division who supported a military coup jump-started by Castro's assassination. FitzGerald at first considered several dubious schemes for killing Castro, including giving him a botulism-infected scuba-diving suit and placing a colorful seashell rigged with explosives in the waters where he regularly went skin diving. Indeed, in an incredible example of poor timing, the CIA chose the most sensitive moments of the December 1962 prisoner negotiations to send Castro a diving suit infected with a deadly poison. Fortunately the American lawyer entrusted with the mission, not knowing that he was carrying what he later denounced as a "nice big germ bag," switched it with another one he purchased. This effort had failed, but FitzGerald was not overly concerned: He thought a coup had more promise because the army contained "the greatest concentration of possibly disillusioned personnel." By early September 1963 Secretary of the Army Cyrus Vance forwarded FitzGerald a study of the previous June setting out a "spectrum of actions" designed "to encourage dissident elements in the military and other power centers of the Regime to bring about the eventual liquidation of the Castro-communist entourage and the elimination of the Soviet presence in Cuba." FitzGerald counted on Cubela to stage the coup.[25]

Thus the revived AMLASH project rested on killing Castro as the chief means for fomenting a coup. Two CIA officials—newly assigned case officer Nestor Sanchez and a colleague—immediately met on September 5 with Cubela in Porto Allegro, Brazil. Sanchez had worked with Harvey on Task Force W before accepting this new assignment and was well aware of his reputation for taking any action deemed necessary. FitzGerald would surely not change the approach. "I did not hear of any plans to assassinate Castro," Sanchez asserted in carefully couched words that failed to conceal the administration's willingness to resort to assassination. It was a military coup against a nation with which the United States was not at war, with Sanchez insisting that the discussion was "not specifically in assassination terms." Thus did still another U.S. official draw an arbitrary distinction between killing Castro in the course of a coup and an outright assassination. As FitzGerald's new special assistant on SAS and his case officer on the AMLASH project, Sanchez declared that his responsibility was "to organize a military coup inside Cuba against Fidel Castro."[26]

If Castro was not aware of Cubela's private dealings with the CIA, he knew of the agency's attempts to kill him, whether directly or during a coup. Just two days after Sanchez met with Cubela in Brazil, Castro bitterly denounced recent U.S.-prompted raids on Cuban territory and publicly warned the Kennedy administration against trying to bring down his government. Was the timing coincidental? Or was Cubela a double agent who had alerted Castro to the plot? Evidence remains inconclusive, but at a party probably staged in the *Brazilian* embassy in Havana, Castro bitterly proclaimed in an impromptu, three-hour interview with AP journalist Daniel Harker that "we are prepared to fight them and answer in kind." American leaders "should think that if they are aiding terrorist plans to eliminate Cuban leaders, they themselves will not be safe." In a warning that establishes Castro's knowledge of the plots, he declared: "Let Kennedy and his brother Robert take care of themselves since they too can be the victims of an attempt which will cause their death."[27]

Not by coincidence did the CIA's private talks with Cubela intensify by late September, just as Washington's policymakers moved toward a military coup that rested on killing Castro either in the assault or by assassination. The Joint Chiefs of Staff had expressed concern with the effectiveness of recent CIA raids on Cuba, and when FitzGerald requested military assistance, they first wanted to know the extent of the covert operations. On September 25 FitzGerald secretly briefed them on further details of the program. Most encouraging, he declared in an allusion to Cubela not shared with the generals that CIA officers had been "getting closer to military personnel who might break with Castro." At least ten high-ranking military figures were "talking with CIA but as yet are not talking to each other." FitzGerald saw a "parallel in history"—"the plot to kill Hitler; and this plot is being studied in detail to develop an approach." Vance considered a coup the "most promising" line of attack, and FitzGerald thought the time right, arguing that Castro's position had "seriously weakened."[28]

Against the advice of his CIA colleagues, FitzGerald took an extraordinary step that starkly personified the administration's obsession with Castro: He decided to *join* Sanchez in a Paris meeting with Cubela on October 29 to assure him that the "U.S. Government was serious about this operation." Cubela was probably a "dangle" (double agent), hotly warned Harold Swenson, the chief of counterintelligence in SAS. From his JMWAVE post in Miami, Shackley cautioned that if Cubela launched a coup, "it's quite likely they'll track you down. You have a high profile." FitzGerald was not concerned about either risk in light of the potential payoff. Cubela wanted confirmation of White House support from someone in high authority—preferably a meeting with the president. That was out of the question, of course, but FitzGerald settled on the next best approach. He would introduce himself to Cubela as the "personal representative of Robert F. Kennedy who traveled to Paris" to promise "full U.S. support with a change of the present government in Cuba." It remains debatable whether the attorney general knew of this unusual arrangement, but it is inconceivable that FitzGerald would have undertaken this approach without first clearing it with him. Whatever the truth, the ploy worked. Posing as James Clark, FitzGerald delivered a personal assurance of help that satisfied Cubela, who asked for rifles, scopes, and explosives "to assassinate Castro from a distance." Three weeks later, FitzGerald authorized Sanchez to provide the weapons along with a poison pen that Cubela rejected with the remark that surely the CIA could "come up with something more sophisticated than that."[29]

In November two assassinations occurred—though neither in Cuba— that stunned the world and suggested a future resting on violence. The generals in the South Vietnamese army launched their long-expected coup on November 1, assassinating President Ngo Dinh Diem and his brother in Saigon while a CIA agent sat at coup headquarters after assuring U.S. support in the event of Diem's overthrow. Then, just three weeks later, on the evening of November 22, as Sanchez and Cubela came out of their second meeting in Paris, they learned of President Kennedy's death that day in Dallas.[30]

"Why do such things happen to good people?" asked Cubela, visibly shaken by the news. He returned to Cuba to organize the coup, although Sanchez claimed that within hours a cable arrived from FitzGerald in Washington, putting the entire Cuban operation on hold until the new administration clarified its policy. For whatever reason, the AMLASH files contain no such cable; but in any case it was too late to stop Cubela. In what Sanchez considered the most important result of the Paris meeting, Cubela continued laying the groundwork for a coup. The CIA's 1967 internal report trenchantly noted the irony "that at the very moment President Kennedy was shot a CIA officer was meeting with a Cuban agent in Paris and giving him an assassination device for use against Castro."[31]

III

The new president was Lyndon B. Johnson, who, years after leaving the White House, told *Atlantic* magazine that in November 1963 he was shocked to learn that "we had been operating a damned Murder, Inc., in the

Caribbean." But if his dismay at the outset was real, it soon changed when he became privy to the attempts to assassinate Castro during the Kennedy years. Johnson had invited Kennedy's advisers to stay, confirming his public promise to continue previous policies and thereby suggesting a private knowledge of the Cuban project that Helms confirmed. When asked if Johnson knew of the "continuing efforts to assassinate Castro," Helms asserted that "the Special Group would have continued to consider these matters, and . . . that whoever was chairing the Special Group would have in turn reported to the President, which was the usual practice."[32]

Shortly after becoming president, Johnson received a plan prepared by the State and Defense departments and the CIA that outlined the U.S. response to a Cuban military coup. Once the coup had occurred, a "special team" would go to Cuba to determine whether the takeover had neutralized top leaders as the prelude to U.S. military intervention. Vance concurred in the plan, and President Johnson expressed great interest in dispatching American troops immediately after a popular uprising—presumably set off by Castro's death. The Joint Chiefs justified the U.S. military involvement as pivotal to the administration's continued effort to overthrow Castro by a "phased and controlled series of political, economic, psychological and military actions."[33]

President Johnson supported the plan. In an early April 1964 meeting in the Oval Office, FitzGerald explained that since an internal uprising was unlikely without a military coup, the CIA had been "trying to penetrate the Cuban regime's power structure." The agency had had little success but, in an unspoken allusion to Cubela, had made "an important penetration in the Cuban army." Up to this moment, Johnson had remained undecided about whether U.S. policy should focus on eliminating the Castro regime or pursuing "some less drastic objective." He had wanted an ongoing program of sabotage raids to continue until there was an "unexpected opportunity" for "US intervention and elimination of the overall Communist threat in Cuba." The new plan seemed to offer that opportunity—so much so that he informed his advisers that in two months he would suspend the raids.[34]

McCone, however, argued that the sabotage efforts had not had a chance to work and warned that putting an end to that program would effectively terminate the June 1963 directive to overthrow the regime. He quoted from the directive in reminding his colleagues of their charge "to encourage dissident elements in the military and other power centers of the regime to bring about the eventual liquidation of the Castro Communist entourage and the elimination of the Soviet presence from Cuba." All parts of the program were interdependent and must be, in the words of the directive, "executed in tandem." The "real issue," McCone repeated in a memo the following day, was whether to continue the push for Castro's "liquidation" or to "abandon" that policy "and thus rely on future events of an undisclosed nature which might accomplish this objective." Shackley confirmed McCone's assessment, insisting that suspending the sabotage program ensured no popular insurrection, no pretext for invading Cuba, no military coup, and no assassination.[35]

Clearly assassination weighed heavily on McCone's mind as his officers secretly continued working with Cubela. *Twice* the CIA director had referred to "liquidation" in advocating Castro's overthrow. Surely he had used the term as a euphemism for either assassinating Castro or killing him in the course of a military coup. But the AMLASH program continued to flounder. Over the next few months, and at FitzGerald's request, JMWAVE operatives dropped weapons and supplies for Cubela, but with little success. Finally, in November 1964 the CIA informed Cubela of its intention to call off the operation. Although disappointed, Cubela indicated that he would continue to work with fellow dissident Manuel Artime in staging a coup. In a series of events closely monitored by McCone, Sanchez met again with Cubela in Paris the following month, where Cubela reiterated his intention to initiate a coup. "The only cure for rabies," he remarked, "is get rid of the dog." By the time Sanchez and Cubela met for the last time (that same December in Madrid), the Artime-Cubela connection had become what a CIA report termed "the Agency back-up."[36]

With so much determination behind it, why didn't the Cubela-Artime plot materialize? Few caches reached their destination, and the CIA was never able to provide a silencer for a high-powered telescopic rifle. But most of all, the dissidents were unable to penetrate Castro's defense perimeter. In the meantime McCone short-circuited Cubela by cutting off support to Artime, because he refused to cooperate and had become a "persistent menace." Bundy agreed, calling Artime "a firecracker in our midst." The State Department recommended that the 303 Committee (the former SGA) notify Artime of the termination. Ambassador-at-Large Llewellyn Thompson emphasized that "there was no U.S. commitment to Cubela via Artime," and FitzGerald agreed, remarking that "Cubela was living on borrowed time."[37]

The CIA terminated the Cubela operation in late June 1965, because it considered "the entire AMLASH group insecure" and a threat to CIA activities in Cuba and agency operatives in Western Europe. The number of Cubans knowledgeable of the plan and the CIA's involvement in it had grown dangerously large, and their circle "ever-widening," forcing the agency "to eliminate contacts ASAP." The CIA had acted with good reason. Less than a year later, Cuban authorities arrested Cubela for plotting to kill Castro, and a public trial resulted during which Cubela confessed to treason and tearfully demanded execution at the wall. But, in a development that raises doubt about whether he was a double agent, he never revealed the help he received from the United States. The court sentenced him to death; surprisingly, Castro commuted the sentence to twenty-five years in jail. Cubela served only ten years, working as a cardiologist in Havana until his release.[38]

Cubela's demise appropriately corresponded with the collapse of America's Cuban policy, for by the autumn of 1965 the growing conflict in Vietnam and continued problems in Laos had combined with a crisis in the Dominican Republic to force the Johnson administration to call off all attempts to overthrow Castro. Helms argued that the mounting difficulties in Vietnam and Laos necessitated the change, and the *New York Times* later charged that the Dominican revolution had led to the June intervention by U.S. marines and prevented Cuban exiles in Spain from training in the Dominican Republic for the planned invasion. Journalist Tad Szulc agreed with the latter assessment, declaring in a 1974 article in *Esquire* magazine that the U.S. involvement in the Dominican Republic had forced the cancellation of a second invasion of Cuba by 750 armed exiles following Castro's assassination. But these explanations provided at best a transparent subterfuge for the hard reality that the White House policy toward Cuba already lay in shambles. "The bearded devil had won the war," declared Shackley.[39]

The AMLASH project, however, did not go away; it spawned the charge that Castro had learned of the plot to kill him and acted first by having Kennedy assassinated. A dubious argument, perhaps—particularly in light of a certain American military response if verified. Yet lingering questions have kept this suspicion alive. No one informed the Warren Commission of the CIA's attempts to kill Castro, including Dulles, who sat on the panel— perhaps because he thought their exposure would cause a war with Cuba or lead to discoveries of other agency operations. Helms likewise revealed nothing to the commission because, he told the Church Committee in 1975, accusing Castro of killing the president could have started a war. Helms insisted that his instructions had been to answer questions and provide requested material and *not* to "initiate any particular thing." "In other words," clarified a Church Committee member, "if you weren't asked for it, you didn't give it." "That's right, sir." Besides, Helms asserted, the Warren Commission should have been aware of Washington's attempts to topple the Havana regime. "My recollection at the time was that it was public knowledge that the United States was trying to get rid of Castro." As for Castro, Helms added, Soviet intelligence had infiltrated the Cuban exile community in Florida, and he had to have known that Cuban exiles wanted to kill him and had U.S. government support. Despite these arguable defenses, some observers have insisted that withholding information was morally wrong and an obstruction of justice.[40]

Several critics have linked the AMLASH operation to the president's death by citing Castro's September 1963 warning to American leaders that their lives were in danger for trying to kill him. But both the CIA and the FBI discerned no threat to President Kennedy, and neither agency launched an investigation. One FBI official, however, later attested that had he known of the CIA's plots or of Castro's warning, he would have immediately instructed his field offices to be "particularly aware of anything that might indicate an assassination attempt" on the president. And the CIA officer (not identified) who coordinated the agency's investigation of the president's death attested that had he been aware of the assassination plots, and most specifically of AMLASH, "I certainly think that that would have become an absolutely vital factor in analyzing the events surrounding the Kennedy assassination." Moreover, Swenson from counterintelligence thought it "logical" that those involved in the assassination efforts should have considered the possibility of "a connection" and should have "explored it on their own." The Senate committee of 1976 investigating the Dallas events failed to understand why there was no inquiry, especially since the president's alleged assassin, Lee Harvey Oswald, had had contacts with both pro-Castro and anti-Castro groups in Cuba.[41]

These discussions raised suspicions within the Church Committee about Castro's involvement in Kennedy's death, but when staff member Jim Johnston attempted to tie the two matters together, he could not refute Sanchez's counterargument. If Castro were behind Kennedy's assassination, Sanchez declared, he surely would not have publicly announced his intention. Then why the extraordinary secrecy about CIA documents relating to AMLASH? Because of their "sensitivity," Sanchez replied. Cubela had returned to Cuba to initiate a coup, and FitzGerald sought "to protect his security." Sanchez saw no connection between the AMLASH project and Kennedy's death and had never heard any discussion in the CIA of the possibility.[42]

Although present findings do not tie the Cubela affair to the events in Dallas, it is difficult to believe that the CIA so readily dismissed any possible relationship. An investigation might have uncovered nothing, but at the least the agency could have maintained credibility by following every lead. Robert Kennedy was virtually incapacitated by his brother's slaying, a despondency doubtless magnified by profound guilt over his pursuing an anti-Castro policy that might have brought about this tragedy.[43] One has the feeling that those in the CIA aware of the Cubela operation (or any of the other assassination attempts) were likewise distraught that their actions might have contributed to the president's death and therefore tried to dismiss the matter as quickly and quietly as possible.

Indeed, President Johnson had suspected from the beginning of his administration that Castro had retaliated against Kennedy; finally, as the charge picked up momentum, he ordered an internal CIA investigation. In early 1967, on the same day he received FBI reports of this accusation and in response to Washington columnist Drew Pearson's article raising the same questions, the president instructed Helms as CIA director to look into the matter. Pearson had touched a national nerve by asserting that "President Johnson is sitting on a political H-Bomb" and asking whether Robert Kennedy had "approved an assassination plot which then possibly backfired against his late brother." The story had further intrinsic interest because it had come from Edmund Morgan, a Washington attorney who had related the account given him by his client, none other than CIA cut-out Robert Maheu. Helms directed Inspector General J. S. Earman to conduct an in-house investigation of the agency that, when submitted two months later, proved so explosive that Helms ordered the destruction of all copies and related papers. The original he put into safekeeping, where it remained classified until 1994 and even then appeared annoyingly encumbered with blacked-out passages. The inspector general's report confirmed the CIA's plots with the Mafia to assassinate Castro and the agency's creation of an executive action program. But it said nothing about any connection between the attempt to kill Castro and the death of Kennedy. Johnson nonetheless tied them together. To domestic affairs adviser Joseph Califano, he declared that "Kennedy tried to kill Castro, but Castro got Kennedy first."[44]

April 17, 1961, marked the beginning of a new and more dangerous era in American foreign relations. Traditional reliance on negotiations had become secondary to a forceful interventionist foreign policy devised by the CIA with White House approval that proved enormously costly, both before and after the Bay of Pigs. Plausible deniability had failed to meet its greatest challenge—revising history—and yet its basic tenet of hiding the truth by euphemistic language has become standard parlance in Washington's governing circles. Presidents Eisenhower, Kennedy, and Johnson bequeathed a long and embittered relationship between the United States and Cuba that continues to block normalized relations.

Cold War fears made America's Cuban policy into a major issue between the United States and the Soviet Union. The Eisenhower administration developed the program to eliminate Castro, the Kennedy administration implemented the plan without putting restrictions on means, and the Johnson administration continued the effort into the summer of 1965. All three executives were hard-line Cold Warriors, the first breaking relations with Cuba, the second attempting to kill Castro as an integral part of overthrowing the regime, and the third continuing his predecessor's post–Bay of Pigs program by supporting a second invasion of Cuba, preceded by an assassination and climaxed by U.S. military intervention.[45] But more pressing matters in Vietnam, Laos, and the Dominican Republic shifted Johnson's attention from Cuba and finally laid an already moribund six-year-long project to rest.

In retrospect, it seems inconceivable that three presidential administrations could have supported a program so clearly laden with warnings of failure. Schlesinger and others cautioned against the political costs even if successful, but President Kennedy and a host of other advisers single-mindedly focused on the chances for a major victory in the Cold War at the dawn of his administration. The CIA took charge of an operation that grew beyond its area of expertise—a highly complex night-time amphibious operation that World War II strategists had not risked and that the 1961 military specialists in the Pentagon would have found difficult to manage even in daylight. General Lemnitzer and his Joint Chiefs colleagues meanwhile conceded leadership to the CIA and sat on the side as observers, failing the president by not demanding control of an operation that fell into their realm of responsibility as the nation's military leaders. Once President Kennedy canceled the D-1 and D-Day air strikes, the small landing brigade had no chance against Castro's planes and ground forces, and it could not count on either a popular uprising, an escape to the mountains, or a switch to guerrilla warfare. Nor could the White House expect to dodge responsibility by resorting to plausible denial.

Then why did the Kennedy administration go ahead? Perhaps because the plan *might* work. Or because the "magic button" of assassination *might* set the overthrow in motion. And, as Dulles, Bissell, and others (including the Cuban exiles) thought, the president *might* approve American military intervention if the alternative was defeat.

But the assassination plot failed, and Castro survived to outlive nine presidents and all three Mafia figures, indeed to recently taunt the White House with the story of how he turned down the gift of a Galápagos turtle when learning that it lived only a hundred years. "That's the problem with pets," he remarked with a smile. "You get attached to them and then they die on you."[46]

More than the Joint Chiefs, President Kennedy criticized the CIA for devising a plan containing multiple defects and not warning him despite knowing about them from the beginning. Not by coincidence did Dulles retire from the agency in September 1961, followed by Bissell's departure six months later. Dulles claimed that President Kennedy never said a harsh word to him after the Bay of Pigs and that he gracefully took the blame for the failure. He also insisted that he had retired near the time he had planned when asked to stay on by the new Kennedy administration. But these assertions cannot conceal the president's determination to make changes in CIA leadership. If Bissell thought that he as chief strategist was safe in the president's shadow by glossing over or concealing flaws in the plan, he found out that when the operation fell apart, he automatically became expendable because of that very closeness. "If this were a parliamentary government," Kennedy told him, "I would have to resign and you, a civil servant, would stay on. But being the system of government it is, a presidential government, you will have to resign." Bissell never received the director's job that the president once said was his when it became available.[47]

The United States paid a heavy price for the Bay of Pigs, the effects of which it still feels today. The invasion shattered relations with Cuba and throughout the Cold War remained a hot issue that further embittered the U.S. rivalry with the Soviet Union. Even today, with the Cold War becoming part of a distant past, the United States still refuses to recognize Cuba, and its 1962 trade embargo remains in effect. The supreme irony of the Cuban debacle is that its architects failed to see the numerous pitfalls in intervention and prepared to try the same remedy again—except that Presidents Kennedy and Johnson felt confident they would do it right the next time by using American troops rather than surrogates.

In a rational world, the outcome at the Bay of Pigs should have guaranteed against repeating such ventures, but the world of the 1960s was not rational. America's top strategists did not grapple with the actual numbers of troops required to fight Castro's thirty-two-thousand-man army and nearly three hundred thousand militia in an unfamiliar tropical morass of jungles and swamps. Nor did they devise an exit strategy in the event that matters did not work out as planned. With an American public fearful of Communism, the president and his brother had become obsessed with eliminating Castro as a means for restoring U.S. dignity as well as that of their own. The U.S. military meanwhile fervently sought an opportunity to regain respect by supporting the broader use of its craft, while the CIA frantically fought for survival against President Kennedy's threat to emasculate its powers. More than a decade afterward, the assassination plots became public and, followed by the Church Committee's revelations and the executive order against assassination, dealt another severe blow to the CIA's credibility. Directly responsible to the president, the CIA remains highly sensitive to the danger in providing unpleasant reports, in general impeded from fulfilling its main mission of independently keeping the White House informed of world events.[48]

Further troubling is the failure of later presidential administrations to learn from the Bay of Pigs fiasco and indeed to so readily adopt its most controversial features of covert warfare. Even with the passing of the Cold War, the almost paranoid fear persists in the highest governing circles that almost any nation opposed to American policy is automatically a threat to U.S. security and thus a legitimate subject for forceful elimination. The Bay of Pigs invasion broadened the executive's war-making powers by helping to institutionalize and massively expand a nearly two-century-long practice of clandestine operations that, if meshed with ample military power and managed correctly, appeared capable of both plausible denial and ultimate success. Critics have called covert methods unconstitutional, insisting that such tactics permit secret little wars by a national security state having no sense of public accountability; supporters have appealed to national security and executive privilege in justifying the concealing of private actions from popular scrutiny. More than a few have questioned whether democracy is compatible with a state so tied to warfare.

Thus did the U.S. disaster at the Bay of Pigs paradoxically point the way to continued covert actions accompanied by outright military intervention in other nettlesome countries. Just as America's strategists in the 1960s failed to adequately assess the number of troops needed to fight Castro, so did they repeat that same mistake later in that same decade and again forty years afterward when sending American troops into Vietnam and Iraq. And, as in Cuba, so have later strategists believed they could decide what is best for the targeted country—in short, manipulate and guide history into paths favorable to the American interest. But as history has repeatedly shown, intervention is far more complicated than it appears at the outset. The United States in April 1961 had embarked on the slippery slope toward a high-risk policy of forceful regime change that did not work in Cuba, nor in Vietnam, nor in Iraq, and remains shaky in Afghanistan.[49]

On March 1, 1962, in a small White House ceremony almost a year after the Bay of Pigs, President Kennedy pinned a National Security Medal on Bissell while asserting that his "high purpose, unbounded energy, and unswerving devotion to duty are benchmarks in the intelligence service." Then, perhaps with a subtle double meaning, the president concluded that Bissell "leaves an enduring legacy."[50]

Notes

ABBREVIATIONS

ARRB	Assassination Records Review Board
CCH	Church Committee Hearings
CIA	Central Intelligence Agency
DCI	Director of Central Intelligence
DOD	Department of Defense
DS	Department of State
FRUS	*Foreign Relations of the United States*
GPO	Government Printing Office
IG Report	Earman, J. S., Inspector General's Report
JCS	Joint Chiefs of Staff
JFK	John F. Kennedy
JFKL	John F. Kennedy Library
LBJ	Lyndon B. Johnson
NA	National Archives, College Park, Maryland
NIE	National Intelligence Estimate
NSAM	National Security Action Memorandum
NSC	National Security Council
RFK	Robert F. Kennedy
RG	Record Group
SNIE	Special National Intelligence Estimate
USIA	United States Information Agency

PROLOGUE

1. Loch K. Johnson, *A Season of Inquiry: Congress and Intelligence* (Lexington: University Press of Kentucky, 1985), 1, 59. Johnson had an inside view of the committee's work, for he was a political scientist on leave from the University of Georgia to serve as staff assistant to the Church Committee. Other Democrats were Philip A. Hart, Michigan; Walter F. Mondale, Minnesota; Walter D. Huddleston, Kentucky; Robert Morgan, North Carolina; and Gary Hart, Colorado. The Republicans were John Tower, Texas, vice-chair; Barry Goldwater, Arizona; Charles Mathias, Maryland; Richard S. Schweiker, Pennsylvania; and Howard H. Baker Jr., Tennessee.

2. Church Committee Assassination Report: U.S. Congress, Senate, Select Committee to Study Governmental Operations with Respect to Intelligence Activities, *Alleged Assassination Plots Involving Foreign Leaders; Interim Report*, 94th Congress, First Session, Senate Report No. 94-465 (Washington: GPO, 1975; rpt. New York: W. W. Norton, 1976), 71, 73–75, 77, 79–82, 85, 88–90; IG Report, 20–34; Johnson, *Season of Inquiry*, 50–51, 73. When the CIA's internal inquiry of 1967 was published after its declassification in 1994, the publisher included an interview with Cuban Division General Fabián Escalante Font, the former chief of Cuban State Security who had countered the attempts by the CIA and numerous groups in Cuba to kill Castro. According to Escalante, there were more than six hundred American and Cuban assassination plots against Castro from 1959 to 1993. See J. S. Earman (Inspector General of CIA), Memorandum for the Record: "Report on Plots to Assassinate Fidel Castro," May 23, 1967, prepared at request of Richard Helms, Director of CIA. Published as *CIA Targets Fidel: Secret 1967 CIA Inspector General's Report on Plots to Assassinate Fidel Castro* (Melbourne, Australia: Ocean Press, 1996), Introduction, 8. The CIA acknowledged that by early 1961 nearly thirty people inside and outside the agency were aware of the Mafia plan. Ibid., 34–36. For the Rockefeller Commission, see David Belin, Executive Director of the Rockefeller Commission on CIA Activities within the United States, "Investigation of CIA Involvement," 1–69, CCH.

3. Robert E. Quirk, *Fidel Castro* (New York: W. W. Norton, 1993), 356.

CHAPTER 1. GENESIS

1. Arthur M. Schlesinger Jr., *A Thousand Days: John F. Kennedy in the White House* (Boston: Houghton Mifflin, 1965), 181. I want to thank Brian Latell, formerly with the CIA, for his assistance with this chapter.

2. Brian Latell, *After Fidel: The Inside Story of Castro's Regime and Cuba's Next Leader* (New York: Palgrave Macmillan, 2002), 111.

3. Castro quoted in Thomas G. Paterson, *Contesting Castro: The United States and the Triumph of the Cuban Revolution* (New York: Oxford University Press, 1994), 242, 255–56.

4. IG Report, 19-20; Castro and other quotes in Paterson, *Contesting Castro*, 235. Castro shut down the casinos again in September 1961. *Alleged Assassination Plots*, 74 n.2.

5. First Nixon quote in Richard M. Nixon, *RN: The Memoirs of Richard Nixon*, 2 vols. (New York: Warner Books, 1978), I, 250; Schlesinger, *Thousand Days*, 180–81; Trumbull Higgins, *The Perfect Failure: Kennedy, Eisenhower and the CIA at the Bay of Pigs* (New York: W. W. Norton, 1987), 44; Philip W. Bonsal, *Cuba, Castro, and the United States* (London: University of Pittsburgh Press, 1971), 29, 40, 67; Bonsal to DS, Oct. 17, 1959, *FRUS, 1958–1960, Volume VI, Cuba* (Washington: GPO, 1991), 627–28; Dulles quoted in NSC Meeting, Dec. 1, 1959, ibid., 684; second Nixon quote in NSC Meeting, Dec. 10, 1959, ibid., 699.

6. Schlesinger, *Thousand Days*, 181, 183; Robert Hurwitch, Oral History Interview, 16–19, JFKL; Latell, *After Fidel*, 110–11.

7. Peter Wyden, *Bay of Pigs: The Untold Story* (New York: Simon and Schuster, 1979), 107; Grayston L. Lynch, *Decision for Disaster: Betrayal at the Bay of Pigs* (Washington: Brassey's, 1998), 4; IG Report, 3, 10–13.

8. Memo of first meeting of Board of Inquiry on Cuban Operations, April 22, 1961, Luis Aguilar (introduction), *Operation Zapata: The "Ultrasensitive" Report and Testimony of the Board of Inquiry on the Bay of Pigs* (Frederick, Md.: University Publications of America, 1981), 56; *Alleged Assassination Plots*, 92; Higgins, *Perfect Failure*, 47. A copy of King's memo appears in a CIA in-house history, on which Dulles penciled in "removal" over "elimination." Neither word, however, could hide the objective of assassination. See Jack B. Pfeiffer, "Official History of the Bay of Pigs Operation, Volume III: Evolution of CIA's Anti-Castro Policies, 1959–January 1961" (Dec. 1979), 30, 298, JFK Assassination Records Collection (NA).

9. Peter Grose, *Gentleman Spy: The Life of Allen Dulles* (New York: Houghton Mifflin, 1994), 501, 517–18, 602; Dulles quote ibid., 501.

10. David Wise, *The Politics of Lying: Government Deception, Secrecy, and Power* (New York: Random House, 1973), 251; FBI memo, May 22, 1961, cited in Belin, "Investigation of CIA Involvement," 20, CCH; ibid., 8; Bissell testimony, June 9, 1975, p. 3, CCH; Richard M. Bissell Jr., *Reflections of a Cold Warrior: From Yalta to the Bay of Pigs* (New Haven: Yale University Press, 1996), 18, 20, 23, 157; Bissell's quotes on assassination in Wyden, *Bay of Pigs*, 23–24. See also Michael R. Beschloss, *The Crisis Years: Kennedy and Khrushchev, 1960–1963* (New York: HarperCollins, 1991), 135.

11. Beschloss, *Crisis Years*, 135; *Alleged Assassination Plots*, 181 n 1; IG Report, 37–38. The Church Committee attempted to conceal Gottlieb's identity by referring to him as Joseph Scheider.

12. Richard M. Nixon, "Cuba, Castro and John F. Kennedy," *Reader's Digest* 85 (Nov. 1964), 283–300; Richard M. Nixon, *Six Crises* (New York: Pocket Books, 1962), 379–80; Bonsal, *Cuba, Castro, and the United States*, 174; Howard Hunt, *Give Us This Day: The Inside Story of the CIA and the Bay of Pigs*

Invasion . . . by One of Its Key Organizers (New Rochelle, N.Y.: Arlington House, 1973), 40; Memo of NSC meeting, Dec. 16, 1959, *FRUS, 1958–1960, VI, Cuba*, 704–5; Higgins, *Perfect Failure*, 51.

13. Higgins, *Perfect Failure*, 38; Narrative of Anti-Castro Cuban Operation Zapata, Aguilar, *Operation Zapata*, 3; Memo of first meeting of Board of Inquiry on Cuban Operations, April 22, 1961, ibid., 55; *FRUS, 1958–1960, VI, Cuba*, 789 n.3; Gen. Gordon Gray testimony, July 9, 1975, pp. 4–5, CCH.

14. Prouty testimony, July 16, 1975, pp. 2, 28–33, CCH. A number of documents, the Rockefeller Commission concluded years later, "referred to the intent on the part of some of the Cuban teams operating inside Cuba to attempt to assassinate Castro." Belin, "Investigation of CIA Involvement," 7–8, CCH. On Helms and assassination, see Higgins, *Perfect Failure*, 51.

15. Memo of discussion at DS-JCS staff meeting in Pentagon, Jan. 8, 1960, *FRUS, 1958–1960, VI, Cuba*, 731–32. Merchant was deputy undersecretary of state for political affairs.

16. Ibid., 732–33; Memo of NSC meeting, Jan. 14, 1960, ibid., 743, 745.

17. *Alleged Assassination Plots*, 93. In late December of that same year of 1960, Dulles changed his stance, asserting his interest in "getting rid of Castro as quickly as possible and in this field he had direct responsibility." Minutes of Special Group meeting, Dec. 22, 1960, in Pfeiffer, "Official History," III, 183–84, 370 n.17.

18. John Dreier, director of DS Office of Inter-American Regional Political Affairs to Roy Rubottom, assistant secretary of state for inter-American affairs, Jan. 28, 1960, *FRUS, 1958–1960, VI, Cuba*, 771; Memo of discussion at DS-JCS staff meeting in Pentagon, Jan. 8, 1960, ibid., 732–34; Burke to Merchant, Feb. 26, 1960, ibid., 813, 819–20; Memo for record by Robert F. Packard of Policy Planning Staff, Jan. 11, 1960, ibid., 737; Burke to Secretary of Defense Thomas Gates, March 2, 1960, ibid., 822. The Defense Department representative was Deputy Assistant Secretary of Defense John Irwin.

19. Hurwitch, Oral History Interview, April 24, 1964, pp. 159–60, JFKL.

20. Aleksandr Fursenko and Timothy Naftali. *"One Hell of a Gamble": Khrushchev, Castro, and Kennedy, 1958–1964* (New York: W. W. Norton, 1997), 40–47, 54, 60; Bonsal, *Cuba, Castro, and the United States*, 133–35.

21. Khrushchev quoted in Stephen Schwab, "U.S.-Cuba Relations: The Enduring Significance of Guantánamo," Ph.D. dissertation (Tuscaloosa: University of Alabama, 2007), chap. 6; Higgins, *Perfect Failure*, 54; Fursenko and Naftali, *"One Hell of a Gamble,"* 44–45, 54; Stephen Clissold, ed., *Soviet Relations with Latin America, 1918–1968: A Documentary Survey* (London: Oxford University Press, 1970), 255–57.

22. Bonsal, *Cuba, Castro, and the United States*, 134; King quoted in *Alleged Assassination Plots*, 93; ibid., 93, 114–15; Memo of NSC meeting, March 10, 1960, *FRUS, 1958–1960, VI, Cuba*, 832–37. The *FRUS* volume contains no reference to Burke's call for a "package plan." For the quote, see Gray testimony, July 9, 1975, p. 14, CCH.

23. Memo of NSC meeting, March 10, 1960, *FRUS, 1958–1960, VI, Cuba*, 832–37; Gray testimony, July 9, 1975, pp. 4, 6–7, 14–15, 17, 45, CCH; Goodpaster testimony, July 17, 1975, pp. 4–5, 10, CCH; Burke cited in *Alleged Assassination Plots*, 116; last Gray quote ibid., 115. In an unconvincing argument, CIA historian Pfeiffer insisted in his in-house history that the accounts of this meeting by its participants demonstrated that "package" did not refer to assassination. See Pfeiffer, "Official History," III, 68 n*. One Dulles biographer believes that he never would have approved any of the Eisenhower administration's assassination efforts without presidential authorization. See Grose, *Gentleman Spy*, 505.

24. Rubottom to Herter, March 9, 1960, *FRUS, 1958–1960, VI, Cuba*, 829; U.S. embassy in Cuba to DS, March 8, 1960, ibid., 825; Higgins, *Perfect Failure*, 49; Bissell testimony, June 9, 1975, p. 11, CCH; Narrative of Anti-Castro Cuban Operation Zapata, Aguilar, *Operation Zapata*, 3–4, 6. President Eisenhower insisted on using the term "program" rather than "plan," arguing that a program was in a stage of development and a plan suggested a final product. Wyden, *Bay of Pigs*, 24*.

25. Narrative of Anti-Castro Cuban Operation Zapata, Aguilar, *Operation Zapata*, 5; Memo of first meeting of Board of Inquiry on Cuban Operations, April 22, 1961, ibid., 58; Memo of meeting with Eisenhower, Aug. 18, 1960, *FRUS, 1958–1960, VI, Cuba*, 1058. By the end of May, Dulles had approved $900,000 for the Cuban project that ran to the remainder of Fiscal Year 1960. But within two weeks, nearly the entire monetary allotment was gone, and the CIA had to inject another million dollars into the fund. Lyman Kirkpatrick, "Inspector General's Survey of the Cuban Operation, October 1961," in Peter Kornbluh, ed., *Bay of Pigs Declassified: The Secret CIA Report on the Invasion of Cuba* (New York: New Press, 1998), 27–28.

26. Narrative of Anti-Castro Cuban Operation Zapata, Aguilar, *Operation Zapata*, 5–6; Kirkpatrick, "Inspector General's Survey," 28; Juan Carlos Rodríguez, *The Bay of Pigs and the CIA* (Melbourne, Australia: Ocean Press, 1999), 35; Patrick Symmes, *The Boys from Dolores: Fidel Castro's Schoolmates from Revolution to Exile* (New York: Pantheon Books, 2007), 221; Wyden, *Bay of Pigs*, 70–71.

27. Schlesinger, *Thousand Days*, 185; Higgins, *Perfect Failure*, 57; Hurwitch, Oral History Interview, 164, JFKL; Narrative of Anti-Castro Cuban Operation Zapata, Aguilar, *Operation Zapata*, 5; Bissell quoted in memo of meeting with President Eisenhower, Aug. 18, 1960, *FRUS, 1958–1960, VI, Cuba*, 1058–59.

28. Memo of NSC meeting, July 25, 1960, *FRUS, 1958–1960, VI, Cuba*, 1029; Bissell quoted in Beschloss, *Crisis Years*, 134. The CIA later provided weapons that Dominican dissidents used in assassinating Trujillo in late May 1961. On Trujillo, see *Alleged Assassination Plots*, 191–215; Bissell testimony, June 11, pp. 84b, 85, July 22, 1975, pp. 70, 121, CCH; Higgins, *Perfect Failure*, 47 (Trujillo), 56, 88 (Castro). For the best account, see Bernard Diederich, *Trujillo: The Death of the Dictator* (Princeton, N.J.: Markus Wiener Publishers,

1990). Originally published in 1978 as *Trujillo: The Death of the Goat.* On Lumumba, see Richard D. Mahoney, *JFK: Ordeal in Africa* (New York: Oxford University Press, 1983), 43–55, 69–74; Lawrence R. Devlin, *Chief of Station, Congo: A Memoir of 1960–67* (New York: Public Affairs, 2007), 94–95, 113, 115, 128–31, 133–35, 137–38, 191; Grose, *Gentleman Spy,* 502-4; Bissell testimony, Sept. 10, 1975, pp. 14–15, 37, 50–51, 61–63, CCH; Sidney Gottlieb (chief scientist of CIA's Technical Services Division) testimony in Bronson Tweedy (chief of CIA's Africa Division) testimony, Oct. 9, 1975, pp. 15–23, CCH; Gottlieb testimony, Oct. 7, 9, 1975, cited in *Alleged Assassination Plots,* 21, 21 n.1; and ibid., 13–70. Evidence compiled by the CIA suggests that in mid-January 1961, a Belgian captain of a mercenary force killed Lumumba when Congolese troops refused to do so. CIA Information Reports from Leopoldville, Feb. 20, 1961 (Exhibit 10), and March 22, 1961 (Exhibit 11), following Victor Hedgeman (pseudonym for Devlin) testimony, Aug. 25, 1975, CCH.

29. *Alleged Assassination Plots,* 74; Memorandum by Howard J. Osborn, Director of Security, for Director of Central Intelligence on Johnny Roselli, Nov. 9, 1970, in Osborn memorandum for Executive Secretary, CIA Management Committee, in "Family Jewels," May 16, 1973, p. 44. The 703 pages comprising this collection of recently released CIA documents are conveniently located on the website of the National Security Archive at George Washington University in Washington, D.C.

30. *Alleged Assassination Plots,* 74; John Prados, *Safe for Democracy: The Secret Wars of the CIA* (Chicago: Ivan R. Dee, 2006), 215–16; John Ranelagh, *The Agency: The Rise and Decline of the CIA* (London: Weidenfeld and Nicolson, 1986), 204.

31. Robert Maheu and Richard Hack, *Next to Hughes: Behind the Power and Tragic Downfall of Howard Hughes by His Closest Advisor* (New York: HarperCollins, 1992), 40, 69–75; *Alleged Assassination Plots,* 74–75, 74 n.4; IG Report, 15–16.

32. Maheu and Hack, *Next to Hughes,* 114; Maheu testimony, July 29, 1975, pp. 6–8, 14, 49, 53–54, 58–60, CCH. The great classical composer Wolfgang Amadeus Mozart popularized Don Giovanni in his masterly opera that premiered in Prague, Czechoslovakia, in 1787 and focused on a young and licentious nobleman.

33. Charles Rappleye and Ed Becker, *All American Mafioso: The Johnny Rosselli Story* (New York: Barricade Books, 1991, 1995), 132; Mario Puzo, *The Godfather* (New York: G. P. Putnam's Sons, 1969; rpt. New York: Penguin, 1978), 66–70. For a discussion of those who dispute the horse story, see Kitty Kelley, *His Way: The Unauthorized Biography of Frank Sinatra* (New York: Bantam Books, 1986), 190–95.

34. Maheu and Hack, *Next to Hughes,* 115; *Alleged Assassination Plots,* 75; Maheu testimony, July 29, 1975, 13, CCH; Roselli testimony, June 24, 1975, p. 8, CCH.

35. Maheu and Hack, *Next to Hughes*, 115; FBI Case: Roselli, FBI File No. 92-3267-7, Feb. 10, 1958, Los Angeles File No. 92-113, p. 36, U.S. Dept. of Justice, Washington. The full name of the Kefauver Committee was the Special Committee to Investigate Organized Crime in Interstate Commerce. McClellan's was the Senate Select Committee on Improper Activities in the Labor or Management Field.
36. Maheu and Hack, *Next to Hughes*, 115–16.
37. *Alleged Assassination Plots*, 76; Roselli testimony, June 24, 1975, pp. 9, 59, CCH.
38. Maheu and Hack, *Next to Hughes*, 116; Roselli testimony, June 24, 1975, 59, CCH. Maheu praised Roselli's and Giancana's patriotism, declaring that they "appeared like angels." Maheu testimony, July 29, 1975, p. 54, CCH.
39. Memo for Record by Sheffield Edwards, May 14, 1962, *FRUS, 1961–1963, Volume X, Cuba, 1961–1962* (Washington: GPO, 1997), 808; Trafficante testimony, Oct. 7, 1976, p. 1, CCH; Antoinette Giancana and Thomas C. Renner, *Mafia Princess: Growing Up in Sam Giancana's Family* (New York: William Morrow, 1984), 16–17, 30, 40, 198. See also Rappleye and Becker, *All American Mafioso*, 158, 184–87, and William Brashler, *The Don: The Life and Death of Sam Giancana* (New York: Harper and Row, 1977), 204–6.
40. Giancana and Roselli quoted in O'Connell testimony, May 30, 1975, pp. 115–16, CCH. See also IG Report, 25. O'Connell claimed he was involved in the preliminary discussion.
41. Trafficante testimony, Oct. 7, 1976, p. 2, CCH; Scott M. Deitche, *The Silent Don: The Criminal Underworld of Santo Trafficante Jr.* (Fort Lee, N.J.: Barricade Books, 2007), 139; Rappleye and Becker, *All American Mafioso*, 177–78, 189.
42. Varona characterization in Rodríguez, *Bay of Pigs and CIA*, 23–24; Varona quoted ibid., 33; O'Connell testimony, May 30, 1975, pp. 19–20, 87, CCH; Roselli testimony, June 24, 1975, pp. 17, 19–25, CCH; FBI File No. 92-3267-1054, Roselli, Los Angeles Field Report No. 92-113, Oct. 8, 1975, pp. 2–3, U.S. Dept. of Justice, Washington; *Alleged Assassination Plots*, 76; Maheu testimony, July 29, 1975, pp. 40–42, CCH; Maheu and Hack, *Next to Hughes*, 123. Roselli found a Cuban who spoke English and informed Trafficante that his services were no longer needed. Trafficante testimony, Oct. 7, 1976, pp. 2–3, CCH; IG Report, 23–27; Prados, *Safe for Democracy*, 217.
43. Higgins, *Perfect Failure*, 56; Wyden, *Bay of Pigs*, 115; Kornbluh, ed., *Bay of Pigs Declassified*, 8. Peter Kornbluh considers assassination an "explicit component" of the Bay of Pigs project. Ibid., 9. See Bissell's January 1968 speech quoted in Victor Marchetti and John D. Marks, *The CIA and the Cult of Intelligence* (New York: Dell, 1974), 368. Years afterward CIA operative Howard Hunt asserted that after a survey visit to Havana in late 1959 or early 1960 he recommended to Bissell that the agency find Cuban patriots to assassinate Castro "*before* or coincident with the invasion." See Hunt's book,

Give Us This Day, 38. Hunt was one of the Watergate conspirators during the Nixon presidency.

44. Esterline role in drafting plan, in Rodríguez, *Bay of Pigs and CIA*, 21; Esterline's interview with Kornbluh, Oct. 10, 1996, in Kornbluh, ed., *Bay of Pigs Declassified*, 10, 207, 258, 264–65; Don Bohning, *The Castro Obsession: U.S. Covert Operations Against Cuba, 1959–1965* (Washington: Potomac Books, 2005), 25; Esterline quote on not signing, ibid.

45. Esterline's interview with Kornbluh, Oct. 10, 1996, in Kornbluh, ed., *Bay of Pigs Declassified*, 265.

46. Ibid., 10, 264–65.

47. On Dulles's approval, see Osborn memo for DCI on Roselli, Nov. 9, 1970, in "Family Jewels," May 16, 1973, p. 44; Bissell testimony, June 9, pp. 20, 22, 24, June 11, p. 24, July 17, 1975, pp. 15–16, CCH; Edwards testimony before Rockefeller Commission, April 9, 1975, p. 5, quoted in *Alleged Assassination Plots*, 96; Edwards testimony, May 30, 1975, pp. 5–7, CCH; Breckinridge testimony, June 2, 1975, pp. 67–68, CCH. Breckinridge noted that Edwards had "doubletalked the meeting," but that Dulles "probably understood" the focus was assassination. Ibid., 68. See also O'Connell testimony, May 30, 1975, pp. 33–34, 58, 60, CCH; IG Report, 17–18; *Alleged Assassination Plots*, 95, 98 n.3. Breckinridge confirmed this version of the briefing, telling the Church Committee that a 1973 memo prepared in the CIA's Office of Security discussed Roselli without mentioning assassination ("doubletalk") but left no doubt that it meant the Mafia operation when asserting that Dulles "was briefed and gave his approval." Breckinridge in Colby testimony, May 23, 1975, pp. 60–61, 64–65, CCH; FBI memo, May 22, 1961, cited in Belin, "Investigation of CIA Involvement," 29, CCH.

48. FBI memo, May 22, 1961, cited in Belin, "Investigation of CIA Involvement," 29, CCH; Bissell testimony, June 9, p. 61, June 11, 1975, pp. 5–6, 10–11, CCH; Goodpaster testimony, July 17, 1975, pp. 5–6, 8, CCH; Parrott testimony, July 10, 1975, p. 14, CCH; Helms cited in *Alleged Assassination Plots*, 264.

49. Bissell quoted in Rappleye and Becker, *All American Mafioso*, 212. For the wiretapping episode without mention of either McGuire or Rowan, see *Alleged Assassination Plots*, 77–79. Dan Rowan and Dick Martin were later stars of the enormously popular *Laugh-In* TV show of the late 1960s and early 1970s.

CHAPTER 2. TRINIDAD

1. JCS to Gates, Sept. 29, 1960, *FRUS, 1958–1960, VI, Cuba*, 1076–77; Herter to Gates, Oct. 14, 1960, ibid., 1087; Memo of DS-JCS meeting at the Pentagon, Sept. 30, 1960, ibid., 1079; Merchant quoted ibid., 1080. The Platt Amendment of 1901 awarded the United States a site on the island for a naval base, and a treaty two years later formalized the agreement.

2. Memo of meeting in DS between Dennison, Merchant, and other department officers, Oct. 10, 1960, ibid., ed. note, 1082; Memo of NSC meeting, Nov. 7, 1960, ibid., 1119.

3. Memo by White House Staff Secretary, Brig. Gen. Andrew Goodpaster, Oct. 20, 1960, ibid., 1093; Memo of NSC meeting, Oct. 20, 1960, ibid., 1094.
4. Rodríguez, *Bay of Pigs and CIA*, 55–57; Bohning to author, April 15, 2008.
5. Hurwitch, Oral History Interview, 22–23, JFKL; Memo of first meeting of Board of Inquiry on Cuban Operations, April 22, 1961, Aguilar, *Operation Zapata*, 59–60; Rodríguez, *Bay of Pigs and CIA*, 41–42; Merchant quoted in *FRUS, 1958–1960, VI, Cuba*, ed. note, 1126.
6. Warren Trest and Donald Dodd, *Wings of Denial: The Alabama Air National Guard's Covert Role at the Bay of Pigs* (Montgomery, Ala.: New South Books, 2001), 26; Schlesinger, *Thousand Days*, 179; Albert C. Persons, *Bay of Pigs* (Birmingham, Ala.: Kingston Press, 1968), 11, 30–31, 42–43. The word *trax* meant training. Rodríguez, *Bay of Pigs and CIA*, 78.
7. Kirkpatrick, "Inspector General's Survey," 90–91; Trest and Dodd, *Wings of Denial*, 26.
8. Narrative of Anti-Castro Cuban Operation Zapata, Aguilar, *Operation Zapata*, 6–7; Lemnitzer testimony in sixteenth meeting of Green Study Group, May 18, 1961, ibid., 333; Memo of first meeting of Board of Inquiry on Cuban Operations, April 22, 1961, ibid., 59; Kirkpatrick, "Inspector General's Survey," 32, 91; Chief of WH/4/PM, CIA (Hawkins) to Chief of WH/4 of Directorate for Plans (J. D. Esterline), Jan. 4, 1961, *FRUS, X, Cuba, 1961–1962*, 16; Schlesinger, *Thousand Days*, 197. Opa-Locka became the pickup point for carting Cuban refugees to Guatemala.
9. Narrative of Anti-Castro Cuban Operation Zapata, Aguilar, *Operation Zapata*, 7; Kirkpatrick, "Inspector General's Survey," 92; Bissell testimony, June 9, 1975, p. 12, CCH.
10. Kornbluh, ed., *Bay of Pigs Declassified*, 2; Ydígoras quoted in Persons, *Bay of Pigs*, 11.
11. Edward B. Ferrer, *Operation Puma: The Air Battle of the Bay of Pigs* (Miami, Fla.: International Aviation Consultants, 1975), 132, 136–37; Rodríguez, *Bay of Pigs and CIA*, 61.
12. Higgins, *Perfect Failure*, 136; Persons, *Bay of Pigs*, 11, 22, 31, 37; Ferrer, *Puma*, 129; Kirkpatrick, "Inspector General's Survey," Memo of second meeting of Green Study Group, April 24, 1961, Aguilar, *Operation Zapata*, 63, 69–70; Memo of first meeting of Board of Inquiry on Cuban Operations, April 22, 1961, ibid., 60; Trest and Dodd, *Wings of Denial*, 50; Somoza quoted ibid., 29; Hawkins to Esterline, Jan. 4, 1961, *FRUS, X, Cuba, 1961–1962*, pp. 15–16. At the beginning of the April 24 meeting, the committee adopted a new title, the "Green Study Group."
13. Merchant and Cabell quoted in Special Group minutes, Nov. 3, 1960, Belin, "Investigation of CIA Involvement," 35, CCH. Others in attendance were Lansdale, Deputy Secretary of Defense James Douglas, and Eisenhower's special assistant for national security and on the Joint Chiefs' staff, General Gordon Gray. In yet another twist to his own story, Bissell told the Church Committee that Cabell's negative reaction raised doubt about whether he

knew of the assassination project. Bissell testimony, July 17, 1975, pp. 17–18, 22–23, CCH. This was an untenable position given the evidence earlier cited, including Bissell's own testimony, that senior CIA officials were aware of the plan.

14. Lansdale to Douglas, Nov. 7, 1960, *FRUS, 1958–1960, VI, Cuba,* 1116, 1118; Lansdale testimony, July 8, 1975, p. 103, CCH. Higgins believes the term "direct positive action" referred to assassination. See his *Perfect Failure,* 65. In early January 1961 the Joint Chiefs of Staff devised an action plan aimed at overthrowing Castro (JCSM-44-61—Annex 7). The list of recommendations made it to the office of the secretary of defense but lost direction in the midst of the administration change. Narrative of Anti-Castro Cuban Operation Zapata, Aguilar, *Operation Zapata,* 8; Gray testimony, July 9, 1975, p. 9, CCH; Parrott testimony, July 10, 1975, pp. 19–21, CCH; Bissell testimony, July 17, 1975, pp. 15–18, 25, CCH; Pfeiffer, "Official History," III, 281–82. Omphaloskepsis refers to the Eastern belief that meditating on one's navel would induce a mystical trance.

15. Memo of conversation in DS, Nov. 29, 1960, *FRUS, 1958–1960, VI, Cuba,* 1132, 1134, 1136–37, 1139.

16. Narrative of Anti-Castro Cuban Operation Zapata, Aguilar, *Operation Zapata,* 8; Memo of second meeting of Green Study Group, April 24, 1961, ibid., 76–77; Interview of Hawkins by Peter Kornbluh, Oct. 10, 1996, in Kornbluh, ed., *Bay of Pigs Declassified,* 262; Trest and Dodd, *Wings of Denial,* 52.

17. Memo of second meeting of Green Study Group, April 24, 1961, Aguilar, *Operation Zapata,* 77–78, 95.

18. Memo for record, May 1, 1961, *FRUS, X, Cuba, 1961–1962,* p. 412; Lynch, *Decision for Disaster,* 24; Memo of seventh meeting of Green Study Group, May 1, 1961, Aguilar, *Operation Zapata,* 170–71, 174–75.

19. Aguilar, *Operation Zapata,* 171; Haynes Johnson, *The Bay of Pigs: The Leaders' Story of Brigade 2506* (New York: W. W. Norton, 1964), 32; Rodríguez, *Bay of Pigs and CIA,* 78–79.

20. Narrative of Anti-Castro Cuban Operation Zapata, Aguilar, *Operation Zapata,* 7; Interview with Goodwin, May 27, 1975, Exhibit No. 7, p. 5, in McNamara testimony, July 11, 1975, CCH.

21. Castro quoted in U.S. Chargé Daniel M. Braddock to DS, Jan. 2, 1961, *FRUS, X, Cuba, 1961–1962,* p. 1 n.1; Braddock to DS, Jan. 3, 1961, ibid., 1, 1 n.2; Higgins, *Perfect Failure,* 71.

22. Ed. note, *FRUS, X, Cuba, 1961–1962,* p. 2; Memo of conversation between Herter and Rusk, Jan. 3, 1961, ibid., 5; Memo of telephone conversation between Herter and Eisenhower, Jan. 3, 1961, ibid., 6; Memo for record, Jan. 3, 1961, ibid., 3–4. The Swiss embassy in Havana could handle American interests in Cuba, and a break would have no impact on the U.S. naval base in Guantanamo. The United States asked Switzerland to act on its behalf, but the request went to the government of Czechoslovakia. Herter to Cuban embassy, Jan. 3, 1961, ibid., 8; Cuban government to U.S. embassy, Jan. 4, 1961, ibid., 9

n.3. For Eisenhower, see U.S. National Archives and Records Administration, *Public Papers of the Presidents of the United States: Dwight D. Eisenhower: Containing the Public Messages, Speeches, and Statements of the President, 1953–1961*, 8 vols. (Washington: GPO, 1960–61), VIII, 891.

23. Persons, *Bay of Pigs*, 12; Wadsworth quoted ibid., and in ed. note, *FRUS, X, Cuba, 1961–1962*, p. 17.

24. Kirkpatrick, "Inspector General's Survey," 98; Persons, *Bay of Pigs*, author page, 2, 5, 9.

25. Memo of conversation in DS, Jan. 13, 1961, *FRUS, X, Cuba, 1961–1962*, p. 33; Hawkins to Esterline, Jan. 4, 1961, ibid., pp. 14–15; Memo of second meeting of Green Study Group, April 24, 1961, Aguilar, *Operation Zapata*, 72; "Policy Decisions Required for Conduct of Strike Operations Against Government of Cuba" (Annex 14), to the chief, WH/4, CIA Western Hemisphere Division, Branch 4, Jan. 4, 1961, in Narrative of Anti-Castro Cuban Operation Zapata, ibid., 15.

26. Hawkins to Esterline, Jan. 4, 1961, *FRUS, X, Cuba, 1961–1962*, pp. 12, 15; "Policy Decisions Required for Conduct of Strike Operations Against Government of Cuba" (Annex 14), to the chief, WH/4, CIA Western Hemisphere Division, Branch 4, Jan. 4, 1961, in Narrative of Anti-Castro Cuban Operation Zapata, Aguilar, *Operation Zapata*, 15.

27. Edward Ahrens, district director of U.S. Border Patrol, quoted in Persons, *Bay of Pigs*, 13, 23–24.

28. Hawkins to Esterline, Jan. 4, 1961, *FRUS, X, Cuba, 1961–1962*, pp. 10–11. Carlos Rodríguez Santana fell off a cliff and died. Victor A. Triay, *Bay of Pigs: An Oral History of Brigade 2506* (Gainesville: University Press of Florida, 2001), 13; Lynch, *Decision for Disaster*, 24.

29. Hawkins to Esterline, Jan. 4, 1961, *FRUS, X, Cuba, 1961–1962*, p. 13; Kirkpatrick, "Inspector General's Survey," 32; Memo of second meeting of Green Study Group, April 14, 1961, Aguilar, *Operation Zapata*, 72–73.

30. Hawkins to Esterline, Jan. 4, 1961, *FRUS, X, Cuba, 1961–1962*, p. 16. The Garcia family controlled the two LCTs.

31. Hawkins to Esterline, Jan. 4, 1961, ibid., p. 14; *New York Times*, Jan. 10, 1961, cited ibid., p. 25 n.1; Merchant to Herter, Jan. 10, 1961, ibid., 25; Press officer R. Lincoln White cited ibid., 25 n.2; Memo of second meeting of Green Study Group, April 24, 1961, Aguilar, *Operation Zapata*, 72–73; Persons, *Bay of Pigs*, 13.

32. Narrative of Anti-Castro Cuban Operation Zapata, Aguilar, *Operation Zapata*, 8; Memo prepared in CIA, Jan. 12, 1961, *FRUS, X, Cuba, 1961–1962*, p. 27; Staff Study Prepared for DOD, "Evaluation of Possible Military Courses of Action in Cuba," Jan. 16, 1961, ibid., 36, 38.

33. Staff Study Prepared for DOD, "Evaluation of Possible Military Courses of Action in Cuba," Jan. 16, 1961, *FRUS, X, Cuba, 1961–1962*, pp. 36–37, 40. The Defense Department thought the Cuban navy had three PF, two PCE, and forty-three small craft. Ibid., 36. See memo from C. Tracy Barnes, Deputy Director (Plans) for Covert Operations, to Esterline, Jan. 18, 1961, ibid., 43.

34. Helms later declared that the invasion operation resulted from the CIA's successes in Iran and Guatemala. Helms testimony, Sept. 12, 1975, p. 11, CCH.

35. Bissell, Oral History Interview, 3, JFKL; Bissell, *Reflections of Cold Warrior*, 160; Narrative of Anti-Castro Cuban Operation Zapata, Aguilar, *Operation Zapata*, 8; Grose, *Gentleman Spy*, 511–12; James Srodes, *Allen Dulles: Master of Spies* (Washington: Regnery, 1999), 510; Schlesinger, *Thousand Days*, 194–95; Dulles, Oral History Interview, 17–18, JFKL; Memo by Clark Clifford, Jan. 24, 1961, and McNamara to Kennedy, Jan. 24, 1961, both in ed. note, *FRUS, X, Cuba, 1961–1962*, p. 44.

36. Bissell testimony, June 9, 1975, pp. 27, 35–36, 39, CCH.

CHAPTER 3. ZAPATA

1. Dulles, Oral History Interview, 16, JFKL; Bissell testimony, June 9, pp. 38–39, June 11, 1975, pp. 5–6, CCH. *From Russia with Love* appeared in 1957.

2. Narrative of Anti-Castro Cuban Operation Zapata, Aguilar, *Operation Zapata*, 8; Assertions by RFK and Maj. Gen. David W. Gray from the Joint Staff of JCS in memo of second meeting of Green Study Group, April 24, 1961, ibid., 102.

3. Memo of second meeting of Green Study Group, April 24, 1961, ibid., 65; Narrative of Anti-Castro Cuban Operation Zapata, ibid., 8; Schlesinger, *Thousand Days*, 195.

4. Arthur M. Schlesinger Jr., *Robert Kennedy and His Times* (Boston: Houghton Mifflin, 1978), 507, 509–11; Schlesinger in James G. Blight and Peter Kornbluh, eds., *Politics of Illusion: The Bay of Pigs Invasion Reexamined* (Boulder, Colo.: Lynne Rienner Publishers, 1998), 86; IG Report, 37; *Alleged Assassination Plots*, 183–87; Bundy testimony, July 11, 1975, 5, 7, 9–10, 15–16, 41, ibid., 119, 186–87; Bissell testimony, June 9, pp. 54, 81–82, June 11, p. 8, July 22, 1975, pp. 31, 33–35, CCH; Belin, "Investigation of CIA Involvement," 26–28. Schlesinger asserted on June 2, 1985, in his recently published private journals that the president "had no knowledge" of "the assassination attempts." Arthur M. Schlesinger Jr., *Journals: 1952–2000* (New York: Penguin, 2007), 596.

5. Belin, "Investigation of CIA Involvement," 27, CCH; Bissell testimony, June 9, pp. 49, 51, 57, 68, 74, 76, July 17, p. 10, July 22, 1975, p. 32, CCH; IG Report, 37–38.

6. Belin, "Investigation of CIA Involvement," 26–28, CCH; Bundy testimony, July 11, 1975, pp. 5, 7, 9–10, 15–16, 41, in *Alleged Assassination Plots*, 119, 186–87.

7. Bundy testimony before Rockefeller Commission in Belin, "Investigation of CIA Involvement," 30, CCH; Bundy testimony, July 8, 1975, pp. 1–2, 8–9, CCH.

8. Fabián Escalante, *The Cuba Project: CIA Covert Operations, 1959–62* (Melbourne, Australia: Ocean Press, 2004), 75. First published as *The Secret War: CIA Covert Operations Against Cuba, 1959–62* (Melbourne, Australia: Ocean Press, 1995). The second edition contains a new preface and additional ma-

terial. Harvey testimony, June 25, 1975, pp. 18, 27, 35–37, 52, 79, 88, July 11, 1975, p. 59, CCH; *Alleged Assassination Plots*, 181, 183; Bissell testimony, June 9, p. 51, July 17, 1975, p. 10, CCH; Bayard Stockton, *Flawed Patriot: The Rise and Fall of CIA Legend Bill Harvey* (Washington: Potomac Books, 2006), 114.

9. Harvey repeated some of these quotes in his testimony before the Church Committee. See his testimony, June 25, 1975, pp. 53–54, CCH. Exhibit 1 at the end of Harvey's testimony is a copy of the handwritten notes, save for those words blacked out. For the entire scrawled note, see CIA Document, n.d., box 36, 104-10178-10391, RG 233, JFK Collection (NA).

10. Memo of conference with JFK, Jan. 25, 1961, *FRUS, X, Cuba, 1961–1962*, p. 54; CIA memo, Jan. 26, 1961, ibid., 55; Burke, Oral History Interview, 21–22, JFKL.

11. JCS to McNamara, Jan. 27, 1961, *FRUS, X, Cuba, 1961–1962*, pp. 57–58; Memo of meeting in Cabinet Room, Jan. 28, 1961, ibid., 63; Meeting in Pentagon, Jan. 28, 1961, ed. note, ibid., 65.

12. JCS to McNamara, Feb. 3, 1961, ibid., 68–69. The study was entitled, JCSM-57-61, "Military Evaluation of the CIA Paramilitary Plan—Cuba."

13. Ibid., 77–78.

14. Bissell, Oral History Interview, 4, 6, JFKL; Bundy memo of meeting with JFK, Feb. 9, 1961, National Security Files, box 35A, Cuba, General, JFKL.

15. Lemnitzer testimony in sixteenth meeting of Green Study Group, May 18, 1961, Aguilar, *Operation Zapata*, 313–15, 322, 324, 326; Burke testimony in eighteenth meeting of Green Study Group, May 19, 1961, ibid., 347.

16. Lemnitzer testimony in sixteenth meeting of Green Study Group, May 18, 1961, ibid., 322, 324, 326; Burke testimony in eighteenth meeting of Green Study Group, May 19, 1961, ibid., 346; Decker testimony in twelfth meeting of Green Study Group, May 8, 1961, ibid., 270–71.

17. Narrative of Anti-Castro Cuban Operation Zapata, June 13, 1961, ibid., 8; testimony of Lt. Gen. Earle G. Wheeler, director of Joint Staff of JCS, in ninth meeting of Green Study Group, May 3, 1961, ibid., 206; testimony of General Thomas White, Air Force Chief of Staff, in twelfth meeting of Green Study Group, May 8, 1961, ibid., 255–56; JCS to McNamara, Feb. 3, 1961, *FRUS, X, Cuba, 1961–1962*, p. 68. White held this position until June 1961. Schlesinger, *Thousand Days*, 199–200.

18. Memo of DS meeting, Feb. 7, 1961, *FRUS, X, Cuba, 1961–1962*, pp. 83, 85.

19. President Kennedy encouraged the establishment of a Revolutionary Council and a junta of exiles opposed to Castro. Memo of second meeting of Green Study Group, at CIA, April 24, 1961, Aguilar, *Operation Zapata*, 65–66; Bundy to JFK, Feb. 8, 1961, *FRUS, X, Cuba, 1961–1962*, p. 89; Memo of meeting with JFK, Feb. 8, 1961, ibid., 90–91. By mid-February the Joint Chiefs had assessed the military plan and set D-Day for March 5. The president also emphasized that he favored reform in Latin America. Ibid.

20. Schlesinger to JFK, Feb. 11, 1961, *FRUS, X, Cuba, 1961–1962*, pp. 92–93; RFK, Oral History Interview, 1, p. 44, JFKL.

21. CIA paper prepared by Bissell, Feb. 17, 1961, ibid., 105–6.
22. Smathers testimony, July 23, 1975, pp. 6–7, 16–19, 25, CCH.
23. Ibid., 21–22; Beschloss, *Crisis Years*, 139; Christopher Andrew, *For the President's Eyes Only: Secret Intelligence and the American Presidency from Washington to Bush* (New York: HarperCollins, 1995), 263.
24. Gray called it the "CIA-Cuban Volunteer Task Force." Memo of second meeting of Green Study Group, April 24, 1961, Aguilar, *Operation Zapata*, 107; ibid., 83–84. The visit was from February 24–27 and approved on March 10. Memo of third meeting of Green Study Group, April 25, 1961, ibid., 134; Wheeler testimony in ninth meeting of Green Study Group, May 3, 1961, ibid., 206; Narrative of Anti-Castro Cuban Operation Zapata, June 13, 1961, ibid., 10–11; JCS to McNamara, Feb. 3, 1961, *FRUS, X, Cuba, 1961–1962*, p. 74; JCS to McNamara, March 10, 1961, ibid., 125.
25. Memo of fifth meeting of Green Study Group, April 27, 1961, Aguilar, *Operation Zapata*, 154–56.
26. CIA paper prepared by Bissell, March 11, 1961, *FRUS, X, Cuba, 1961–1962*, pp. 138–39.
27. Ibid., 141–42; Schlesinger, *Thousand Days*, 202.
28. White House meeting, March 11, 1961, ed. note, *FRUS, X, Cuba, 1961–1962*, p. 143; Narrative of Anti-Castro Cuban Operation Zapata, June 13, 1961, Aguilar, *Operation Zapata*, 11–13; Memo of second meeting of Green Study Group, April 24, 1961, ibid., 79; JFK quote in Burke, Oral History Interview, 24, JFKL; Schlesinger, *Thousand Days*, 203.
29. Lansdale, Oral History Interview, 9–10, JFKL; CIA paper prepared by Bissell, "Revised Cuban Operation," March 15, 1961, *FRUS, X, Cuba, 1961–1962*, p. 145; Narrative of Anti-Castro Cuban Operation Zapata, June 13, 1961, Aguilar, *Operation Zapata*, 13–14.
30. Wyden, *Bay of Pigs*, 105; Persons, *Bay of Pigs*, 52; Rodríguez, *Bay of Pigs and CIA*, 115; Higgins, *Perfect Failure*, 98; CIA paper prepared by Bissell, March 15, 1961, *FRUS, X, Cuba, 1961–1962*, pp. 146–47.
31. JCS to McNamara, March 15, 1961, *FRUS, X, Cuba, 1961–1962*, pp. 149–50; Appendix C, ibid., 154–55; Wyden, *Bay of Pigs*, 103; Memo of seventeenth meeting of Green Study Group, May 18, 1961, Aguilar, *Operation Zapata*, 316–17; Memo of ninth meeting of Green Study Group, May 3, 1961, ibid., 206–8; Narrative of Anti-Castro Cuban Operation Zapata, June 13, 1961, ibid., 13, 80. Bissell later declared that the "airfield requirement was what led us into Zapata." Ibid., 80.
32. Johnson, *Bay of Pigs*, 82; Wyden, *Bay of Pigs*, 102; Symmes, *Boys from Dolores*, 226.
33. Shoup testimony in twelfth meeting of Green Study Group, May 8, 1961, Aguilar, *Operation Zapata*, 243–44, 246–47.
34. Schlesinger to JFK, March 15, 1961, *FRUS, X, Cuba, 1961–1962*, p. 157.
35. Bundy to JFK, March 15, 1961, ibid., 158.
36. Schlesinger, *Thousand Days*, 203; Memo of second meeting of Green Study Group, April 24, 1961, Aguilar, *Operation Zapata*, 67; Memo of fourth

meeting of Green Study Group, April 26, 1961, ibid., 145. President Kennedy also approved the creation of a special Working Group assigned to coordinate all interdepartmental action within the Executive Branch. A week later, the Interdepartmental Task Force (IDTF) presented a paper that for the first time formalized the steps prepared by the Joint Staff and assigned to the various departments. The issues were so sensitive that the IDTF kept few written records and prohibited the distribution of papers discussed at its meetings. The IDTF was composed of State, Defense, and CIA representatives. Narrative of Anti-Castro Cuban Operation Zapata, June 13, 1961, ibid., 14–16; White House meeting, March 15, 1961, ed. note, *FRUS, X, Cuba, 1961–1962*, p. 159; White House meeting, March 16, 1961, ed. note, ibid., 160.

37. Bissell's view on Cuba, Feb. 17, 1961, National Security Files, box 35A, Cuba, General, JFKL; Bissell testimony, June 9, 1975, p. 12, CCH; Bissell, Oral History Interview, 25, 29–30, JFKL; Schlesinger, *Thousand Days*, 206–7, 209; RFK, Oral History Interview, 1, p. 57, JFKL.

38. Wyden, *Bay of Pigs*, 103; Higgins, *Perfect Failure*, 105–6; Rodríguez, *Bay of Pigs and CIA*, 115, 118–19; Johnson, Bay of Pigs, 82–83; Aguilar, *Operation Zapata*, xiii. The account did not identify the adviser. On Castro's helicopters, see Grayston Lynch, After Action Report on Operation, May 4, 1961, *FRUS, X, Cuba, 1961–1962*, p. 246.

39. RFK, Oral History Interview, 1, p. 58, JFKL; Pepe quotes in Johnson, *Bay of Pigs*, 224, 68*.

40. Memo of second meeting of Green Study Group, April 24, 1961, Aguilar, *Operation Zapata*, 68, 84, 109; Schlesinger, *Thousand Days*, 209.

41. Gray's statement in fourth meeting of Green Study Group, April 26, 1961, Aguilar, *Operation Zapata*, 143–44; Memo of second meeting of Green Study Group, April 24, 1961, ibid., 108–9; Gray's testimony in tenth meeting of Green Study Group, at Pentagon, May 4, 1961, ibid., 215. One other landing spot came under brief consideration—on the islands near the Isle of Pines. But Dulles later remarked that that proposal fell by the wayside when it became clear that rebel supporters in Cuba would have to swim out to the site to join the force. Ibid., 108.

42. Burke testimony in eighteenth meeting of Green Study Group, May 19, 1961, ibid., 343–45; Gray testimony in tenth meeting of Green Study Group, May 4, 1961, ibid., 213–14. For the questionable claim that the Joint Chiefs strongly favored the Trinidad Plan but that McNamara apparently never made this clear to the president, see L. James Binder, *Lemnitzer: A Soldier for His Time* (Washington: Brassey's, 1997), 263.

43. Memo of second meeting of Green Study Group, April 24, 1961, ibid., 85, 109–10.

44. Burke, Oral History Interview, 21–22, 24, JFKL; Bissell, Oral History Interview, 24–25, JFKL; Unsigned note for Bissell, May 10, 1961, Papers of Theodore Sorensen, Classified Subject Files, box 48, Cuba, General, JFKL; Helms testimony, June 13, p. 18, Sept. 12, 1975, p. 11, CCH; Johnson, *Bay of Pigs*, 104–5.

45. Schlesinger, *Thousand Days*, 196; Burke, Oral History Interview, 25, JFKL.
46. Bissell, Oral History Interview, 10, JFKL; Memo of second meeting of Green Study Group, April 24, 1961, Aguilar, *Operation Zapata*, 85.
47. White House meeting, March 17, 1961, ed. note, *FRUS, X, Cuba, 1961–1962*, p. 160.
48. Lynch, After Action Report on Operation, May 4, 1961, ibid., 238.
49. Dennison to Lemnitzer, March 28, 1961, ibid., 175–76.
50. Narrative of Anti-Castro Cuban Operation Zapata, June 13, 1961, Aguilar, *Operation Zapata*, 16; Schlesinger, *Thousand Days*, 198; Kirkpatrick, "Inspector General's Survey," 93–95.
51. Kirkpatrick, "Inspector General's Survey," 97; *U.S. News and World Report*, March 27, 1961, pp. 44, 45, cited in Trest and Dodd, *Wings of Denial*, 36–37.
52. Schlesinger, *Thousand Days*, 207–8; Kirkpatrick, "Inspector General's Survey," 95–97.
53. Unsigned memo (by Fulbright) on Cuba policy, March 29, 1961, pp. 1, 3–4, 6, 10, President's Office Files, box 114a, Countries, Cuba, General, JFKL.
54. Schlesinger, *Thousand Days*, 246; JFK and Acheson quoted in Richard Reeves, *President Kennedy: Profile of Power* (New York: Simon and Schuster, 1993), 76–77.
55. Tad Szulc and Karl E. Meyer, *The Cuban Invasion: The Chronicle of a Disaster* (New York: Ballantine Books, 1962); Schlesinger, *Thousand Days*, 218; Kornbluh, ed., *Bay of Pigs Declassified*, 2.
56. Bowles to Rusk, March 31, 1961, *FRUS, X, Cuba, 1961–1962*, pp. 178–80; Galbraith to JFK, April 3, 1961, James Goodman, ed., *Letters to Kennedy: John Kenneth Galbraith* (Cambridge: Harvard University Press, 1998), 64.
57. Meeting in DS, April 4, 1961, ed. note, *FRUS, X, Cuba, 1961–1962*, p. 185; Mann, Oral History Interview, 18, 20, JFKL; Berle quoted in Bissell, Oral History Interview, 27, JFKL. Robert Kennedy claimed that Fulbright eased his opposition in a subsequent meeting after the Joint Chiefs and others briefed him in more detail. RFK, Oral History Interview, 1, p. 44, JFKL.
58. Schlesinger to JFK, April 5, 1961, *FRUS, X, Cuba, 1961–1962*, pp. 186–87.
59. Schlesinger to JFK, April 10, 1961, ibid., 196–99, 202.
60. White House meeting, April 6, 1961, ed. note, ibid., 191–92; Narrative of Anti-Castro Cuban Operation Zapata, June 13, 1961, Aguilar, *Operation Zapata*, 16; Bowles quoted in Higgins, *Perfect Failure*, 108.
61. News stories cited in Wyden, *Bay of Pigs*, 154–55; JFK quoted ibid., 155. Pierre Salinger was the press secretary.
62. CIA paper prepared by Bissell, April 12, 1961, *FRUS, X, Cuba, 1961–1962*, pp. 214–15; Bissell briefing in Narrative of Anti-Castro Cuban Operation Zapata, June 13, 1961, Aguilar, *Operation Zapata*, 16–17. These air strike plans caused problems later because the instructions were verbal and unclear rather than written and signed as orders. Unidentified person's testimony in third meeting of Green Study Group, April 25, 1961, ibid., 130. The person called the instructions "fuzzy." Ibid.

63. White House meeting, April 12, 1961, ed. note, *FRUS, X, Cuba, 1961–1962*, p. 213; JFK at White House press conference, April 12, 1961, *Public Papers of the Presidents of the United States: John F. Kennedy, 1961* (Washington: GPO, 1962), 258; Higgins, *Perfect Failure*, 100; Johnson, *Bay of Pigs*, 72.

64. Bundy to Rusk, April 13, 1961, *FRUS, X, Cuba, 1961–1962*, p. 218; Lemnitzer to Dennison, April 13, 1961, ibid., 219.

65. Lemnitzer to Dennison, April 7, 1961, Encl. F, ibid., 194–95; White House meeting, April 5, 1961, ed. note, ibid., 190; Lemnitzer to Dennison, April 1, 1961, ibid., 182; Wheeler to Dennison, April 13, 1961, ibid., 220; Memo of second meeting of Green Study Group, April 24, 1961, Aguilar, *Operation Zapata*, 113; Higgins, *Perfect Failure*, 117, 138.

66. Rodríguez, *Bay of Pigs and CIA*, 149; Johnson, *Bay of Pigs*, 76, 80–81.

67. Kornbluh, ed., *Bay of Pigs Declassified*, 210, 258; Narrative of Anti-Castro Cuban Operation Zapata, June 13, 1961, Aguilar, *Operation Zapata*, 17; RFK, Oral History Interview, 1, p. 43, JFKL; Hawkins to Esterline, April 13, 1961, in CIA memo for Gen. Maxwell Taylor (then chair of Cuba Study Group discussed later), April 26, 1961, *FRUS, X, Cuba, 1961–1962*, pp. 221–22. Air Force Col. George Gaines thought the B-26 squadron "equal to the best U.S. Air Force squadron." Ibid., 222.

68. Dulles quoted in Theodore C. Sorensen, *Kennedy* (New York: Harper and Row, 1965), 296; RFK, Oral History Interview, 1, pp. 43–44, JFKL.

69. Schlesinger, *Thousand Days*, 225; Hawkins in Bohning, *Castro Obsession*, 39.

70. Persons, *Bay of Pigs*, 43, 45; Johnson, *Bay of Pigs*, 77.

71. Lynch, After Action Report, May 4, 1961, *FRUS, X, Cuba, 1961–1962*, p. 239; Schlesinger, *Thousand Days*, 225–26.

72. Lynch, After Action Report, May 4, 1961, *FRUS, X, Cuba, 1961–1962*, pp. 238–39.

73. Rodríguez, *Bay of Pigs and CIA*, 148–49; Higgins, *Perfect Failure*, 64, 128, 139, 149; Wyden, *Bay of Pigs*, 31, 56; Johnson, *Bay of Pigs*, 85–86; Bender quoted ibid., 85.

74. Memo of second meeting of Green Study Group, April 24, 1961, Aguilar, *Operation Zapata*, 80; Unidentified person's testimony, ibid., 95; Memo of third meeting of Green Study Group, April 25, 1961, ibid., 114, 133; Kirkpatrick, "Inspector General's Survey," 38–39; JCS to McNamara, Feb. 3, 1961, *FRUS, X, Cuba, 1961–1962*, p. 70.

75. Rodríguez, *Bay of Pigs and CIA*, 150.

76. Burke, Oral History Interview, 21, JFKL; Memo of second meeting of Green Study Group, April 24, 1961, Aguilar, *Operation Zapata*, 88, 114; Schlesinger, *Thousand Days*, 190; Schlesinger to JFK, March 20, 1961, *FRUS, X, Cuba, 1961–1962*, p. 162; Barnes to Dulles, March 21, 1961, ibid., 164; Trest and Dodd, *Wings of Denial*, 58–59; Johnson, *Bay of Pigs*, 26, 30; Rodríguez, *Bay of Pigs and CIA*, 24–25; Triay, *Bay of Pigs*, 9.

77. Persons, *Bay of Pigs*, 48–49.

CHAPTER 4. POLITICS

1. Ferrer, *Puma*, 136; Lynch, *Decision for Disaster*, 124; Lemnitzer testimony in seventeenth meeting of Green Study Group, May 18, 1961, Aguilar, *Operation Zapata*, 313–17, 320–21.

2. Memo of conversation between Taylor and unidentified air commander, May 6, 1961, Aguilar, *Operation Zapata*, 233; Memo of eighteenth meeting of Green Study Group, May 19, 1961, ibid., 346; Ferrer, *Puma*, 143; Bissell, *Reflections of Cold Warrior*, 171.

3. Burke testimony in eighteenth meeting of Green Study Group, May 19, 1961, Aguilar, *Operation Zapata*, 346–47; Persons, *Bay of Pigs*, 50, 60; Lynch, *Decision for Disaster*, 75; Ferrer, *Puma*, 135–36. Castro also had three C-47 transports, a single amphibious PBY, several smaller planes, and the potentially deadly though not yet functional Soviet MIGs. Ibid., 136.

4. Ferrer, *Puma*, 132, 140; Persons, *Bay of Pigs*, 49–50.

5. Persons, *Bay of Pigs*, 50–51.

6. Triay, *Bay of Pigs*, 68; Kornbluh's interview of Hawkins and Esterline, Oct. 10, 1996, Kornbluh, ed., *Bay of Pigs Declassified*, 263; Bohning, *Castro Obsession*, 32; Bohning e-mail to author, June 24, 2007.

7. Bohning, *Castro Obsession*, 31–34; Bohning e-mail to author, June 24, 2007. In his book, Bohning quotes from a letter from Hawkins dated August 27, 2001.

8. Kornbluh's interview of Hawkins and Esterline, Oct. 10, 1996, Kornbluh, ed., *Bay of Pigs Declassified*, 263–64.

9. Bohning e-mail to author, June 24, 2007; Bissell, *Reflections of Cold Warrior*, 183; CIA paper, April 12, 1961, *FRUS, X, Cuba, 1961–1962*, p. 214.

10. Bohning, *Castro Obsession*, 36–37.

11. Persons, *Bay of Pigs*, 49–50; Kirkpatrick, "Inspector General's Survey," 38; Ferrer, *Puma*, 140. The two men killed in action were Capt. Daniel Fernández-Mon and Navigator Gastón Pérez. Ibid., 153–54.

12. Operations Center, April 15, 1961, ed. note, *FRUS, X, Cuba, 1961–1962*, p. 227; Johnson, *Bay of Pigs*, 85, 95; Triay, *Bay of Pigs*, 69; Rodríguez, *Bay of Pigs and CIA*, 155–58.

13. Narrative of Anti-Castro Cuban Operation Zapata, June 13, 1961, Aguilar, *Operation Zapata*, 18; Ferrer, *Puma*, 150–51, 157, 161; Memo by Col. Stanley W. Beerli of U.S. Air Force, April 15, 1961, *FRUS, X, Cuba, 1961–1962*, pp. 227–28; Rodríguez, *Bay of Pigs and CIA*, 151.

14. Memo of conversation between Taylor and unidentified air commander, May 6, 1961, Aguilar, *Operation Zapata*, 234; Doster quoted in Ferrer, *Puma*, 162.

15. Narrative of Anti-Castro Cuban Operation Zapata, June 13, 1961, Aguilar, *Operation Zapata*, 18; Memo of conversation between Taylor and unidentified air commander, May 6, 1961, ibid., 128, 234; Memo for Record, April 16, 1961, *FRUS, X, Cuba, 1961–1962*, p. 232; Persons, *Bay of Pigs*, 50; Kirkpatrick, "Inspector General's Survey," 37.

16. Johnson, *Bay of Pigs*, 91–92; Kornbluh, ed., *Bay of Pigs Declassified*, 304; Rodríguez, *Bay of Pigs and CIA*, 133; Castro communiqué from Havana, April 15, 1961, ed. note, *FRUS, X, Cuba, 1961–1962*, pp. 228–29.

17. UN General Assembly discussion, April 15, 1961, ed. note, *FRUS, X, Cuba, 1961–1962*, p. 229; Johnson, *Bay of Pigs*, 92.

18. Higgins, *Perfect Failure*, 130–31; Bohning, *Castro Obsession*, 43; Evan Thomas, *The Very Best Men: Four Who Dared: The Early Years of the CIA* (New York: Simon and Schuster, 1995), 205; Kornbluh, ed., *Bay of Pigs Declassified*, 2–3, 18 n.3; Ferrer, *Puma*, 160.

19. Stevenson to Rusk and Dulles, April 16, 1961, *FRUS, X, Cuba, 1961–1962*, p. 230; ibid., 230 n.1; Bissell, *Reflections of Cold Warrior*, 183; Wyden, *Bay of Pigs*, 189.

20. Johnson, *Bay of Pigs*, 95–96; Castro quoted 96; Symmes, *Boys from Dolores*, 224; Kornbluh, ed., *Bay of Pigs Declassified*, 4.

21. Narrative of Anti-Castro Cuban Operation Zapata, June 13, 1961, Aguilar, *Operation Zapata*, 18; Johnson, *Bay of Pigs*, 65–66; Adam B. Ulam, *The Rivals: America and Russia Since World War II* (New York: Viking, 1971), 319; Schlesinger, *Thousand Days*, 215–16.

22. McNamara testimony in ninth meeting of Green Study Group, May 3, 1961, Aguilar, *Operation Zapata*, 200–201. In arguing for military escalation in Vietnam in July 1965, McNamara declared it might "stave off defeat in the short run and offer a good chance of producing a favorable settlement in the longer run." George C. Herring, *America's Longest War: The United States and Vietnam, 1950–1975* (Boston: McGraw-Hill, 1979; 4th ed., 2002), 164.

23. McNamara testimony in ninth meeting of Green Study Group, May 3, 1961, Aguilar, *Operation Zapata*, 202–3; Tim Weiner, *Legacy of Ashes: The History of the CIA* (New York: Doubleday, 2007), 173.

24. Kornbluh's interview of Hawkins and Esterline, Oct. 1996, Kornbluh, ed., *Bay of Pigs Declassified*, 263; Bissell, *Reflections of Cold Warrior*, 184.

25. Narrative of Anti-Castro Cuban Operation Zapata, June 13, 1961, Aguilar, *Operation Zapata*, 20; Higgins, *Perfect Failure*, 132–33; Charles P. Cabell, ed., *Memoirs of War, Peace, and the CIA* (Colorado Springs, Colo.: Impavide Publications, 1997), 366; Kirkpatrick, "Inspector General's Survey," 38.

26. Bundy to Taylor, May 4, 1961, in tenth meeting of Green Study Group, Aguilar, *Operation Zapata*, 179; Johnson, *Bay of Pigs*, 96–97; Higgins, *Perfect Failure*, 132.

27. Cabell, *Memoirs*, 364, 366; Narrative of Anti-Castro Cuban Operation Zapata, June 13, 1961, Aguilar, *Operation Zapata*, 20. Several writers consider the decision to call off the D-Day strikes a major factor in the invasion's failure. See, for example, Bohning, *Castro Obsession*, 13; Lynch, *Decision for Disaster*, 77–79; and Persons, *Bay of Pigs*, 97. Capt. Edward Ferrer of the rebel air force criticized President Kennedy for moving the invasion site from Trinidad to

Zapata, and canceling all air strikes after the first phase of the D-2 operation. The latter decision "doomed the invasion to failure." Ferrer, *Puma*, 233–35.

28. Cabell, *Memoirs*, 366–67.
29. Lynch, *Decision for Disaster*, 77–78; Bissell, *Reflections of Cold Warrior*, 186; Cabell, *Memoirs*, 370; Narrative of Anti-Castro Cuban Operation Zapata, June 13, 1961, Aguilar, *Operation Zapata*, 20.
30. Cabell, *Memoirs*, 360, 371–72.
31. Ibid., 372–73.
32. Ibid., 373–74; Cabell to Taylor, May 9, 1961, *FRUS, X, Cuba, 1961–1962*, pp. 236–37.
33. Cabell, *Memoirs*, 374; Narrative of Anti-Castro Cuban Operation Zapata, Aguilar, *Operation Zapata*, 20–21.
34. Lyman Kirkpatrick, Oral History Interview, 10, JFKL; Bissell, *Reflections of Cold Warrior*, 185.
35. Shoup, Oral History Interview, 16, JFKL; Howard Jablon, *David M. Shoup: A Warrior Against War* (Lanham, Md.: Rowman and Littlefield, 2005), 79–80.
36. Kirkpatrick, Oral History Interview, April 26, 1967, p. 11, JFKL.
37. CIA Paper, "Cuban Operation," April 12, 1961, *FRUS, X, Cuba, 1961–1962*, p. 215; Cabell, *Memoirs*, 376.
38. Lynch, *Decision for Disaster*, 79; Narrative of Anti-Castro Cuban Operation Zapata, June 13, 1961, Aguilar, *Operation Zapata*, 21.
39. Narrative of Anti-Castro Cuban Operation Zapata, June 13, 1961, Aguilar, *Operation Zapata*, 21.
40. Ibid.; Memo of third meeting of Green Study Group, April 25, 1961, ibid., 131; Cabell, *Memoirs*, 376–77.
41. Bissell, *Reflections of Cold Warrior*, 184; Bissell, Oral History Interview, 38, JFKL.
42. Cabell, *Memoirs*, 384–85.
43. Rusk testimony in tenth meeting of Green Study Group, May 4, 1961, Aguilar, *Operation Zapata*, 221–22.
44. Memo of third meeting of Green Study Group, April 25, 1961, ibid., 130.
45. Ed. note, White House meeting, April 12, 1961, *FRUS, X, Cuba, 1961–1962*, pp. 213–14; Bissell, *Reflections of Cold Warrior*, 183.
46. Bundy testimony in seventh meeting of Green Study Group, May 1, 1961, Aguilar, *Operation Zapata*, 181; Rusk testimony in tenth meeting of Green Study Group, May 4, 1961, ibid., 223.
47. Memo for Record (probably by Taylor) of president's luncheon meeting with Cuban Study Group (Taylor, RFK, Burke, Dulles), May 16, 1961, *FRUS, X, Cuba, 1961–1962*, p. 526; Memo by Burke of same, ibid., 528.
48. Edwards testimony before Rockefeller Commission, Belin, "Investigation of CIA Involvement," 14, CCH; Edwards testimony, May 30, 1975, p. 12, CCH; IG Report, 27–28; Maheu testimony, July 29, 1975, pp. 42–44, 60–61, CCH; words "cold feet" in both Roselli testimony, June 24, 1975, p. 24, CCH, and

Maheu testimony, July 29, 1975, p. 33, CCH. Orta returned the pills. O'Connell testimony, May 30, 1975, p. 44, CCH. When Venezuela and Cuba broke relations in November, Orta secured refuge in the Mexican embassy until Castro permitted him to leave for Mexico in 1964. Orta moved to Miami in February 1965. IG Report, 28; Trafficante testimony, Oct. 7, 1976, p. 3, CCII; Gerardo Reyes, "From Aide to Assassin Plotter," *Miami Herald*, July 8, 2007 (posted online); "Castro Says U.S.-Mafia Assassin Had Little Chance," *Reuters India*, July 8, 2007; "Castro Says US Assassin Lacked Access," *Boston Globe*, July 9, 2007 (Reuters, posted online); Bohning, *Castro Obsession*, 179.

49. Belin, "Investigation of CIA Involvement," 15, CCH; Breckinridge in Colby testimony, May 21, 1975, pp. 60–61, CCH; Ted Shackley, with Richard A. Finney, *Spymaster: My Life in the CIA* (Dulles, Va.: Potomac Books, 2005), 57. See also David Corn, *Blond Ghost: Ted Shackley and the CIA's Crusades* (New York: Simon and Schuster, 1994), 118–19.

50. Elder to Bundy, April 13, 1961, encl.: UPI article of April 13, 1961, in President's Office Files, box 114a, Countries, Cuba, General, JFKL.

51. For the president's March 1961 discussion with Smathers, see chapter 3. On this point of assassination, see Beschloss, *Crisis Years*, 139.

52. Halpern interview, April 7, 1998, pp. 5–6, CIA Misc. Files, box 9, JFK-M-10 (F3) Halpern (NA). Halpern was on two CIA committees promoting Castro's collapse.

53. Hawkins quoted in Bohning, *Castro Obsession*, 39–40. Hawkins' reference to an earlier attempt to stop the invasion meant the April 9 meeting, which Bissell never acknowledged as having taken place. Kornbluh's interview of Hawkins, Oct. 10, 1996, Kornbluh, ed., *Bay of Pigs Declassified*, 262.

54. Lemnitzer testimony in seventeenth meeting of Green Study Group, May 18, 1961, Aguilar, *Operation Zapata*, 327.

55. Dulles, Oral History Interview, 28, JFKL. For an example of the traditional story, see Taylor, Oral History Interview, 3, JFKL.

56. President's press conference of Jan. 1963 in *Public Papers of the Presidents of the United States: John F. Kennedy, 1963* (Washington: GPO, 1964), 92.

CHAPTER 5. D-DAY

1. Kornbluh, ed., *Bay of Pigs Declassified*, 38–39, 87–88.

2. Ferrer, *Puma*, 144–45; Wyden, *Bay of Pigs*, 131; Rodríguez, *Bay of Pigs and CIA*, 10–11, 84; Lynch, *Decision for Disaster*, 26.

3. Kirkpatrick, "Inspector General's Survey," 38, 84, 88; Johnson, *Bay of Pigs*, 86, 97, 103; Ferrer, *Puma*, 145; Rodríguez, *Bay of Pigs and CIA*, 149.

4. Ferrer, *Puma*, 105, 145.

5. Ibid., 143–44; Cuba Study Group to JFK, June 13, 1961, *FRUS, X, Cuba, 1961–1962*, p. 597.

6. Cuba Study Group to JFK, June 13, 1961, *FRUS, X, Cuba, 1961–1962*, p. 597.

7. Ibid., 599; Rodríguez, *Bay of Pigs and CIA*, 22; Wheeler testimony in ninth meeting of Green Study Group, May 3, 1961, Aguilar, *Operation Zapata*, 209;

Memo of sixth meeting of Green Study Group, April 28, 1961, ibid., 165. The two officers were Air Force lieutenant colonel George Gaines and Navy captain Jacob Scapa. Ibid.

8. Unidentified foreign intelligence officer in DS, in ninth meeting of Green Study Group, May 3, 1961, Aguilar, *Operation Zapata*, 199–200.

9. Johnson, *Bay of Pigs*, 110, 113–14; Ferrer, *Puma*, 167–68; Kirkpatrick, "Inspector General's Survey," 39.

10. Wyden, *Bay of Pigs*, 131; Rodríguez, *Bay of Pigs and CIA*, 7; Lynch, *Decision for Disaster*, 83–84; Kirkpatrick, "Inspector General's Survey," 39.

11. Lynch, *Decision for Disaster*, v, xv, 50, 187; Wyden, *Bay of Pigs*, 83–84; Higgins, *Perfect Failure*, 34; Johnson, *Bay of Pigs*, 106; Lynch, After Action Report, May 4, 1961, *FRUS*, X, *Cuba, 1961–1962*, p. 238.

12. Gray quoted in Lynch, *Decision for Disaster*, 83; ibid., 84; Johnson, *Bay of Pigs*, 83, 103–4; Lynch, After Action Report, May 4, 1961, *FRUS*, X, *Cuba, 1961–1962*, pp. 239–40; Memo of sixth meeting of Green Study Group, April 28, 1961, Aguilar, *Operation Zapata*, 161.

13. Wyden, *Bay of Pigs*, 219; Lynch, *Decision for Disaster*, 85, 87; Lynch, After Action Report, May 4, 1961, *FRUS*, X, *Cuba, 1961–1962*, p. 240; Rodríguez, *Bay of Pigs and CIA*, 166–67.

14. Lynch, After Action Report, May 4, 1961, *FRUS*, X, *Cuba, 1961–1962*, p. 240; Lynch, *Decision for Disaster*, 85–86.

15. Bissell quoted in John J. Nutter, *The CIA's Black Ops: Covert Action, Foreign Policy, and Democracy* (Amherst, N.Y.: Prometheus Books, 2000), 17; Johnson, *Bay of Pigs*, 103.

16. Quotes in Lynch, *Decision for Disaster*, 88; Wyden, *Bay of Pigs*, 221.

17. Johnson, *Bay of Pigs*, 104; Narrative of Anti-Castro Cuban Operation Zapata, June 13, 1961, Aguilar, *Operation Zapata*, 21–22; Lynch, *Decision for Disaster*, 88; Lynch, After Action Report, May 4, 1961, *FRUS*, X, *Cuba, 1961–1962*, p. 241; Wyden, *Bay of Pigs*, 221.

18. Memo of sixth meeting of Green Study Group, April 28, 1961, Aguilar, *Operation Zapata*, 161; Lynch, *Decision for Disaster*, 86, 89; Wyden, *Bay of Pigs*, 220; Johnson, *Bay of Pigs*, 105; Lynch, After Action Report, May 4, 1961, *FRUS*, X, *Cuba, 1961–1962*, p. 241.

19. Rodríguez, *Bay of Pigs and CIA*, 159–61; Johnson, *Bay of Pigs*, 109–10; Symmes, *Boys from Dolores*, 227.

20. Ferrer, *Puma*, 178, 180; Memo of sixth meeting of Green Study Group, April 28, 1961, Aguilar, *Operation Zapata*, 161; Pepe testimony in sixteenth meeting of Green Study Group, May 17, 1961, ibid., 290; Lynch, *Decision for Disaster*, 107–8; Lynch, After Action Report, May 4, 1961, *FRUS*, X, *Cuba, 1961–1962*, p. 241.

21. Lynch, After Action Report, May 4, 1961, *FRUS*, X, *Cuba, 1961–1962*, p. 242; Lynch, *Decision for Disaster*, 108–111.

22. Ferrer, *Puma*, 185; Lynch, *Decision for Disaster*, 108–12; Lynch, After Action Report, May 4, 1961, *FRUS*, X, *Cuba, 1961–1962*, pp. 241–42.

23. Narrative of Anti-Castro Cuban Operation Zapata, June 13, 1961, Aguilar, *Operation Zapata*, 22–24; Memo of second meeting of Green Study Group, April 24, 1961, ibid., 96; Testimony of Armando López-Estrada of 1st Airborne Battalion in sixteenth meeting of Green Study Group, May 17, 1961, ibid., 296; Johnson, *Bay of Pigs*, 112, 114.

24. Narrative of Anti-Castro Cuban Operation Zapata, June 13, 1961, Aguilar, *Operation Zapata*, 22; Memo of third meeting of Green Study Group, April 25, 1961, ibid., 131; Pepe testimony in sixteenth meeting of Green Study Group, May 17, 1961, ibid., 290–91; Memo of sixth meeting of Green Study Group, April 28, 1961, ibid., 161; Lynch, *Decision for Disaster*, 88, 109.

25. Narrative of Anti-Castro Cuban Operation Zapata, June 13, 1961, Aguilar, *Operation Zapata*, 22; Memo of seventh meeting of Green Study Group, May 1, 1961, ibid., 171; testimony of [?] Royorosa of Underwater Demolition Team in sixteenth meeting of Green Study Group, May 17, 1961, ibid., 297, 299–300.

26. Pepe testimony in sixteenth meeting of Green Study Group, May 17, 1961, Aguilar, *Operation Zapata*, 291; Narrative of Anti-Castro Cuban Operation Zapata, June 13, 1961, ibid., 23; Lopez-Estrada testimony in sixteenth meeting of Green Study Group, May 17, 1961, ibid., 301.

27. Lynch, *Decision for Disaster*, 92–93.

28. Ibid., 93; Testimony by one of those on board the *Barbara J*, in eighth meeting of Green Study Group, May 2, 1961, Aguilar, *Operation Zapata*, 184–85; Lynch, After Action Report, May, 4, 1961, *FRUS, X, Cuba, 1961–1962*, pp. 246–47; William Robertson, After Action Report, May 4, 1961, ibid., 250–51; Johnson, *Bay of Pigs*, 106; Rodríguez, *Bay of Pigs and CIA*, 16.

29. Johnson, *Bay of Pigs*, 106; Kirkpatrick, "Inspector General's Survey," 98; Wyden, *Bay of Pigs*, 86; Rodríguez, *Bay of Pigs and CIA*, 86.

30. Memo of eighth meeting of Green Study Group, May 2, 1961, Aguilar, *Operation Zapata*, 187; Testimony of Rómulo Betancourt, air liaison officer with 2nd Battalion at Red Beach, in sixteenth meeting of Green Study Group, May 17, 1961, ibid., 303; Narrative of Anti-Castro Cuban Operation Zapata, June 13, 1961, 23; Robertson, After Action Report, May 4, 1961, *FRUS, X, Cuba, 1961–1962*, p. 251.

31. Narrative of Anti-Castro Cuban Operation Zapata, June 13, 1961, Aguilar, *Operation Zapata*, 23; Betancourt testimony in sixteenth meeting of Green Study Group, May 17, 1961, ibid., 304; Robertson quoted in Lynch, *Decision for Disaster*, 94–95; Robertson, After Action Report, May 4, 1961, *FRUS, X, Cuba, 1961–1962*, p. 251.

32. Memo of eighth meeting of Green Study Group, May 2, 1961, Aguilar, *Operation Zapata*, 187; Robertson, After Action Report, May 4, 1961, *FRUS, X, Cuba, 1961–1962*, p. 251; Wyden, *Bay of Pigs*, 222.

33. Narrative of Anti-Castro Cuban Operation Zapata, June 13, 1961, Aguilar, *Operation Zapata*, 23; Memo of third meeting of Green Study Group, April 25, 1961, ibid., 132; Memo of eighth meeting of Green Study Group, May 2, 1961, ibid., 185–86; Wyden, *Bay of Pigs*, 228–29; Betancourt testimony in sixteenth

meeting of Green Study Group, May 17, 1961, ibid., 305; Persons, *Bay of Pigs*, 52; Robertson, After Action Report, May 4, 1961, *FRUS, X, Cuba, 1961–1962*, pp. 251–53; Lynch, After Action Report, May 4, 1961, ibid., 242, 248–49.

34. Wyden, *Bay of Pigs*, 229–30; Narrative of Anti-Castro Cuban Operation Zapata, June 13, 1961, Aguilar, *Operation Zapata*, 22; Lynch, After Action Report, May 4, 1961, *FRUS, X, Cuba, 1961–1962*, p. 242; Lynch, *Decision for Disaster*, 113–14.

35. Lynch, After Action Report, May 4, 1961, *FRUS, X, Cuba, 1961–1962*, p. 242; Wyden, *Bay of Pigs*, 230, 255.

36. Narrative of Anti-Castro Cuban Operation Zapata, June 13, 1961, Aguilar, *Operation Zapata*, 23–24; Memo of third meeting of Green Study Group, April 25, 1961, ibid., 132; Kirkpatrick, "Inspector General's Survey," 40.

37. Johnson, *Bay of Pigs*, 114, 131.

38. Memo of eighth meeting of Green Study Group, May 2, 1961, Aguilar, *Operation Zapata*, 187; Narrative of Anti-Castro Cuban Operation Zapata, June 13, 1961, ibid., 22; Robertson, After Action Report, May 4, 1961, *FRUS, X, Cuba, 1961–1962*, p. 254; Lynch, *Decision for Disaster*, 114; Crutchfield quoted ibid., 116; Wyden, *Bay of Pigs*, 231; Rodríguez, *Bay of Pigs and CIA*, 141.

39. Lynch, After Action Report, May 4, 1961, *FRUS, X, Cuba, 1961–1962*, p. 243; Unidentified testimony in eighth meeting of Green Study Group, May 2, 1961, Aguilar, *Operation Zapata*, 191; Narrative of Anti-Castro Cuban Operation Zapata, June 13, 1961, ibid., 25; Lynch, *Decision for Disaster*, 120–21; Wyden, *Bay of Pigs*, 232; Trest and Dodd, *Wings of Denial*, 75; Johnson, *Bay of Pigs*, 129.

40. Robertson, After Action Report, May 4, 1961, *FRUS, X, Cuba, 1961–1962*, p. 255.

41. Narrative of Anti-Castro Cuban Operation Zapata, June 13, 1961, Aguilar, *Operation Zapata*, 23–24; Memo of third meeting of Green Study Group, April 25, 1961, ibid., 132; Kirkpatrick, "Inspector General's Survey," 40.

42. Memo of third meeting of Green Study Group, April 25, 1961, *Operation Zapata*, 135; Sorensen, *Kennedy*, 300; Cabell, *Memoirs*, 379.

43. Narrative of Anti-Castro Cuban Operation Zapata, June 13, 1961, Aguilar, *Operation Zapata*, 24; Memo of third meeting of Green Study Group, April 25, 1961, ibid., 135; Memo of conversation between Taylor and unidentified air commander in eleventh meeting of Green Study Group, May 6, 1961, ibid., 234; Lynch, *Decision for Disaster*, 125–26.

44. Narrative of Anti-Castro Cuban Operation Zapata, June 13, 1961, Aguilar, *Operation Zapata*, 24; Memo of third meeting of Green Study Group, April 25, 1961, ibid., 128, 134–35; Kirkpatrick, "Inspector General's Survey," 40; Wyden, *Bay of Pigs*, 203; Lynch, *Decision for Disaster*, 75, 116; Lynch, After Action Report, May 4, 1961, *FRUS, X, Cuba, 1961–1962*, p. 242; Bissell testimony on T-33s in Memo for Record, April 26, 1961, ibid., 369; Ferrer, *Puma*, 135–36; Persons, *Bay of Pigs*, 50.

45. Rodríguez, *Bay of Pigs and CIA*, 57, 60, 168, 173–75, 181; Bohning to author, April 15, 2008; Johnson, *Bay of Pigs*, 84–85, 115, 116, 120–21.

46. Johnson, *Bay of Pigs*, 168; Persons, *Bay of Pigs*, 53.

CHAPTER 6. REQUIEM

1. Narrative of Anti-Castro Cuban Operation Zapata, June 13, 1961, Aguilar, *Operation Zapata*, 25–26; Memo of third meeting of Green Study Group, April 25, 1961, ibid., 132; Lynch, *Decision for Disaster*, 124.

2. Pepe testimony in sixteenth meeting of Green Study Group, May 17, 1961, Aguilar, *Operation Zapata*, 291–93; Memo of third meeting of Green Study Group, April 25, 1961, ibid., 133; Narrative of Anti-Castro Cuban Operation Zapata, June 13, 1961, ibid., 26.

3. Estrada testimony in sixteenth meeting of Green Study Group, May 17, 1961, ibid., 296; Rodríguez, *Bay of Pigs and CIA*, 195; Symmes, *Boys from Dolores*, 234.

4. Narrative of Anti-Castro Cuban Operation Zapata, June 13, 1961, Aguilar, *Operation Zapata*, 25; Commander McGriffin's testimony in seventh meeting of Green Study Group, May 1, 1961, ibid., 167–68; Robertson, After Action Report, May 4, 1961, *FRUS, X, Cuba, 1961–1962*, p. 252.

5. CIA to its personnel in Nicaragua, April 18, 1961, *FRUS, X, Cuba, 1961–1962*, p. 287; Kirkpatrick, "Inspector General's Survey," 40, 98; Persons, *Bay of Pigs*, 53; Narrative of Anti-Castro Cuban Operation Zapata, June 13, 1961, Aguilar, *Operation Zapata*, 26–27; Lynch, *Decision for Disaster*, 126.

6. Memo of seventeenth meeting of Green Study Group, May 18, 1961, Aguilar, *Operation Zapata*, 329–30.

7. Memo of seventh meeting of Green Study Group, May 1, 1961, ibid., 168.

8. Khrushchev to JFK, encl. in U.S. embassy in Moscow to DS, April 18, 1961, *FRUS, X, Cuba, 1961–1962*, pp. 264–65; JFK to Khrushchev, April 18, 1961, ibid., 283–84.

9. Memo of conversation regarding cabinet meeting, April 18, 1961, ibid., 274; Bundy to JFK, April 18, 1961, President's Office Files, box 114a, Countries, Cuba, General, JFKL; Gen. Earle Wheeler, Oral History Interview, 17, JFKL.

10. Memo of conversation regarding cabinet meeting, April 18, 1961, *FRUS, X, Cuba, 1961–1962*, pp. 274–75; Wheeler, Oral History Interview, 17, JFKL.

11. Memo of conversation regarding cabinet meeting, April 18, 1961, *FRUS, X, Cuba, 1961–1962*, pp. 275, 275 n.5.

12. Burke's directive in Gray to Dennison and Clark, April 18, 1961, ibid., 275–76; Burke to Dennison, April 18, 1961, ibid., 277.

13. Clark to Dennison, April 18, 1961, ibid., 278.

14. Dennison to Neil H. McElroy, Commander of Key West Forces, April 18, 1961, ibid., 279; Dennison to JCS, April 18, 1961, ibid., 281; JFK quoted in Lynch, *Decision for Disaster*, 128; Burke quoted in Ferrer, *Puma*, 210.

15. Narrative of Anti-Castro Cuban Operation Zapata, June 13, 1961, Aguilar, *Operation Zapata*, 32.

16. Ferrer, *Puma*, 210.
17. Clark to Dennison, April 18, 1961, *FRUS, X, Cuba, 1961–1962*, p. 279.
18. Ibid., 287; Kirkpatrick, "Inspector General's Survey," 40.
19. Kirkpatrick, "Inspector General's Survey," 40; Narrative of Anti-Castro Cuban Operation Zapata, June 13, 1961, Aguilar, *Operation Zapata*, 27–29, 31, 32; Memo of third meeting of Green Study Group, April 25, 1961, ibid., 133, 135.
20. Narrative of Anti-Castro Cuban Operation Zapata, June 13, 1961, Aguilar, *Operation Zapata*, 28, 32–33; Unidentified person quoted in Kirkpatrick, Oral History Interview, 13, JFKL; JCS to Dennison, April 19, 1961, *FRUS, X, Cuba, 1961–1962*, p. 290.
21. Burke to Dennison, April 19, 1961, *FRUS, X, Cuba, 1961–1962*, p. 291; Narrative of Anti-Castro Cuban Operation Zapata, June 13, 1961, Aguilar, *Operation Zapata*, 31.
22. Trest and Dodd, *Wings of Denial*, 11–13; Memo of second meeting of Green Study Group, April 24, 1961, Aguilar, *Operation Zapata*, 121; Lynch, *Decision for Disaster*, 129. Cuban Gonzalo Herrera commanded the B-26 that hit San Blas. Ibid. See also Ferrer, *Puma*, 213–16.
23. Trest and Dodd, *Wings of Denial*, 13; Lynch, *Decision for Disaster*, 129.
24. Lynch, *Decision for Disaster*, 129. The two Americans killed near Playa Larga were Capt. Thomas Willard "Pete" Ray and Navigator Leo Francis Baker. Ibid. Trest and Dodd argue that the other two Americans, Major Riley Shamburger and Navigator Wade Gray, perished in the fiery crash into the water. *Wings of Denial*, 85. Two other writers, both pilots at the time, agree. See Persons (American), *Bay of Pigs*, 2, and Ferrer (Cuban), *Puma*, 215–16. But Lynch's argument about their execution is more persuasive. A CIA study was noncommittal. See Kirkpatrick, "Inspector General's Survey," 40, 98. The four American deaths remained secret for years, although all pilots knew they were operating under U.S. auspices. The pilots kept this knowledge from their families, just as Washington's officials concealed this information from the families in the course of resolving legal and moral claims. Ibid., 98–99.
25. RFK to Kenneth P. O'Donnell (JFK's aide), April 19, 1961, President's Office File, box 114a, Countries, Cuba, General, JFKL. Not until almost two years later did Robert Kennedy admit that the CIA had planned the invasion and that the administration had approved it. Trest and Dodd, *Wings of Denial*, 96.
26. Trest and Dodd, *Wings of Denial*, 83; Kirkpatrick, Oral History Interview, 13, JFKL; Lynch, *Decision for Disaster*, 129; Schlesinger, *Thousand Days*, 233; Ferrer, *Puma*, 218; Narrative of Anti-Castro Cuban Operation Zapata, June 13, 1961, Aguilar, *Operation Zapata*, 29; Searcy quoted in interview with Wyden. See Wyden's work, *Bay of Pigs*, 299.
27. Esterline's memo (containing Hawkins' concurrence) to Bohning, Dec. 15, 1998. I want to thank Don Bohning for sharing this memo with me. The interpretation regarding Bissell's responsibility is mine.
28. Persons, *Bay of Pigs*, 63.

29. Gray's briefing before JCS, April 19, 1961, ed. note, *FRUS, X, Cuba, 1961–1962*, pp. 291–92; Clark to Dennison, April 19, 1961, ibid., 292.

30. Lemnitzer testimony in seventeenth meeting of Green Study Group, May 18, 1961, Aguilar, *Operation Zapata*, 330.

31. McGriffin testimony in seventh meeting of Green Study Group, May 1, 1961, ibid., 168; Pepe testimony in sixteenth meeting of Green Study Group, May 17, 1961, ibid., 293; CIA officers in Nicaragua to CIA, April 19, 1961, *FRUS, X, Cuba, 1961–1962*, p. 298.

32. Clark to Dennison, April 19, 1961, *FRUS, X, Cuba, 1961–1962*, p. 294 n.1, top of page; ibid., 294 n.1, bottom of page; Lynch, After Action Report, May 4, 1961, ibid., 245; Kirkpatrick, "Inspector General's Survey," 41.

33. Clark to Dennison, April 19, 1961, *FRUS, X, Cuba, 1961–1962*, p. 300; Lynch, *Decision for Disaster*, 55, 66, 67.

34. Clark to Dennison, April 19, 1961, *FRUS, X, Cuba, 1961–1962*, p. 301; Kirkpatrick, "Inspector General's Survey," 41.

35. Betancourt testimony in sixteenth meeting of Green Study Group, May 17, 1961, Aguilar, *Operation Zapata*, 309–10. Betancourt did not identify the type of aircraft.

36. Memo of seventh meeting of Green Study Group, May 1, 1961, ibid., 168; JCS to Dennison, April 19, 1961, *FRUS, X, Cuba, 1961–1962*, 302; Lynch, After Action Report, May 4, 1961, ibid., 245–46; Kirkpatrick, "Inspector General's Survey," 41.

37. Clark to Dennison, April 19, 1961, *FRUS, X, Cuba, 1961–1962*, p. 300; Kornbluh, ed., *Bay of Pigs Declassified*, 2–3; Ferrer, *Puma*, 203–4, 218; Aguilar, *Operation Zapata*, xiv; Higgins, *Perfect Failure*, 176; Triay, *Bay of Pigs*, 6. A Cuban Military Tribunal sentenced the prisoners to thirty years of hard labor for treason but set ransom at $62 million. Verdict by Cuban Military Tribunal, April 8, 1962, *FRUS, X, Cuba, 1961–1962*, ed. note, 783. Castro rejected a proposed settlement of $26 million in food as a violation of the tribunal's stipulated amount. Rusk to JFK, April 18, 1962, ibid., 794. A late December 1962 agreement led to the release of the captives for a $53 million ransom in food and drugs. The final twenty-five Americans in Cuba did not leave until the spring of 1963. *FRUS, 1961–1963, Volume XI, Cuban Missile Crisis and Aftermath* (Washington: GPO, 1996), ed. note, 773. On Cuban casualties, see Johnson, *Bay of Pigs*, 179. For the brigade's struggle to survive, see ibid., 181–82.

38. Persons, *Bay of Pigs*, preface, 2, 78, 80, 87, 89, 97; Ferrer, *Puma*, 233–34; Kornbluh interview of Hawkins, Oct. 10, 1996, in Kornbluh, ed., *Bay of Pigs Declassified*, 266.

39. Pepe testimony in sixteenth meeting of Green Study Group, May 17, 1961, Aguilar, *Operation Zapata*, 294; Betancourt testimony in sixteenth meeting of Green Study Group, May 17, 1961, ibid., 310.

40. Unidentified speaker (Lynch) in sixth meeting of Green Study Group, April 28, 1961, ibid., 160, 162; White testimony in twelfth meeting of Green Study

Group, May 8, 1961, ibid., 256, 259; Memo of second meeting of Green Study Group, April 24, 1961, ibid., 86–87; Bissell, Oral History Interview, 13–14, JFKL; Bissell, *Reflections of Cold Warrior*, 183–84; Rodríguez, *Bay of Pigs and CIA*, 199–200. For names excised from the Aguilar edition, see *FRUS, X, Cuba, 1961–1962*, pp. 334–56 (Bissell's view on 352).

41. Kirkpatrick, "Inspector General's Survey," 56–57.

42. Rodríguez, *Bay of Pigs and CIA*, 199–200; Bissell, *Reflections of Cold Warrior*, 195.

43. Memo of second meeting of Green Study Group, April 24, 1961, Aguilar, *Operation Zapata*, 80 (Bissell quote), 98; White testimony in twelfth meeting of Green Study Group, May 8, 1961, ibid., 259–60; Memo of sixth meeting of Green Study Group, April 28, 1961, ibid., 162; Bissell's views in Memo for record, April 26, 1961, *FRUS, X, Cuba, 1961–1962*, p. 369.

44. Bonsal, *Cuba, Castro, and the United States*, 184–85; Higgins, *Perfect Failure*, 104; Wyden, *Bay of Pigs*, 292, 311.

45. Cabell, *Memoirs*, 383; Castro's remarks on June 15, 1961, in informational memo, probably drafted by CIA, June 22, 1961, *FRUS, X, Cuba, 1961–1962*, pp. 608–9.

46. Rodríguez, *Bay of Pigs and CIA*, 141–42.

47. Kirkpatrick, Oral History Interview, 14–15, JFKL; Cuba Study Group to JFK, June 13, 1961, *FRUS, X, Cuba, 1961–1962*, p. 600; Narrative of Anti-Castro Cuban Operation Zapata, June 13, 1961, Aguilar, *Operation Zapata*, 34–35; RFK statement in seventeenth meeting of Green Study Group, May 18, 1961, ibid., 330–31.

48. Sorensen, *Kennedy*, 302–5.

49. Ibid., 306–7.

50. Bundy to Taylor, May 4, 1961, in tenth meeting of Green Study Group, Aguilar, *Operation Zapata*, 178–80; JCS to McNamara, March 10, 1961, *FRUS, X, Cuba, 1961–1962*, p. 125; Memo for Record, April 26, 1961, ibid., 369; Memo for record (probably by Taylor) of JFK's luncheon meeting with Cuba Study Group (Taylor, RFK, Burke, Dulles), May 16, 1961, ibid., 526; Memo by Burke of JFK's luncheon meeting with Taylor, RFK, Burke, Dulles), May 16, 1961, ibid., 528.

CHAPTER 7. INQUISITION

1. Richard M. Nixon, *RN: The Memoirs of Richard Nixon*, 2 vols. (New York: Warner Books, 1978), I, 289; JFK's public quotes in Kornbluh, ed., *Bay of Pigs Declassified*, 3; JFK's private quotes in Reeves, *President Kennedy*, 103, Cabell, *Memoirs*, 388, and Sorensen, *Kennedy*, 309; John F. Kennedy, *Profiles in Courage* (New York: Harper, 1956); Schlesinger, *Thousand Days*, 244, 248. See Jack Anderson's articles enclosed in FBI File No. 92-3267-1043, Roselli, Los Angeles Field Report No. 92-113, March 17, 1971, p. 12, U.S. Dept. of Justice, Washington.

2. *Public Papers of Presidents: JFK, 1961*, p. 304 (April 20, 1961).

3. Kornbluh, ed., *Bay of Pigs Declassified*, 3; Schlesinger to JFK, May 3, 1961, President's Office Files, box 114a, Countries, Cuba, General, JFKL.
4. Schlesinger to JFK, May 3, 1961, President's Office Files, box 114a, Countries, Cuba, General, JFKL.
5. Walt Rostow, Deputy Special Asst. for National Security Affairs, to JFK, April 21, 1961, *FRUS, X, Cuba, 1961–1962*, p. 311; RFK to JFK, April 19, 1961, ibid., 303–4.
6. Bowles's notes on Cabinet and Oval Office meetings, April 20, 1961, ibid., 304–5; David Halberstam, *The Best and the Brightest* (New York: Random House, 1969).
7. Bowles's notes on Cabinet and Oval Office meetings, April 20, 1961, *FRUS, X, Cuba, 1961–1962*, pp. 305–6.
8. McNamara to Lemnitzer, April 20, 1961, ibid., 306–7.
9. Memo by Burke of McNamara's meeting with JCS and Secretaries of the Services, April 21, 1961, ed. note, ibid., 309–10.
10. Bowles' notes on NSC Meeting, April 22, 1961, ibid., 313–14.
11. Record of actions of NSC Meeting, April 22, 1961, ibid., 316, 316 n.1.
12. Maxwell D. Taylor, *Swords and Plowshares: A Memoir* (New York: W. W. Norton, 1972), 180; Taylor testimony, July 9, 1975, pp. 3–5, CCH.
13. JFK to Taylor, April 22, 1961, Exhibit No. 1 in Appendix, Taylor testimony, July 9, 1975, CCH.
14. Taylor to JFK, June 13, 1861, Aguilar, *Operation Zapata*, 1; Memo of first meeting of Board of Inquiry on Cuban Operations, April 22, 1961, ibid., 54–61; Memo for record, April 22, 1961, *FRUS, X, Cuba, 1961–1962*, pp. 318–24; Author's interview with Joe Shannon, American B-26 pilot at the Bay of Pigs, May 24, 2006.
15. IG Report, 33–34, 43; Belin, "Investigation of CIA Involvement," 37, CCH.
16. Bissell testimony, June 9, 1975, pp. 27, 33, 35–36, 38, June 11, pp. 5–6, CCH.
17. Ibid., June 9, pp. 44–46, June 11, p. 27, July 22, 1975, pp. 53–54, 56, CCH; Taylor testimony, July 9, 1975, pp. 72–73, CCH; Burke affidavit, Aug. 25, 1975, cited in *Alleged Assassination Plots*, 122.
18. Rusk testimony, July 10, 1975, pp. 51, 42, CCH; Taylor testimony, July 9, 1975, pp. 7–8, CCH; Belin, "Investigation of CIA Involvement," 53, CCH.
19. IG Report, 33–34; Colby testimony, May 21, 1975, p. 29, CCH; Helms testimony, April 28, 1975, p. 2494, CCH; Belin, "Investigation of CIA Involvement," 54–55, CCH.
20. Schlesinger, *RFK*, 507; Schlesinger in Blight and Kornbluh, eds., *Politics of Illusion*, 86; Taylor testimony, July 9, 1975, p. 5, CCH.
21. Memo of second meeting of Green Study Group, April 24, 1961, Aguilar, *Operation Zapata*, 90, 99.
22. Ibid., 86, 88–89, 101–2, 116; Gray testimony in fifth meeting of Green Study Group, April 27, 1961, ibid., 152–53.
23. Memo of second meeting of Green Study Group, April 24, 1961, ibid., 81–83, 104; Decker, Oral History Interview, 10–11, JFKL.

24. Rusk testimony in tenth meeting of Green Study Group, May 4, 1961, Aguilar, *Operation Zapata*, 221.
25. Shoup testimony in twelfth meeting of Green Study Group, May 8, 1961, ibid., 247–48; Decker testimony, ibid., 273.
26. Lemnitzer testimony in seventeenth meeting of Green Study Group, May 18, 1961, ibid., 317.
27. Shoup testimony in twelfth meeting of Green Study Group, May 8, 1961, ibid., 253–54; Rusk testimony in tenth meeting of Green Study Group, May 4, 1961, ibid., 220. As related earlier, Acheson had warned President Kennedy about sending such a small force against Castro's legions. See chapter 3.
28. Dulles, Gray, and Cabell in Memo of second meeting of Green Study Group, April 24, 1961, ibid., 86–87, 111; Lemnitzer testimony in seventeenth meeting of Green Study Group, May 18, 1961, ibid., 334; Higgins, *Perfect Failure*, 93–94, 103; Kirkpatrick, "Inspector General's Survey," 55; Cabell, *Memoirs*, 387.
29. Memo of sixth meeting of Green Study Group, April 28, 1961, Aguilar, *Operation Zapata*, 158.
30. Memo of second meeting of Green Study Group, April 24, 1961, ibid., 86, 99, 110–12; Shoup testimony in twelfth meeting of Green Study Group, May 8, 1961, ibid., 252.
31. Wheeler testimony in seventh meeting of Green Study Group, May 3, 1961, ibid., 208; Bundy testimony in seventh meeting of Green Study Group, May 1, 1961, ibid., 177–78.
32. Rusk testimony in tenth meeting of Green Study Group, May 4, 1961, ibid., 220; Lemnitzer testimony in seventeenth meeting of Green Study Group, May 18, 1961, ibid., 317–18.
33. Lemnitzer testimony in seventeenth meeting of Green Study Group, May 18, 1961, ibid., 318–19.
34. Ibid., 319.
35. Shoup testimony in twelfth meeting of Green Study Group, May 8, 1961, ibid., 248.
36. Ibid., 248–50.
37. Burke testimony in eighteenth meeting of Green Study Group, May 19, 1961, ibid., 350–51.
38. Conclusions of Cuban Study Group, ibid., 42; Burke, Oral History Interview, 22, JFKL; Taylor to JFK, Sept. 1, 1961, National Security Files, box 35a, Cuba, General, JFKL.
39. Shoup, Oral History Interview, 19, 21–23, JFKL.
40. Lemnitzer testimony in seventeenth meeting of Green Study Group, May 18, 1961, Aguilar, *Operation Zapata*, 333; Shoup testimony in twelfth meeting of Green Study Group, May 8, 1961, ibid., 254; Bundy to Taylor, May 4, 1961, in seventh meeting of Green Study Group, ibid., 180; Bundy testimony in seventh meeting of Green Study Group, May 1, 1961, ibid., 181; Conclusions of Cuban Study Group, ibid., 40; Rusk testimony in tenth meeting of Green

Study Group, May 4, 1961, ibid., 223; Kirkpatrick, "Inspector General's Survey," 49–50, 55.

41. Bissell, Oral History Interview, 7–9, JFKL.

42. Conclusions of Cuban Study Group, Aguilar, *Operation Zapata*, 43; Recommendations of Cuban Study Group, ibid., 44–46, 48–53.

43. Kornbluh, ed., *Bay of Pigs Declassified*, 13–14, 41–47, 99–101; Bissell, "An Analysis of the Cuban Operation," Jan. 18, 1962, ibid., 136–37, 145–46; Memo for record, April 26, 1961, *FRUS, X, Cuba, 1961 1962,* p. 370; Kirkpatrick, Oral History Interview, 13, JFKL; Berle, Oral History Interview, 40, JFKL. The reader will recall that Bissell, in another characteristic change of stance, more than five years later asserted that air cover would *not* have ensured success. Bissell, Oral History Interview, 14, JFKL.

44. JCS to McNamara, April 26, 1961, *FRUS, X, Cuba, 1961–1962*, pp. 371–72, 381–83.

45. Ibid., 372–73, 375.

46. CIA Paper for NSC, April 26, 1961, ibid., 389–90.

47. McNamara to JCS, May 1, 1961, ibid., 405–6; Recommendations of Cuban Study Group, Aguilar, *Operation Zapata*, 53.

48. Mansfield to JFK, May 1, 1961, President's Office Files, box 114a, Countries, Cuba, General, JFKL; Pell to Rusk, May 5, 1961, *FRUS, X, Cuba, 1961–1962*, p. 410 n.1.

49. Paper prepared for NSC by Interagency Task Force on Cuba, May 4, 1961, *FRUS, X, Cuba, 1961–1962*, p. 463; Record of Action No. 2422 at 483rd meeting of NSC, May 5, 1961, ibid., 482; Notes on 483rd meeting of NSC, May 5, 1961, ibid., 479–80; Schlesinger to Political Warfare Subcommittee of Cuban Task Force, May 8, 1961, ibid., 492; McNamara to special assistant Adam Yarmolinsky, May 5, 1961, ibid., 489; JCS to Dennison, May 9, 1961, ibid., 516.

50. Shoup, Oral History Interview, 26, JFKL; Kornbluh, ed., *Bay of Pigs Declassified*, 16–17.

EPILOGUE

1. Interview of Sam Halpern, Oct. 30, 1987, CIA Misc. Files, box 8, JFK-M-10 (F1), Halpern (NA); Interview of Helms, Jan. 30, 1998, ARRB, Files of K. Michele Combs, box 10, folder interview (NA); Goodwin to JFK, Nov. 1, 1961, *FRUS, X, Cuba, 1961–1962,* p. 664. Robert Kennedy had earlier discussed this idea with his brother. Also in attendance at this November 3 meeting, according to the President's Appointment Book, were McNamara, Edward Lansdale, and Paul Nitze from the Defense Department; George Ball, U. Alexis Johnson, Wymberley Coerr, and Robert Hurwitch from the State Department; Robert Amory from the CIA; and Goodwin from the president's staff. White House meeting, Nov. 3, 1961, ibid., ed. note, 666.

2. *FRUS, X, Cuba, 1961–1962*, ed. note, 666; Halpern testimony, June 19, 1975, p. 5, CCH; Taylor testimony, July 9, 1975, pp. 19–20, CCH; Lansdale testimony,

July 8, 1975, pp. 3–6, CCH. Lansdale had recommended that the administration support South Vietnamese premier Ngo Dinh Diem and develop a counterinsurgency program to combat the Vietcong. See Jones, *Death of a Generation*, 13, 20–22.

3. White House meeting, Nov. 3, 1961, *FRUS, X, Cuba, 1961–1962*, ed. note, 667; Taylor testimony, July 9, 1975, pp. 20–22, CCH; *Alleged Assassination Plots*, 140.

4. Lansdale testimony, July 8, 1975, pp. 9, 12–13, 22, 136, CCH; Breckinridge testimony, June 2, 1975, pp. 42, 45–46, CCH; Helms deposition to Belin, April 23, 1975, p. 154, CCH; Helms testimony, June 13, 1975, p. 73, CCH; Lansdale, Oral History Interview, 18, JFKL; Lansdale testimony, July 8, 1975, pp. 41, 11, CCH; *FRUS, X, Cuba, 1961–1962*, ed. note, 666–67; McNamara testimony, July 11, 1975, pp. 61, 93, CCH.

5. Szulc testimony, June 10, 1975, pp. 24, 26–27, CCH; Szulc's notes on conversation, Nov. 9, 1961, after ibid. See also *FRUS, X, Cuba, 1961–1962*, p. 807 n.1.

6. Szulc testimony, June 10, 1975, pp. 27–29, CCH; Szulc's notes on conversation, Nov. 9, 1961, after ibid.; Goodwin testimony, July 18, 1975, pp. 3–4, 11, CCH; Goodwin reference in Szulc testimony, June 10, 1975, ibid., 27. Dulles was still CIA director at this time, not replaced by McCone until November 29, 1961. Bissell remained deputy director of plans, and Helms and Harvey were in the CIA as well.

7. JFK address before U. of Washington, Nov. 16, 1961, *Public Papers of the President, John F. Kennedy, 1961*, p. 725; Interview of Goodwin, May 27, 1975, Exhibit No. 7, p. 2, in McNamara testimony, July 11, 1975, CCH. Years afterward, Szulc published the president's pledge against assassination in a February 1974 article in *Esquire* magazine, entitled "Cuba on Our Mind." Copy of article after Szulc's testimony, June 10, 1975, CCH.

8. Memo by McCone, Nov. 22, 1961, *FRUS, X, Cuba, 1961–1962*, pp. 684–85, 686; *Alleged Assassination Plots*, 144, 145 n.1.

9. IG Report, 3; Memo of Mongoose meeting by George McManus, Richard Helms's executive assistant, Jan. 19, 1962, after Helms testimony, July 17, 1975, CCH.

10. Carter testimony, Sept. 19, 1975, pp. 18, 74, CCH; Bissell testimony, July 22, 1975, p. 65, CCH; Halley (alias for Shackley) testimony, Aug. 19, 1975, pp. 25–26, CCH; Shackley, *Spymaster*, x, 50–51, 53, 55–56, 68–72.

11. Helms testimony, June 13, pp. 26, 57, 88, 137, July 17, pp. 13–15, 18, 25, 60–61, Sept. 11, 1975, p. 7, CCH; Helms testimony to Belin of Rockefeller Commission, April 23, 1975, pp. 159–60, CCH.

12. Osborn to DCI, June 24, 1966, p. 6, ARRB, T. Jeremy Dunn Files, box 9, Folder RP/Castro Assassination Plots (NA); Harvey testimony, July 11, 1975, p. 65, CCH; Harvey's note quoted in Bissell testimony, June 9, 1975, p. 74, CCH; Bissell testimony, June 11, pp. 17–18, 49, 52–53, July 17, 1975, pp. 12–13, CCH; CIA director William Colby testimony, May 21, 1975, p. 30, CCH.

Harvey tried to hide executive action capability under the ZR/RIFLE title when assigned the task of developing the program. Memo by Joseph Seltzer, April 16, 1975, box 36, 104-10178-10379, RG 233, JFK Collection (NA); CIA document, n.d., pp. 1–2, box 36, 104-10178-10012, ibid.; *Alleged Assassination Plots*, 83, 83 n.2; Harvey testimony, June 25, 1975, pp. 69,77, CCH; O'Connell testimony, May 30, 1975, p. 90, CCH; IG Report, 40; Bissell testimony, June 11, 1975, p. 47, CCH.

13. Harvey testimony, June 25, pp. 22, 24, 31, 69, 76, July 11, 1975, p. 66, CCH.

14. O'Connell testimony, May 30, 1975, pp. 19–20, 46–48, 52, CCH; Harvey testimony, June 25, pp. 63–64, 91-92, Sept. 22, 1975, p. 41, CCH; Memo of conversation in DS, Feb. 27, 1962, *FRUS, X, Cuba, 1961–1962*, p. 763; Memo of conversation in DS, March 29, 1962, ibid., 778; Roselli testimony, June 24, 1975, pp. 21, 23–24, 29, 31, 33–34, 39, CCH; IG Report, 7, 29–33, 45–47; *Alleged Assassination Plots*, 84, 131; Stockton, *Flawed Patriot*, 176–78; Corn, *Blond Ghost*, 67. Roselli inspected one of Varona's speedboats and dipped into his personal funds to give an unidentified Cuban at the dock eight hundred dollars for gas money. Roselli refused reimbursement because, he asserted, "it was a government project and this would be my donation towards it." Roselli testimony, June 24, 1975, pp. 36–37, CCH. Varona intended to kill Raúl Castro as well as Che Guevara. O'Connell returned the money to his home office; Varona kept the equipment O'Connell testimony, May 30, 1975, pp. 20, 54, CCH. See Bohning, *Castro Obsession*, 179–81. For Castro's account of this second poison attempt, see Fidel Castro and Ignacio Ramonet, *Fidel Castro: My Life, a Spoken Autobiography* (New York: Scribner, 2008), 253. Originally published in Spain in 2006 as *Fidel Castro: Biografía a dos voces*. See also Weiner, *Legacy of Ashes*, 173.

15. Dennison to JCS, Feb. 24, 1962, *FRUS, X, Cuba, 1961–1962*, 750–56; Hilsman to U. Alexis Johnson, Feb. 20, 1962, ibid., 747–48; Tasks in Lansdale, "Program Review" for Operation Mongoose, Jan. 18, 1962, ibid., 715–18; Lansdale to Goodwin, March 6, 1962, ibid., 767; Lansdale to SGA, March 12, 1962, ibid., 767–68. In light of the small number of volunteers, the Defense Department terminated the plan for allowing Cuban nationals into the U.S. armed services, effective June 30, 1962. Gilpatric to Lemnitzer, March 13, 1962, ibid., 770; Guidelines for Operation Mongoose by Taylor, March 14, 1962, ibid., 771; Lansdale to Brig. Gen. William H. Craig, DOD Project Officer for Operation Mongoose, March 5, 1962, in "Justification for U.S. Military Intervention in Cuba" (TS), JCS 1969/303, JCS Central Files 1962, box 29, JCS Record Case, Code Name Northwoods, Record No. 202-10002-10104, Agency File No. 3360, Feb. 7, 1962, NA (hereafter Northwoods File); Report by DOD and JCS Representative on Caribbean Survey Group, Brig. Gen. Craig, to JCS on Cuba Project, March 9, 1962, p. 3, ibid.; Lemnitzer to McNamara, March 13, 1962, cover letter for "Justification for U.S. Military Intervention in Cuba (TS)," pp, 2, 5, JCS Central Files 1962, ibid.; note by secretaries, March 14, 1962, JCS 1969/321, ibid.

16. Taylor memo, March 16, 1962, Exhibit No. 3 in Appendix, Taylor testimony, July 9, 1975, CCH; Bundy testimony, July 8, 1975, pp. 4–5, CCH; "Guidelines for Operation Mongoose," March 14, 1962, *FRUS, X, Cuba, 1961–1962*, p. 771; McCone, "Memorandum on Operation Mongoose," April 12, 1962, ibid., 791–92. The editors of this volume did not include the Northwoods File, claiming it was "Not found." Ibid., 792 n.3. James Bamford erroneously argues that the White House opposed military force and therefore discarded the Joint Chiefs' plan. See James Bamford, *Body of Secrets: Anatomy of the Ultra-Secret National Security Agency from the Cold War Through the Dawn of a New Century* (New York: Doubleday, 2001), 87. Lemnitzer quoted ibid., 81–82; Report quoted ibid., 82.

17. Goodwin testimony, July 18, 1975, p. 5, CCH; *Alleged Assassination Plots*, 321–22; David W. Belin, *Final Disclosure: The Full Truth About the Assassination of President Kennedy* (New York: Scribner's, 1980), 113; Richard N. Goodwin, *Remembering America: A Voice from the Sixties* (Boston: Little, Brown, 1988), 189; Goodwin in McNamara testimony, July 11, 1975, p. 70, CCH; IG Report, 7, 113–14, 118.

18. CIA operative (alias Weatherby) testimony, Aug. 1, 1975, p. 34, CCH; CIA Report, Nov. 1963, unit 4, box 102, 104-10215-10216, RG 233, JFK Collection (NA); Thomas, *Very Best Men*, 298–99; McCone to JMWAVE, June 15, 1962, box 101, 104-10215-10108, RG 233, JFK Collection (NA); McCone to JMWAVE, June 15, 1962, box 101, 104-10215-10110, ibid.; McCone to JMWAVE, June 29, 1962, box 101, 104-10215-10092, ibid. Cubela had machine-gunned Batista's security chief in a Havana night club in 1956 and instantly won favor in the Castro camp. McCone did not personally sign the dispatches affixed with his stamped signature, but even if the remote possibility exists that he knew nothing of the Cubela connection, he bears responsibility because the business occurred under his watch.

19. Nikita Khrushchev, *Khrushchev Remembers* (Boston: Little, Brown, 1970), 493–94; Fursenko and Naftali, *"One Hell of a Gamble,"* 182–83, 186–87.

20. Dennison to JCS, Feb. 24, 1962, *FRUS, X, Cuba, 1961–1962*, p. 750; KGB (Soviet security and intelligence service) quoted in Fursenko and Naftali, *"One Hell of a Gamble,"* 150–51.

21. Helms testimony, June 13, p. 23, Sept. 11, 1975, p. 9, CCH; First RFK quote in *Alleged Assassination Plots*, 147; SGA quoted ibid.; Memo by McCone, Oct. 4, 1962, *FRUS, 1961–1963, XI, Cuban Missile Crisis and Aftermath*, 12; McCone memo of discussion with Bundy, Oct. 5, 1962, ibid., 13; McCone memo of Oct. 10 meeting, Oct. 11, 1962, ibid., 18; Helms memo, Oct. 16, 1962, ibid., 46. President Kennedy objected only to mining Cuba's harbors because the move might alienate other Latin American states. Fursenko and Naftali, *"One Hell of a Gamble,"* 228.

22. Circular telegram to all Latin American posts, Dec. 22, 1962, *FRUS, 1961–1963, XI, Cuban Missile Crisis and Aftermath*, 635; Bundy to JFK, Jan. 4, 1963, ibid., 650; Memo for Taylor from Lt. Gen. Joseph F. Carroll, USAF, on DIA-

CIA Assessment of Status of Soviet Military Personnel in Cuba, Oct. 24, 1963, box 5, RG 218, JCS Records, JFK Assassination Records Collection (NA); Memo for Taylor from W. Y. S., "Future Policy Toward Cuba," Jan. 24, 1963, Taylor Papers, box 7, box 3, ibid. For the prisoner negotiations and settlement, see note 37 of chapter 6 above.

23. Halpern interview, Jan. 15, 1998, p. 38, CIA Misc. Files, box 9, JFK-M-10 (F2), Halpern (NA). Supporting Halpern's argument is Michael L. Kurtz, *The JFK Assassination Debates: Lone Gunman Versus Conspiracy* (Lawrence: University Press of Kansas, 2006), 194. For an opposing view, see Peter Kornbluh, "JFK and Castro: The Secret Quest for Accommodation," *Cigar Aficionado Online*, Sept./Oct. 1999, p. 13.

24. Jones, *Death of a Generation*, 314 ff.; Helms testimony, June 13, 1975, pp. 24–25, CCH.

25. IG Report, 75–77; "Highly Sensitive Activities," CIA-DDP Files, CIA Misc. Files, box 6, JFK-M-07 (F1), ZR/RIFLE, Harvey, Sept. 3, 1975 (NA); Memo by Col. Walter M. Higgins, Jr., Executive Officer, SACSA, briefing of JCS by Fitzgerald, Aug. 5, 1963, box 1, RG 218, JCS Records, JFK Assassination Records Collection (NA); Vance to Fitzgerald, Sept. 3, 1963, ibid.; Vance quoted from CIA Paper for NSC, June 8, 1963, *FRUS, 1961–1963, XI, Cuban Missile Crisis and Aftermath*, 828. For the diving suit story, see Prados, *Safe for Democracy*, 312–13.

26. U.S. Senate, 94th Congress, 2nd Session, *The Investigation of the Assassination of President John F. Kennedy: Performance of the Intelligence Agencies, Book V: Final Report of the Select Committee to Study Governmental Operations with Respect to Intelligence Activities* (Washington: GPO, 1976), 3, 13 (hereafter *Final Report*); AMLASH Case Officer (Sanchez) testimony, July 29, 1975, pp. 11–15, 18, 40, Feb. 11, 1976, p. 4, CCH (hereafter Sanchez testimony); Weiner, *Legacy of Ashes*, 208–9.

27. Castro quoted in Sanchez testimony, Feb. 11, 1976, 89–90, CCH; Castro story in *New Orleans Times Picayune*, Sept. 9, 1963, in Helms testimony, July 18, 1975, pp. 32–33, CCH; AP account of Castro interview quoted in Kurtz, *JFK Assassination Debates*, 193; Intelligence Documents on Plots to Assassinate Castro, Russell Holmes Papers, box 52, folder RH18, F02c, AMLASH (NA).

28. Joseph A. Califano, *Inside: A Public and Private Life* (New York: Public Affairs, 2004), 124; Memo by Col. Higgins, briefing of JCS by Fitzgerald on CIA Cuban Operations and Planning, Sept. 25, 1963, box 1, RG 218, JCS Records, JFK Assassination Records Collection (NA); Vance memo for chair of Joint Chiefs of Staff, Gen. Taylor, on draft of State-Defense Contingency Plan for Coup in Cuba, Oct. 1, 1963, box 5, ibid.; Vance memo for Taylor on special operations, Oct. 10, 1963, ibid.

29. Belin, "Investigation of CIA Involvement," 62, CCH; Swenson (referred to by pseudonym of Joseph Langosch) and Shackley quotes in Thomas, *Very Best Men*, 299–300; Shackley testimony, Aug. 19, 1975, pp. 79–80, CCH; Califano, *Inside*, 125; Contact plan quoted in Helms testimony, June 13, 1975,

pp. 116–17, CCH; Sanchez testimony, July 29, 1975, pp. 57, 72, 92, 104, CCH; *Final Report*, 18–19; CIA comment on charge of plot in 1965, Donald Chamberlain, CIA Inspector General, box 105, RG 233, JFK Collection (NA); Halpern testimony, June 18, 1975, p. 17, CCH. Swenson appears in some of the documents as Joseph Langosch.

30. On Diem's and his brother's assassinations, see Jones, *Death of a Generation*, chap. 17.

31. *Alleged Assassination Plots*, 89; IG Report, 90, 93a–94; Sanchez testimony, July 29, 1975, pp. 114–15, 117, Feb. 11, 1976, pp. 76, 84–85, CCH; CIA Report, box 102, RG 233, JFK Collection (NA); Memo for record, March 29, 1965, ibid. AMLASH files among CIA materials, ibid.

32. Leo Janis, "The Last Days of the President," *Atlantic*, July 1973, pp. 35, 39, quoted in *Alleged Assassination Plots*, 180 n.1; ibid., 179–80; Robert Dallek, *Flawed Giant: Lyndon Johnson and His Times, 1961–1973* (New York: Oxford University Press, 1998), 53; Randall B. Woods, *LBJ: Architect of American Ambition* (New York: Free Press, 2006), 428; Goodwin testimony, July 18, 1975, p. 24, CCH; Helms testimony, June 13, 1975, pp. 35–36, 139, CCH; Helms testimony, Aug. 9, 1978, p. 35, House Select Committee on Assassinations, RG233 (NA). The SGA became known as Special Group 5412 after Kennedy's death. On June 2, 1964, NSAM No. 303 changed the name of the Cuban advisory group to the 303 Committee, the room in which it met. Bundy to Rusk, McNamara, and McCone, June 2, 1964, *FRUS, 1964–1968, Volume XXXIII, Organization and Management of U.S. Foreign Policy; United Nations* (Washington: GPO, 2004), 453. The 303 Committee consisted of Bundy as chair, McCone, Deputy Secretary of Defense Cyrus Vance, and Acting Deputy Undersecretary of State for Political Affairs Llewellyn Thompson. Ibid., n.2.

33. JCS 2304/205-2, JCS Central Files 1963, Joint Secretariat to JCS, "Draft State-Defense Plan for a Coup in Cuba," 19–22, Appendix, 10, Dec. 4, 1963, box 4, RG 218, JCS Records, JFK Assassination Records Collection (NA); Vance to McNamara, "A Contingency Plan for a Coup in Cuba," Nov. 30, 1963, ibid.; Memo by Col. W. C. Chamberlin, USMC, Latin American Branch, talking paper for meeting of Dec. 19, 1963, on contingency planning in Cuba, box 1, ibid.; Woods, *LBJ*, 495.

34. Memo by Gen. Wheeler on meeting with LBJ on Cuba, Dec. 19, 1963, box 1, Joseph Califano Papers, RG 335, Records of Office of Sec. of Army, JFK Collection (NA); Memo of meeting with LBJ, Dec. 19, 1963, *FRUS, 1961–1963, XI, Cuban Missile Crisis and Aftermath*, 905; Briefing sheet by Col. P. A. Wyman, Special Operations Division, SACSA, Jan. 29, 1964, box 1, RG 218, JCS Records, JFK Assassination Records Collection (NA); Taylor memo of JCS meeting with LBJ on Feb. 28, 1964 (memo dated March 1, 1964), box 5, ibid.; Taylor to LBJ on possible actions against Castro government, March 21, 1964, ibid.; Fitzgerald memo of White House meeting, April 7, 1964, *FRUS, 1964–1968, Volume XXXII, Dominican Republic; Cuba; Haiti; Guyana* (Washington: GPO, 2005), 627, 629.

35. Helms testimony, Sept. 11, 1975, p. 25, CCH; Fitzgerald memo of White House meeting, April 7, 1964, *FRUS, 1964–1968, XXXII, Dominican Republic; Cuba; Haiti; Guyana,* 628; McCone memo, April 8, 1964, attachment, ibid., 630; McCone quoted from CIA Paper for NSC, June 8, 1963, *FRUS, 1961–1963, XI, Cuban Missile Crisis and Aftermath,* 828; Shackley, *Spymaster,* 76.

36. Sanchez testimony, July 29, 1975, pp. 119–20, 127, 132, 136, Feb. 11, 1976, pp. 84–85, CCH; IG Report, 96–97, 100–103; *Alleged Assassination Plots,* 89–90; Prados, *Safe for Democracy,* 321–22; Memo by C/RR to C/FI, March 29, 1965, box 103, RG 233, JFK Collection (NA); CIA comment on charge of plot in 1965, Chamberlain, box 105, ibid.; Memo by Sanchez, Dec. 20, 1964, ibid.; McCone to Madrid, Dec. 23, 1964, ibid.; Cable to McCone, Dec. 8, 1964, ibid.; C/WH/COG, memo on CIA connections with Cubela, Jan. 10, 1974, box 105, ibid.; Sanchez to McCone, Feb. 3, 1965, box 104, ibid.; Memo by WH/SA/EOB (Sanchez), Aug. 28, 1964, box 102, ibid.; Memo by Sanchez on meeting between Artime and Cubela in Madrid, Dec. 27, 1964, Jan. 3, 1965, box 104, ibid.

37. For cache deliveries, see CIA comment on charge of plot in 1965, Chamberlain, box 105, RG 233, JFK Collection (NA); CIA Report, April 16, 1964, box 102, ibid.; COS, JMWAVE, to Fitzgerald, April 17, 1964, ibid.; JMWAVE to McCone, Aug. 1, 1964, box 103, ibid. For failure to develop a silencer, see Paris Station to McCone, May 3, 1964, box 102, ibid. See also memo by TSD/KB, July 1, 1964, box 103, ibid.; Memo by WH/SA/EOB (Sanchez), Aug. 28, 1964, ibid.; Murat Williams, Deputy Director for Coordination of Bureau of Intelligence and Research, to Mann, Jan. 8, 1965, *FRUS, 1964–1968, XXXII, Dominican Republic; Cuba; Haiti; Guyana,* 703; Memo by Peter Jessup, Jan. 13, 1965, ibid., 704; Memo to 303 Committee, Feb. 23, 1965, ibid., 705; Williams to Robert Adams, Deputy Asst. Sec. of State for Inter-American Affairs, March 8, 1965, ibid., 707–8. Artime disbanded his paramilitary team. Memo to 303 Committee, March 22, 1965, ibid., 716.

38. *Final Report,* 78; Breckinridge in Colby testimony, May 23, 1975, p. 79, CCH; IG Report, 103–6; Ed. note, *FRUS, 1964–1968, XXXII, Dominican Republic; Cuba; Haiti; Guyana,* 743; CIA comment on charge of plot in 1965, Chamberlain, box 105, RG 233, JFK Collection (NA). Great numbers of students and others had demonstrated against the Castro regime and issued death threats if Cubela died, perhaps making Castro realize he did not need a martyr and should spare Cubela. The CIA concluded that Castro perhaps found it "politically imprudent" to execute "someone so close to his inner circle, who had merely plotted without acting." As late as 2005, Cubela was living in Madrid. Sanchez testimony, July 29, 1975, pp. 65, 70, Feb. 11, 1976, p. 36, CCH; *Washington Post,* March 8, 11, 1966, box 104, RG 233, JFK Collection (NA); Unnamed New York press article, March 8, 1966, ibid.; Castro's letter quoted in Reuters article, March 8, 1966, ibid.; UPI reports of student unrest in CIA director William Raborn to JMWAVE, March 10, 1966, box 104, ibid; Raborn to JMWAVE, March 12, 1966, ibid.; JMWAVE to Raborn, March 9,

1966, ibid; George Bush to [withheld], Oct. 6, 1976, box 105, ibid.; IG Report, 111.

39. Rusk to Bundy, Aug. 30, 1965, *FRUS, 1964–1968, XXXII, Dominican Republic; Cuba; Haiti, Guyana,* 727; Jessup to LBJ, Sept. 22, 1965, ibid., 729; Belin, "Investigation of CIA Involvement," pp. 63–64, CCH; Helms testimony, June 13, 1975, pp. 24–25, CCH; *New York Times,* March 6, 1966, clipping in box 104, RG 233, JFK Collection (NA); Tad Szulc, "Cuba on Our Mind," *Esquire,* Feb. 1974, copy after Szulc testimony, June 10, 1975, CCH; Higgins, *Perfect Failure,* 175; Shackley, *Spymaster,* 76.

40. Srodes, *Dulles,* 553; Grose, *Gentleman Spy,* 552; Weiner, *Legacy of Ashes,* 227–30; *Final Report,* 67–68; Helms testimony, June 13, 1975, pp. 81–82, CCH.

41. Anthony Summers, *Conspiracy* (New York: McGraw-Hill, 1980), 437; *Final Report,* 5–6, 27–28, 37–40, 73.

42. Sanchez testimony, July 29, 1975, pp. 90–91, 93, 96–97, Feb. 11, 1976, pp. 98–99, CCH; Fitzgerald's directive of secrecy in Sanchez's memo for record, Nov. 19, 1963, in SAS/SO/NS Report, box 102, RG 233, JFK Collection (NA).

43. Woods, *LBJ,* 428.

44. William Sullivan (longtime head of FBI's Domestic Intelligence Division) testimony, April 21, 1976, p. 22, CCH; *Final Report,* 6; Pearson quoted in Bohning, *Castro Obsession,* 177; Edmund Morgan testimony, March 19, 1976, pp. 5, 8–13, 20–21, 28–30, 33, 38–40, 44–50, CCH; IG Report; LBJ quote to Califano in Califano, *Inside,* 126; Dallek, *Flawed Giant,* 51-53. See also Robert Dallek, *An Unfinished Life: John F. Kennedy, 1917–1963* (Boston: Little, Brown, 2003), 698. Morgan claimed that one of his other clients, Mafia figure John Roselli, later agreed with Maheu's account but had not been responsible for the story related to Pearson. Morgan testimony, March 19, 1976, pp. 48–50.

45. Shackley, *Spymaster,* 72.

46. Basil Ince, "Castro Among the Family Jewels," *Trinidad and Tobago Express,* July 18, 2007. Giancana was murdered in his Oak Park, Illinois, home in June 1975, just days before his scheduled appearance before the Church Committee, and a year or so later, fishermen spotted a barrel off the Florida coast, chained shut but containing Roselli's body sawed into pieces. Both murders remain unresolved but carried the same message. Giancana's death came gangland execution style—a single shot in the back of the head followed by six bullets fired circular fashion into his mouth and face to signify that he talked too much. Roselli had testified four times before the committee, paying the ultimate price for his candor. Trafficante died by natural causes. He had refused to go before the committee, although several members interviewed him and provided a summary of the meeting. Maheu testified at length and is still alive at the time of this writing. Giancana and Renner, *Mafia Princess,* 18, 273; Report of Special Investigative Division of FBI, Aug. 9, 1976, encl. in FBI Case: [?] Roskil, FBI File No. 92-3267-1071, March 22, 1977, Miami File 92-517, U.S. Dept. of Justice, Washington; FBI Bureau File No. 72, 2382, cover

page, ibid. Roselli testified before the Church Committee in June and September 1975 (twice) and April 1976.

47. Higgins, *Perfect Failure*, 87, 161; Wyden, *Bay of Pigs*, 96; Bissell, *Reflections of Cold Warrior*, 204; JFK quoted ibid., 191; Dulles, Oral History Interview, 33, JFKL.

48. Weiner, *Legacy of Ashes*, xiii–xv, 179; John Prados, *Lost Crusader: The Secret Wars of CIA Director William Colby* (New York: Oxford University Press, 2003), 343.

49. Stephen F. Knott, *Secret and Sanctioned: Covert Operations and the American Presidency* (New York: Oxford University Press, 1996) 3–4, 7-8.

50. JFK quoted in Bissell, *Reflections of Cold Warrior*, 204.

BIBLIOGRAPHY

PRIMARY SOURCES

Unpublished Sources

John F. Kennedy Library, Boston, Massachusetts
  George W. Ball Papers
  McGeorge Bundy Papers
  John Kenneth Galbraith Papers
  Roswell L. Gilpatric Papers
  Roger Hilsman Papers
  John F. Kennedy Papers
    National Security Files
      Cuba, General
    President's Office Files
      Countries, Cuba, General
    National Security Council Meetings
  Theodore Sorensen Papers
  Oral History Interviews
    Adolf A. Berle
    Richard M. Bissell
    Chester B. Bowles
    McGeorge Bundy
    Arleigh A. Burke
    George H. Decker
    Roswell L. Gilpatric
    Richard M. Helms

Roger Hilsman
Robert A. Hurwitch
Robert H. Johnson
U. Alexis Johnson
Robert F. Kennedy
Lyman B. Kirkpatrick
Edward G. Lansdale
Lyman L. Lemnitzer
Thomas Mann
John A. McCone
Robert S. McNamara
Mike Mansfield
Walt W. Rostow
Dean Rusk
David M. Shoup
Theodore C. Sorensen
Maxwell D. Taylor
Earle Wheeler

National Archives, College Park, Maryland
  Assassination Records Review Board
    Files of K. Michelle Combs
    Files of T. Jeremy Dunn
  Belin, David, Executive Director of CIA Commission. "Investigation of CIA In-
    volvement in Plans to Assassinate Foreign Leaders," June 5, 1975, Record No.
    157-10005-10153, Record Group 233, box 435-8, Church Committee Hearings
  Califano, Joseph, Papers
  CIA Miscellaneous Files
  CIA Reports Record Group 233, Records of the U.S. House of Representatives,
    Select Committee on Assassination, JFK Task Force, Segregated CIA Collection,
    Records of the JFK Collection
  FBI Case Files Arranged by Individual Surnames, HSCA Subject Files, HQ Main
    Files
  FBI Case Files Arranged by Individual Surnames, HSCA Subject Files, Misc. Files
  Holmes, Russell, Papers
  Joint Chiefs of Staff Central Files
  Pfeiffer, Jack B. "Official History of the Bay of Pigs Operation, Volume III:
    Evolution of CIA's Anti-Castro Policies, 1959–January 1961" (Dec. 1979), JFK
    Assassination Records Collection
  Taylor, Maxwell D., Papers

U.S. Senate Intelligence Committee Select Committee to Study Governmental
    Operations with Respect to Intelligence Activities—Record Group 46, Church
    Committee Hearings
  AMLASH Case Officer (Nestor Sanchez) Testimony

Richard M. Bissell Testimony
Scott Breckinridge Testimony
McGeorge Bundy Testimony
Marshall Carter Testimony
William E. Colby Testimony
Sheffield Edwards Testimony
Walter Elder Testimony
Roswell Gilpatric Testimony
Andrew Goodpaster Testimony
Richard Goodwin Testimony
Gordon Gray Testimony
Halley (alias for Ted Shackley) Testimony
Samuel Halpern Testimony
William Harvey Testimony
Richard Helms Testimony
Howard Hunt Testimony
Robert Johnson Testimony
Edward Lansdale Testimony
Robert Maheu Testimony
John A. McCone Testimony
Robert McNamara Testimony
James O'Connell Testimony
Thomas Parrott Testimony
Fletcher Prouty Testimony
John Roselli Testimony
Walt Rostow Testimony
Dean Rusk Testimony
George Smathers Testimony
William Sullivan Testimony
Tad Szulc Testimony
Santo Trafficante Testimony
Maxwell D. Taylor Testimony
Weatherby (alias for CIA operative) Testimony

Published Sources

Aguilar, Luis (introduction). *Operation Zapata: The "Ultrasensitive" Report and Testimony of the Board of Inquiry on the Bay of Pigs.* Frederick, Md.: University Publications of America, 1981.

Earman, J. S. (Inspector General of CIA). Memorandum for the Record: "Report on Plots to Assassinate Fidel Castro," May 23, 1967, prepared at request of Richard Helms, Director of CIA (declassified in 1994). Record Series JFK, Record Number 104-10213-10101, CIA Files, National Archives, College Park, Md. Published as *CIA Targets Fidel: Secret 1967 CIA Inspector General's Report on Plots to Assassinate Fidel Castro.* Melbourne, Australia: Ocean Press, 1996.

Kirkpatrick, Lyman. "Inspector General's Survey of the Cuban Operation, October 1961." In Peter Kornbluh, ed., *Bay of Pigs Declassified: The Secret CIA Report on the Invasion of Cuba,* 23–132. New York: New Press, 1998.

Kornbluh, Peter, ed. *Bay of Pigs Declassified: The Secret CIA Report on the Invasion of Cuba.* New York: New Press, 1998.

Documentary Collections, Congressional Documents, and Periodicals

Church Committee Assassination Report: U.S. Congress, Senate, Select Committee to Study Governmental Operations with Respect to Intelligence Activities. *Alleged Assassination Plots Involving Foreign Leaders; Interim Report.* 94th Congress, 1st Session, Senate Report No. 94-465. Washington: GPO, 1975; rpt. New York: W. W. Norton, 1976.

Clissold, Stephen, ed. *Soviet Relations with Latin America, 1918–1968: A Documentary Survey.* London: Oxford University Press, 1970.

Goodman, James, ed. *Letters to Kennedy: John Kenneth Galbraith.* Cambridge: Harvard University Press, 1998.

May, Ernest R., and Philip D. Zelikow, eds. *The Kennedy Tapes: Inside the White House During the Cuban Missile Crisis.* Cambridge: Harvard University Press, 1997.

Naftali, Timothy, Philip Zelikow, and Ernest May, eds. *The Presidential Recordings: John F. Kennedy, the Great Crises.* 3 vols. New York: W. W. Norton, 2001.

Rockefeller, Nelson A., et al. *Report to the President by the Commission on CIA Activities Within the United States.* Washington: GPO, 1975.

U.S. Department of Justice. FBI Files (reports, correspondence, interviews).

U.S. Department of State. *Foreign Relations of the United States, 1958–1960, Volume V: American Republics.* Washington: GPO, 1991.

———. *Foreign Relations of the United States, 1958–1960, Volume VI: Cuba.* Washington: GPO, 1991.

———. *Foreign Relations of the United States, 1961–1963, Volume X, Cuba, 1961–1962.* Washington: GPO, 1997.

———. *Foreign Relations of the United States, 1961–1963, Volume XI, Cuban Missile Crisis and Aftermath.* Washington: GPO, 1996.

———. *Foreign Relations of the United States, 1964–1968, Volume XXXII, Dominican Republic; Cuba; Haiti; Guyana.* Washington: GPO, 2005.

———. *Foreign Relations of the United States, 1964–1968, Volume XXXIII, Organization and Management of U.S. Foreign Policy; United Nations.* Washington: GPO, 2004.

U.S. National Archives and Records Administration. *Public Papers of the Presidents of the United States: Dwight D. Eisenhower: Containing the Public Messages, Speeches, and Statements of the President, 1953–1961.* 8 vols. Washington: GPO, 1960–61.

———. *Public Papers of the Presidents of the United States: John F. Kennedy: Containing the Public Messages, Speeches, and Statements of the President, 1961–1963.* 3 vols. Washington: GPO, 1962–64.

U.S. Senate. 94th Congress, 1st Session. *Hearings Before the Select Committee to Study Governmental Operations with Respect to Intelligence Activities, Volume 6: Federal Bureau of Investigation.* Washington: GPO, 1976.

———. 94th Congress, 2nd Session. *Foreign and Military Intelligence, Book I: Final Report of the Select Committee to Study Governmental Operations with Respect to Intelligence Activities.* Washington: GPO, 1976.

———. 94th Congress, 2nd Session. *Supplementary Detailed Staff Reports on Intelligence Activities and the Rights of Americans, Book III: Final Report of the Select Committee to Study Governmental Operations with Respect to Intelligence Activities.* Washington: GPO, 1976.

———. 94th Congress, 2nd Session. *The Investigation of the Assassination of President John F. Kennedy: Performance of the Intelligence Agencies, Book V: Final Report of the Select Committee to Study Governmental Operations with Respect to Intelligence Activities.* Washington: GPO, 1976.

Memoirs and Personal Accounts

Belin, David W. *Final Disclosure: The Full Truth About the Assassination of President Kennedy.* New York: Scribner's, 1980.

Bissell, Richard M. Jr. *Reflections of a Cold Warrior: From Yalta to the Bay of Pigs.* New Haven: Yale University Press, 1996.

Bonsal, Philip W. *Cuba, Castro, and the United States.* London: University of Pittsburgh Press, 1971.

Cabell, Charles P., ed. *Memoirs of War, Peace, and the CIA.* Colorado Springs, Colo.: Impavide Publications, 1997.

Califano, Joseph A. *Inside: A Public and Private Life.* New York: Public Affairs, 2004.

Castro, Fidel, and Ignacio Ramonet. *Fidel Castro: My Life, a Spoken Autobiography.* New York: Scribner, 2008. Originally published in Spain as *Fidel Castro: Biografía a dos voces.* 2006.

Colby, William, and Peter Forbath. *Honorable Men: My Life in the CIA.* New York: Simon and Schuster, 1978.

Devlin, Lawrence R. *Chief of Station, Congo: A Memoir of 1960–67.* New York: Public Affairs, 2007.

Escalante, Fabián. *The Cuba Project: CIA Covert Operations, 1959–62.* Melbourne, Australia: Ocean Press, 2004. First published as *The Secret War: CIA Covert Operations Against Cuba, 1959–62.* Melbourne, Australia: Ocean Press, 1995.

Ferrer, Edward B. *Operation Puma: The Air Battle of the Bay of Pigs.* Miami, Fla.: International Aviation Consultants, 1975, 1982.

Giancana, Antoinette, and Thomas C. Renner. *Mafia Princess: Growing Up in Sam Giancana's Family.* New York: William Morrow, 1984.

Goodwin, Richard N. *Remembering America: A Voice from the Sixties.* Boston: Little, Brown, 1988.

Halberstam, David. *The Best and the Brightest.* New York: Random House, 1969.

Helms, Richard, with William Hood. *A Look Over My Shoulder: A Life in the Central Intelligence Agency.* New York: Random House, 2003.

Hunt, Howard. *Give Us This Day: The Inside Story of the CIA and the Bay of Pigs Invasion . . . by One of Its Key Organizers.* New Rochelle, N.Y.: Arlington House, 1973.

Johnson, Haynes. *The Bay of Pigs: The Leaders' Story of Brigade 2506.* New York: W. W. Norton, 1964.

Johnson, U. Alexis. *The Right Hand of Power.* Englewood Cliffs, N.J.: Prentice-Hall, 1984.

Kennedy, John F. *Profiles in Courage.* New York: Harper, 1956.

Kennedy, Robert F. *The Enemy Within: The McClellan Committee's Crusade Against Jimmy Hoffa and Corrupt Labor Unions.* New York: Harper, 1960.

———. *Thirteen Days: A Memoir of the Cuban Missile Crisis.* New York: W. W. Norton, 1969.

Khrushchev, Nikita. *Khrushchev Remembers.* Boston: Little, Brown, 1970.

Lechuga, Carlos. *In the Eye of the Storm: Castro, Khrushchev, Kennedy, and the Missile Crisis.* Melbourne, Australia: Ocean Press, 1995.

Lynch, Grayston L. *Decision for Disaster: Betrayal at the Bay of Pigs.* Washington: Brassey's, 1998.

Maheu, Robert, and Richard Hack. *Next to Hughes: Behind the Power and Tragic Downfall of Howard Hughes by His Closest Advisor.* New York: HarperCollins, 1992.

Nixon, Richard M. *RN: The Memoirs of Richard Nixon.* 2 vols. New York: Warner Books, 1978.

———. *Six Crises.* New York: Pocket Books, 1962.

Persons, Albert C. *Bay of Pigs: A Firsthand Account of the Mission by a U.S. Pilot in Support of the Cuban Invasion Force in 1961.* Birmingham, Ala.: Kingston Press, 1968.

Schlesinger, Arthur M., Jr. *Journals: 1952–2000.* New York: Penguin, 2007.

———. *A Thousand Days: John F. Kennedy in the White House.* Boston: Houghton Mifflin, 1965.

Shackley, Ted, with Richard A. Finney. *Spymaster: My Life in the CIA.* Dulles, Va.: Potomac Books, 2005.

Sorensen, Theodore C. *Kennedy.* New York: Harper and Row, 1965.

Taylor, Maxwell D. *The Uncertain Trumpet.* New York: Harper and Brothers, 1960.

———. *Swords and Ploughshares: A Memoir.* New York: W. W. Norton, 1972.

Triay, Victor A. *Bay of Pigs: An Oral History of Brigade 2506.* Gainesville: University Press of Florida. 2001.

Author Interviews

Col. Joe Grady, May 24, 2006
Col. Joe Shannon, May 24, 2006

SECONDARY SOURCES

Books

Andrew, Christopher. *For the President's Eyes Only: Secret Intelligence and the American Presidency from Washington to Bush.* New York: HarperCollins, 1995.

Bamford, James. *Body of Secrets: Anatomy of the Ultra-Secret National Security Agency from the Cold War Through the Dawn of a New Century.* New York: Doubleday, 2001.

Beschloss, Michael R. *The Crisis Years: Kennedy and Khrushchev, 1960–1963.* New York: HarperCollins, 1991.

Binder, L. James. *Lemnitzer: A Soldier for His Time.* Washington: Brassey's, 1997.

Blight, James G., and Peter Kornbluh, eds. *Politics of Illusion: The Bay of Pigs Invasion Reexamined.* Boulder, Colo.: Lynne Rienner Publishers, 1998.

Bohning, Don. *The Castro Obsession: U.S. Covert Operations Against Cuba, 1959–1965.* Washington: Potomac Books, 2005.

Brashler, William. *The Don: The Life and Death of Sam Giancana.* New York: Harper and Row, 1977.

Corn, David. *Blond Ghost: Ted Shackley and the CIA's Crusades.* New York: Simon and Schuster, 1994.

Currey, Cecil B. *Edward Lansdale: The Unquiet American.* Boston: Houghton Mifflin, 1988.

Dallek, Robert. *An Unfinished Life: John F. Kennedy, 1917–1963.* New York: Little, Brown, 2003.

———. *Flawed Giant: Lyndon Johnson and His Times, 1961–1973.* New York: Oxford University Press, 1998.

Deitche, Scott M. *The Silent Don: The Criminal Underworld of Santo Trafficante Jr.* Fort Lee, N.J.: Barricade Books, 2007.

Diederich, Bernard. *Trujillo: The Death of the Dictator.* Princeton, N.J.: Markus Wiener Publishers, 1990. Originally published in 1978 as *Trujillo: The Death of the Goat.*

Fox, Stephen. *Blood and Power: Organized Crime in Twentieth-Century America.* New York: William Morrow, 1989.

Frankel, Max. *High Noon in the Cold War: Kennedy, Khrushchev, and the Cuban Missile Crisis.* New York: Ballantine Books, 2004.

Freedman, Lawrence. *Kennedy's Wars: Berlin, Cuba, Laos, and Vietnam.* New York: Oxford University Press, 2000.

Furiati, Claudia. *ZR Rifle: The Plot to Kill Kennedy and Castro.* Melbourne, Australia: Ocean Press, 1994.

Fursenko, Aleksandr, and Timothy Naftali. *"One Hell of a Gamble": Khrushchev, Castro, and Kennedy, 1958–1964.* New York: W. W. Norton, 1997.

Giglio, James N. *The Presidency of John F. Kennedy.* Lawrence: University Press of Kansas, 1991.

Grose, Peter. *Gentleman Spy: The Life of Allen Dulles.* New York: Houghton Mifflin, 1994.

Herring, George C. *America's Longest War: The United States and Vietnam, 1950–1975*. Boston: McGraw–Hill, 1979; 4th ed., 2002.

Hersh, Seymour M. *The Dark Side of Camelot*. Boston: Little, Brown, 1997.

Higgins, Trumbull. *The Perfect Failure: Kennedy, Eisenhower, and the CIA at the Bay of Pigs*. New York: W. W. Norton, 1987.

Jablon, Howard. *David M. Shoup: A Warrior Against War*. Lanham, Md.: Rowman and Littlefield, 2005.

Johnson, Loch K. *A Season of Inquiry: Congress and Intelligence*. Lexington: University Press of Kentucky, 1985.

Jones, Howard. *Death of a Generation: How the Assassinations of Diem and JFK Prolonged the Vietnam War*. New York: Oxford University Press, 2003.

Kelley, Kitty. *His Way: The Unauthorized Biography of Frank Sinatra*. New York: Bantam Books, 1986.

Knott, Stephen F. *Secret and Sanctioned: Covert Operations and the American Presidency*. New York: Oxford University Press, 1996.

Kurtz, Michael L. *The JFK Assassination Debates: Lone Gunman Versus Conspiracy*. Lawrence: University Press of Kansas, 2006.

Latell, Brian. *After Fidel: The Inside Story of Castro's Regime and Castro's Next Leader*. New York: Palgrave Macmillan, 2002.

Mahoney, Richard D. *JFK: Ordeal in Africa*. New York: Oxford University Press, 1983.

Marchetti, Victor, and John D. Marks. *The CIA and the Cult of Intelligence*. New York: Dell, 1974.

Nutter, John J. *The CIA's Black Ops: Covert Action, Foreign Policy, and Democracy*. Amherst, N.Y.: Prometheus Books, 2000.

Parmet, Herbert S. *JFK: The Presidency of John F. Kennedy*. New York: Dial Press, 1983.

Paterson, Thomas G. *Contesting Castro: The United States and the Triumph of the Cuban Revolution*. New York: Oxford University Press, 1994.

Powers, Thomas. *The Man Who Kept the Secrets: Richard Helms and the CIA*. New York: Knopf, 1979.

Prados, John. *Lost Crusader: The Secret Wars of CIA Director William Colby*. New York: Oxford University Press, 2003.

———. *Safe for Democracy: The Secret Wars of the CIA*. Chicago: Ivan R. Dee, 2006.

Quirk, Robert E. *Fidel Castro*. New York: W. W. Norton, 1993.

Ranelagh, John. *The Agency: The Rise and Decline of the CIA*. London: Weidenfeld and Nicolson, 1986.

Rappleye, Charles, and Ed Becker. *All American Mafioso: The Johnny Rosselli Story*. New York: Barricade Books, 1991, 1995.

Reeves, Richard. *President Kennedy: Profile of Power*. New York: Simon and Schuster, 1993.

Rodríguez, Juan Carlos. *The Bay of Pigs and the CIA*. Melbourne, Australia: Ocean Press, 1999.

Schlesinger, Arthur M., Jr. *Robert Kennedy and His Times.* Boston: Houghton Mifflin, 1978.

Srodes, James. *Allen Dulles: Master of Spies.* Washington: Regnery, 1999.

Stockton, Bayard. *Flawed Patriot: The Rise and Fall of CIA Legend Bill Harvey.* Washington: Potomac Books, 2006.

Summers, Anthony. *Conspiracy.* New York: McGraw-Hill, 1980.

Symmes, Patrick. *The Boys from Dolores: Fidel Castro's Schoolmates from Revolution to Exile.* New York: Pantheon Books, 2007.

Szulc, Tad. *A Compulsive Spy: The Strange Career of E. Howard Hunt.* New York: Viking, 1974.

Szulc, Tad, and Karl E. Meyer. *The Cuban Invasion: The Chronicle of a Disaster.* New York: Ballantine Books, 1962.

Thomas, Evan. *The Very Best Men: Four Who Dared: The Early Years of the CIA.* New York: Simon and Schuster, 1995.

Trento, Joseph J. *The Secret History of the CIA.* Roseville, Calif.: Forum, 2001.

Trest, Warren, and Donald Dodd. *Wings of Denial: The Alabama Air National Guard's Covert Role at the Bay of Pigs.* Montgomery, Ala.: NewSouth Books, 2001.

Tully, Andrew. *CIA: The Inside Story.* New York: William Morrow, 1962.

Ulam, Adam B. *The Rivals: America and Russia Since World War II.* New York: Viking, 1971.

Weiner, Tim. *Legacy of Ashes. The History of the CIA.* New York: Doubleday, 2007.

Welch, Richard E., Jr. *Response to Revolution: The United States and the Cuban Revolution, 1959–1961.* Chapel Hill: University of North Carolina Press, 1985.

Woods, Randall B. *LBJ: Architect of American Ambition.* New York: Free Press, 2006.

Wyden, Peter. *Bay of Pigs: The Untold Story.* New York: Simon and Schuster, 1979.

Articles and Essays

Gleijeses, Piero. "Ships in the Night: The CIA, the White House, and the Bay of Pigs." *Journal of Latin American Studies* 27 (Feb. 1995): 1–42.

Kirkpatrick, Lyman B. "Paramilitary Case Study: The Bay of Pigs." *Naval War College Review* 25 (Nov.–Dec. 1972): 32–42.

Kornbluh, Peter. "JFK and Castro: The Secret Quest for Accommodation." *Cigar Aficionado Online*, Sept./Oct. 1999, 1–15.

Dissertations

Schwab, Stephen. "U.S.-Cuba Relations: The Enduring Significance of Guantánamo." Ph.D. dissertation. Tuscaloosa: University of Alabama, 2007.

Novels

Puzo, Mario. *The Godfather.* New York: G. P. Putnam's Sons, 1969.

Index